Data to Decision

A Guide to Applied Statistics and Machine Learning

Written by Daniel Carr
Published by Cornell-David Publishing House

INDEX

2. Essential Statistics: Probability, Descriptive and Inferential Analysis

1. Introduction to Statistics, Forecasting, and Machine Learning in Real Life

Welcome to *Applying Statistics, Forecasting, and Machine Learning IRL*! This book is designed to help you understand the importance of these three concepts and how they can be incorporated into real-life scenarios to improve decision making, predictions, and understanding of complex situations. In the following subsection, we will dive deeper into the essence of each of these concepts and learn about their various applications in modern life.

1.1 Understanding the Importance of Statistics in Real Life

1.1.1 What are Statistics?

Statistics is a branch of mathematics that deals with the collection, analysis, interpretation, presentation, and organization of quantitative data. It is used to draw conclusions, make predictions, and test hypotheses based on empirical data. In essence, statistics is all about translating raw data or information into meaningful insights.

1.1.2 Applications of Statistics in Real Life

Statistics play a crucial role in several real-life applications, including but not limited to:

1. **Healthcare**: In the field of medicine, statistics help researchers understand the relationship between various factors, such as diet, exercise, and medication, that can impact our overall health. Statistics are also used extensively in clinical trials to test the effectiveness of new treatments and medical interventions. They help to determine the appropriate sample size for a study to ensure the validity of the results and to track the success of treatments over time.
2. **Economics**: Governments and organizations use economic statistics to create policies, forecast economic trends, and allocate resources efficiently. By analyzing historical data related to variables such as inflation, unemployment, and GDP, policymakers can make informed decisions about the future direction of an economy.
3. **Sports**: In the sports world, statistics help to analyze the performance of individual athletes and teams. Metrics such as batting averages, on-base percentage, and player efficiency rating (PER) are commonly used to evaluate the abilities and skills of players in various sports. Furthermore, coaches and analysts rely on statistical data to help with game strategy, player management, and roster planning.
4. **Quality Control**: Companies use statistical quality control methods to detect defective products or services and implement corrective measures. By analyzing the performance of the production process and identifying areas of improvement, organizations can continuously improve the quality of their offerings.
5. **Marketing**: In marketing and advertising, statistics help to identify patterns in consumer behavior, assess the efficacy of marketing strategies, and optimize the allocation of resources. By analyzing customer demographics, preferences, and responses to

marketing campaigns, marketers can create more targeted marketing efforts to reach the desired audience.

1.2 The Power of Forecasting in Real Life

1.2.1 What is Forecasting?

Forecasting is the process of predicting a future event or outcome based on historical data, trends, patterns, or other relevant factors. It is widely used in various fields to help organizations and individuals make informed decisions about the future.

1.2.2 Applications of Forecasting in Real Life

Some notable applications of forecasting in real-life scenarios include:

1. **Weather Forecasting**: Meteorologists use sophisticated models and tools to analyze historical weather data and predict future weather conditions. Accurate weather forecasting helps people plan their activities and can also be vital for emergency management and disaster preparedness.
2. **Stock Market Predictions**: In the finance world, market analysts and investors use forecasting techniques to predict the future prices of stocks or other securities. By analyzing historical data and using statistical models or machine learning algorithms, they attempt to identify trends and patterns that could indicate future movements in the market.

3. **Supply Chain Management**: Businesses rely on forecasting to predict demand for their products or services and manage their supply chain accordingly. By accurately forecasting customer demand, organizations can ensure that they have enough inventory to meet customer needs while minimizing overstock or stockouts.
4. **Human Resources**: HR departments use forecasting to predict future employee needs, such as anticipating the number of new hires required, and identifying potential skill gaps in the workforce. This enables organizations to plan their recruitment strategies effectively and ensure they have the right staff in place to meet future demands.

1.3 Harnessing the Power of Machine Learning in Real Life

1.3.1 What is Machine Learning?

Machine learning is a subfield of artificial intelligence that focuses on teaching computers to learn from data without being explicitly programmed. The primary goal of machine learning is to create algorithms that can learn from experience and make predictions or decisions based on that learned knowledge.

1.3.2 Applications of Machine Learning in Real Life

Machine learning has found numerous applications in real life, including:

1. **Speech Recognition**: Virtual assistants like Siri, Google Assistant, and Alexa use machine learning

algorithms to process and understand spoken language. These algorithms are trained on large datasets of human speech, which help them recognize different accents, dialects, and languages.

2. **Image Recognition**: Machine learning algorithms are used to automatically recognize objects, people, or activities in images or videos. This technology powers applications like Google Photos, which can automatically tag and organize your photos based on the people or objects in the image.
3. **Fraud Detection**: Financial institutions use machine learning to detect patterns of fraudulent activity in credit card transactions, bank account activity, or stock trades. By analyzing large amounts of transactional data, these algorithms can identify suspicious behaviors indicative of fraud and alert the relevant authorities.
4. **Healthcare**: Machine learning is being used to design more effective treatment plans, predict patient outcomes, and discover new drug compounds. One promising application is the analysis of medical images, such as X-rays or MRIs, to diagnose diseases or conditions early.
5. **Autonomous Vehicles**: Self-driving cars leverage machine learning algorithms to analyze data from sensors, cameras, and radars in real-time. This enables the vehicle to make informed decisions about navigation, obstacle detection, and avoidance, and overall control of the car.

In conclusion, the trilogy of statistics, forecasting, and machine learning plays a critical role in shaping our understanding of the world and empowering us to make informed decisions. By embracing these concepts in real-life scenarios, organizations can not only stay competitive but also create a more dynamic, efficient, and inclusive world.

1. Introduction to Statistics, Forecasting and Machine Learning in Real Life

In the era of big data, analytics and artificial intelligence, statistics, forecasting, and machine learning have become essential tools for quantifying, evaluating, and predicting complex systems and phenomena. From businesses optimizing their operations to researchers exploring new frontiers, these methods help us analyze and interpret data, generate insights, and facilitate more informed decision-making. In this section, we will introduce the fundamentals of these powerful tools and demonstrate how they can be applied across various real-life scenarios.

1.1 Why is it Important to Learn about Statistics, Forecasting and Machine Learning in Real Life?

Both experts and professionals of various fields face increasingly complex decision-making problems in today's world. To solve these problems, utilizing the appropriate analytical tools is crucial. Consequently, it's important to understand and apply statistics, forecasting, and machine learning to improve decision efficiency and effectiveness.

1.1.1 Benefits of Applying Statistics and Forecasting

Statistics and forecasting play a significant role in understanding the world around us. By harnessing the power of these methods in real life, we can:

1. Identify patterns and trends: Demystify complex data and reveal underlying structure.
2. Test and verify theories: Through hypothesis testing, we can validate or refute claims about variables' relationships.
3. Make informed decisions: Make predictions and adjust future actions based on the analysis of past data.
4. Enhance communication: Represent data visually and concisely, facilitating better understanding and interpretation.

1.1.2 Benefits of Applying Machine Learning

Machine learning is a rapidly evolving field that leverages computers' abilities to make decisions and predictions from data. Some key benefits of applying machine learning in real life include:

1. Automating tasks: Machines can learn to perform tasks without explicit programming, freeing up time for humans to focus on more complex problems.
2. Enhanced decision-making: Machine learning algorithms can help businesses make more informed decisions based on data-driven predictions and recommendations.
3. Improved customer experience: Machine learning can offer personalized and tailored experiences to

customers by analyzing their behavior and preferences.

4. Continuous improvement: Unlike static models, machine learning models can learn and adapt as new data becomes available, leading to better and more accurate predictions over time.

1.2 Real-Life Applications of Statistics, Forecasting, and Machine Learning

The applications of these methods are vast, spanning various industries and sectors. Some notable examples of their real-life utility include:

1.2.1 Sales Forecasting and Inventory Management

Sales forecasting involves estimating future sales over a specified period. By employing statistics, forecasting, and machine learning, businesses can better anticipate demand, optimize inventory levels, and reduce stockouts or overstock situations.

1.2.2 Healthcare and Medical Research

Researchers can leverage statistics and machine learning to uncover relationships between patient characteristics, medical treatments, and health outcomes. These insights improve patient care, reduce medical costs, and inform public health policy.

1.2.3 Financial Markets

Market participants such as banks, hedge funds, and individual investors use machine learning to predict stock prices, identify trade opportunities, manage risk, and optimize portfolio allocations.

1.2.4 Fraud Detection and Prevention

Machine learning models can analyze vast amounts of transaction data, identifying unusual patterns that may signal fraudulent activities. By detecting and preventing fraud quickly, businesses can reduce losses and protect their customers.

1.2.5 Natural Language Processing (NLP)

Machine learning algorithms process and analyze large volumes of text data, enabling automatic text summarization, sentiment analysis, machine translation, and plagiarism detection.

1.3 Challenges and Considerations

While the potential benefits of applying statistics, forecasting, and machine learning in real life are immense, there are inherent challenges:

1. Quality of data: Ensuring data is accurate and representative of the problem at hand is crucial for drawing reliable conclusions and making accurate predictions.
2. Technical and ethical considerations: Balancing the potential benefits against the risks, such as biased algorithms, privacy issues, and misuse of the technology, is essential.

3. Complexity and interpretability: Complex models sometimes produce "black-box" outputs, making it difficult for non-experts to understand the underlying mechanics and results of the analysis.

Despite these challenges, the future of statistics, forecasting, and machine learning promises continued innovation and growth. As more industries and sectors recognize these methods' potential, their real-life applications will become increasingly valuable and ubiquitous.

1. Introduction to Statistics, Forecasting and Machine Learning in Real Life

In today's data-driven world, with the exponential growth of information being created and processed, methods for analyzing and making sense of this data have become more important than ever. Statistics, forecasting, and machine learning are three closely related disciplines that form the backbone of modern data analysis techniques. In this section, we will provide an overview of these concepts and how they are applied in real-life situations, enabling us to make data-driven decisions, predict future events, and automate complex tasks.

1.1 The Role of Statistics in Real Life

Statistics is the science and practice of collecting, organizing, analyzing, and interpreting numerical data to gain insight into a wide variety of phenomena. Real-life applications of statistics are vast and include various fields such as economics, business, healthcare, sports, and social sciences.

In these contexts, statistics helps us uncover patterns and trends, understand the relationships between variables, and make informed decisions based on empirical evidence. Some common real-life applications of statistics include:

- Estimating average salary, the living cost in different cities, and inflation rates
- Analyzing customer preferences and satisfaction levels to drive business growth
- Assessing the effectiveness of medication and treatment methods in healthcare
- Measuring the performance and skill of athletes or sports teams
- Evaluating the impact of public policies on socio-economic indicators

1.2 Forecasting: Predicting the Future with Data

Forecasting is a statistical technique that aims to predict future events or conditions by analyzing historical data. It plays a crucial role in various fields, including economics, finance, climate science, and many more. Accurate forecasting helps individuals, businesses, and governments make better decisions and prepare for future challenges.

Some real-life applications of forecasting include:

- Weather prediction: Forecasting weather patterns to help with agriculture, event planning, and natural disaster preparedness

- Economic forecasting: Predicting trends in economic indicators such as GDP, inflation rate, and unemployment to aid policy-making and financial planning
- Stock market prediction: Forecasting future stock prices to enable better financial investment decisions
- Demand forecasting: Estimating future demand for products or services to guide inventory management and production planning

1.3 Machine Learning: Teaching Computers to Learn from Data

Machine learning is a subfield of artificial intelligence (AI) that focuses on developing algorithms that enable computers to learn and improve their performance on specific tasks through experience (i.e., by analyzing data). In real life, machine learning offers an increasingly powerful tool to automate complex tasks, discover hidden patterns, and make predictions based on large-scale data.

Some prominent real-life applications of machine learning include:

- Natural language processing: Machines learning to understand human languages, powering applications such as speech recognition, machine translation, and sentiment analysis
- Image and video processing: Automating tasks such as object detection, facial recognition, and video classification
- Recommender systems: Predicting users' preferences and recommending items, as seen in online shopping, movie, and music recommendation platforms like Amazon, Netflix, and Spotify

- Fraud detection: Analyzing large volumes of financial transactions to detect unusual patterns, potentially indicating fraudulent activity
- Personalized medicine: Developing tailored treatment plans for patients using machine learning algorithms that analyze patient-specific data, such as genetic information, medical history, and lifestyle factors

1.4 The Intersection of Statistics, Forecasting, and Machine Learning

The fields of statistics, forecasting, and machine learning share a common goal: to extract meaningful insights from data. While these techniques are closely related, they are distinct in terms of their underlying methodologies, assumptions, and applications.

Statistics focus on making inferences about population characteristics based on a sample of data, using methods such as hypothesis testing, estimation, and regression analysis. Forecasting, on the other hand, primarily deals with time-series data, aiming to predict future events or conditions by modeling historical trends and patterns. Machine learning differs from both of these fields in that it involves developing algorithms that can automatically learn from data and improve their performance on tasks without being explicitly programmed to do so.

Despite these differences, the three disciplines often intersect and complement one another in real-life applications. For example, advanced machine learning techniques such as deep learning and reinforcement learning are built upon the foundations of statistical theory. Furthermore, some applications require a combination of forecasting and machine learning approaches, such as predicting stock prices or demand for products in a dynamic, fast-changing environment.

1.5 Challenges and Limitations in Real-Life Applications

Applying statistics, forecasting, and machine learning in real-life situations is not without challenges. Some of the common difficulties practitioners face include:

- Data quality: Incomplete, inconsistent, or biased data can lead to misleading or inaccurate results
- Model complexity: Striking the right balance between model simplicity and accuracy is essential to avoid overfitting (capturing noise in the data) and underfitting (failing to capture essential patterns)
- Causality vs. correlation: Identifying causal relationships between variables is crucial for making informed decisions, but disentangling causality from mere association is often challenging
- Ethical considerations: The use of these techniques can raise ethical concerns, such as potential bias, discrimination, and privacy issues

Keeping these challenges and limitations in mind, practitioners must exercise caution when interpreting results and implementing data-driven strategies in real-life contexts.

1.6 Conclusion

In conclusion, the application of statistics, forecasting, and machine learning in real life enables us to make sense of the ever-growing volumes of data generated by our modern world. With these powerful tools, we can better understand complex phenomena, predict future events, and automate tasks—ultimately empowering individuals, businesses, and governments to make more informed decisions and improve their decision-making processes.

1. Introduction to Statistics, Forecasting and Machine Learning in Real Life

In today's data-driven world, statistical analysis, forecasting, and machine learning have found their place in diverse aspects of our daily lives. From healthcare to marketing, finance to sports, and politics to social media, these techniques have ushered in a new era of data comprehension that is continuously evolving. In this section, we will discuss the importance and application of these techniques in real-life scenarios, and their role in empowering individuals and organizations with valuable information.

1.1 Real-life Applications of Statistical Analysis

Statistical analysis involves collecting, analyzing, interpreting, presenting, and organizing data. It helps us understand trends, patterns, and relationships among variables within the data, which guides decision-making and facilitates problem-solving. Here are some real-life applications that demonstrate the importance of statistical analysis:

1. **Healthcare**: Health professionals use statistical analysis to study the efficacy of new drugs, the causes of diseases, and the effectiveness of various treatments. For example, it helps determine the success of clinical trials, the prevalence of certain conditions, and the accuracy of diagnostic tests. This information can be utilized to improve patient care and inform public health policies.
2. **Finance**: Investors, banks, and insurers rely on statistical analysis to analyze financial risks, assess the performance of investment portfolios, and make informed decisions. Tools like regression analysis, time-series forecasting, and Monte Carlo simulations help them comprehend complex financial models, forecast future trends, and manage risk effectively.
3. **Marketing**: Statisticians help businesses analyze customer data to identify trends, preferences, and needs. By understanding customer behavior, companies can target their advertising, segment their markets, and fine-tune their pricing strategies. Techniques like A/B testing, clustering, and sentiment analysis provide actionable insights to enhance sales performance and grow market share.
4. **Sports**: Coaches, teams, and athletes leverage statistical analysis to evaluate performance, refine game strategies, and make data-driven decisions. Advanced analytics helps uncover hidden patterns, areas of improvement, and potential competitive advantages, revolutionizing the way sports are played, coached, and managed.
5. **Politics**: Political campaigns and polling organizations use statistical analysis to gauge public opinion, monitor voter behavior, and devise strategies

to persuade undecided voters. By analyzing polling data, campaign managers can target key demographics, refine campaign messages, and allocate resources more efficiently.

1.2 Forecasting in Real Life

Forecasting is the art and science of predicting future events based on historical data. It plays a pivotal role in planning, decision-making, and risk assessment across various domains. Let's explore some real-life applications of forecasting techniques:

1. **Weather Forecasting**: Meteorologists rely on computer models, historical data, and other inputs to predict weather conditions days, weeks, or even months in advance. Accurate forecasts inform emergency planning, agriculture operations, energy management, and transportation systems.
2. **Economic Forecasting**: Economists use forecasting models to predict key economic indicators such as inflation, unemployment rates, and GDP growth. Governments and businesses can then use these predictions to formulate fiscal and monetary policies, or to prepare for potential economic downturns.
3. **Inventory and Supply Chain Management**: Companies use demand forecasting to estimate future customer demand for their products, allowing them to maintain optimal levels of inventory, minimize stockouts, and improve customer satisfaction. Likewise, forecasting can inform decisions about procurement, production planning, and distribution across the supply chain.
4. **Human Resources**: Forecasting can help organizations anticipate their future staffing needs,

allowing them to make data-driven decisions about hiring, training, and retention strategies. Accurate workforce forecasting can minimize skill gaps, reduce employee turnover, and ensure the right people are in the right roles at the right time.

1.3 Machine Learning in Real-Life Applications

Machine learning is the process of enabling computers to learn and make decisions, without being explicitly programmed. It has become an essential tool for solving complex problems in real-world applications. Here are some examples:

1. **Fraud Detection**: Banks, credit card companies, and payment processors use machine learning algorithms to identify suspicious transactions, flagging them for further investigation. By analyzing massive datasets, these algorithms can quickly identify patterns and behaviors that indicate fraudulent activity.
2. **Healthcare**: Machine learning algorithms can analyze medical images to detect diseases or abnormalities, predict patient outcomes, and identify high-risk individuals. These techniques can help doctors make faster, more accurate diagnoses, and enable more personalized treatment plans.
3. **Natural Language Processing**: Machine learning has enabled significant advancements in understanding and generating human language. Applications such as speech recognition, sentiment analysis, and machine translation have transformed the way businesses interact with customers and analyze textual data.

4. **Autonomous Vehicles**: Self-driving cars rely on machine learning algorithms to understand their environment, make decisions, and navigate the roads safely. By processing data from sensors, cameras, and radar systems, these vehicles can anticipate and respond to complex traffic situations, improving safety and reducing congestion on our roads.
5. **Recommender Systems**: Online businesses like Amazon, Netflix, and Spotify use machine learning to analyze user behavior, preferences, and browsing history to generate personalized product recommendations. This enhances customer experience and increases the likelihood of repeat purchases.

In conclusion, statistics, forecasting, and machine learning are powerful tools that enhance our understanding of the world and help us make more informed decisions. By embracing these techniques and integrating them into our lives, individuals and organizations can unlock new opportunities, refine their strategies, and ultimately, drive progress in various domains. The real-life applications highlighted in this section merely scratch the surface of what's possible, as new techniques and advancements continue to emerge.

1. Introduction to Statistics, Forecasting, and Machine Learning in Real Life

As we progress in the age of information, data has become a key component of our decision-making process. Whether in finance, healthcare, or any other industry, understanding trends and patterns in the data at hand can help us make informed conclusions and consequently achieve more desirable results in our personal or professional lives. In this regard, having a solid understanding of statistics, forecasting, and machine learning is crucial. These powerful fields not only help us analyze and understand the data available but also provide the framework and tools for developing models that can make predictions and aid in decision-making. This chapter serves as an introduction to the real-life relevance of these fields and how they are applied across various domains.

1.1 Statistical Analysis and its Real-Life Applications

Statistical analysis is concerned with the collection, organization, analysis, interpretation, and presentation of data. It deals with the idea of extracting meaningful insights from raw data and using it to draw valid conclusions. Appropriate statistical methods can help to identify patterns and trends, as well as evaluate relationships between variables. Here are a few real-life applications of statistics:

1. *Healthcare:* In medicine, statistical methods are employed to evaluate the effectiveness of new drugs, treatments, or preventive measures. They help in determining whether the observed effects are significant or simply due to chance. Clinical trials,

cohort studies, and meta-analyses are examples of research designs that use statistics in healthcare.

2. *Government & Policy-Making:* Governments rely on data-driven decisions to allocate resources or formulate policies. Statistical analysis can help in understanding the needs of a population, improving infrastructure, optimizing resource allocation, determining crime rates or environmental issues, and much more, which aids in better decision-making.
3. *Finance & Economics:* Statistics play a vital role in finance and economics, from financial planning and risk management to economic forecasting. For instance, regression analysis is a common statistical technique used to study relationships between variables, such as the stock market index, interest rates, and GDP growth.
4. *Sports:* Coaches, analysts, and teams use statistical data and analytics to gauge team performance, track their progress, and make strategic decisions to maximize their chances of winning.

1.2 Forecasting and its Real-Life Applications

Forecasting is the process of making predictions about future events based on historical data, patterns, trends, and current conditions with the help of statistical methods, computational algorithms, or judgment. Accurate forecasting can be very beneficial in various domains as it helps in strategic planning, resource management, and decision-making. Here are a few real-life applications of forecasting:

1. *Weather Forecasting:* Weather forecasting is one of the most well-known examples of forecasting. Meteorologists use a combination of historical data, statistical models, and atmospheric simulations to predict the weather accurately. This helps in early warnings of hazardous weather conditions such as hurricanes, tornadoes, and floods, potentially saving lives and property.
2. *Business & Finance:* In business, forecasting is crucial in areas such as demand forecasting, sales forecasting, financial forecasting, and workforce planning. It enables businesses to predict market trends, allocate resources, and streamline their operations, as well as mitigate risks and uncertainties.
3. *Agriculture:* Accurate weather and crop yield forecasts help farmers make better decisions regarding crop selection, planting, and harvesting times. This information can directly impact food prices, supply chain management, and global hunger.
4. *Energy Sector:* Forecasting is essential for energy management and planning, which includes predicting electricity demand, renewable energy production, and optimizing the operation of power plants.

1.3 Machine Learning and its Real-Life Applications

Machine learning is a subset of artificial intelligence that focuses on training computers to learn from data and autonomously improve their performance through experience, rather than explicitly programming them to do so. As a result, machine learning algorithms can detect patterns, trends, or anomalies in data, make predictions, and help in optimal decision-making. Here are a few real-life applications of machine learning:

1. *Automated Fraud Detection:* Machine learning models can analyze vast amounts of transaction data in real-time and detect anomalies or discrepancies, reducing the likelihood of fraudulent activities and enhancing the security of financial systems.
2. *Natural Language Processing:* Machine learning has enabled the development of intelligent chatbots, voice assistants, and translation systems by processing and understanding human language. These applications are widely used in customer support and communication, resulting in a more efficient and personalized user experience.
3. *Healthcare:* Machine learning algorithms have found their use in various domains within healthcare, such as diagnosing diseases by analyzing medical images, predicting patient outcomes, and developing personalized treatment plans.
4. *Autonomous Vehicles:* Self-driving cars rely on advancements made in machine learning, particularly computer vision and sensor fusion, which allow the vehicle to "see" its surroundings and make safe driving decisions.

In conclusion, the fields of statistics, forecasting, and machine learning play crucial roles in various aspects of our daily lives, influencing the decisions we make and the systems we interact with. Fundamental knowledge of these fields, coupled with practical applications, can help individuals and professionals alike make better decisions and unlock the full potential of the data-driven world in which we live.

A Comprehensive Guide to Real-World Applications of Statistics, Forecasting, and Machine Learning

The advancements in technology and our growing reliance on data have made understanding statistics, forecasting, and machine learning more important than ever before. These fields have real-world applications in numerous domains, including business, healthcare, sports, finance, climate change, and many more. In this guide, we will explore some of the leading use cases of these fields and provide a practical perspective on how they can be applied to gain valuable insights and make informed decisions that drive success in various industries.

I. Business Applications

1. **Sales Forecasting** - By analyzing historical sales data, businesses can predict future sales, manage inventory levels, and identify patterns in consumer behavior. This helps them allocate resources efficiently and stay ahead of competitors. Machine learning models, such as time series forecasting and regression analysis, can provide accurate sales forecasts to ensure smooth operations and reduce uncertainties.
2. **Marketing and Customer Segmentation** - Leveraging statistical analysis and machine learning algorithms, businesses can better understand their target audience by identifying patterns and trends in customer data. Techniques like clustering and decision trees can help companies understand customer preferences, create personalized marketing

campaigns, and optimize their marketing strategies based on customer segments.

3. **Risk Management and Fraud Detection** - Statistical and machine learning models can identify anomalies and potential fraud in vast amounts of transactional data. By building and training algorithms on historical cases of fraud, companies can predict and prevent fraudulent activities from happening, minimizing financial loss and enhancing security in their processes.

II. Healthcare Applications

1. **Disease Diagnosis and Treatment** - Machine learning techniques, like supervised learning and neural networks, can be applied to analyze medical images and health records for more accurate disease identification and treatment recommendations. These algorithms help physicians make data-driven decisions that ultimately lead to better patient outcomes.
2. **Predicting Disease Outbreaks** - By analyzing historical data and current health events, using methods such as time-series analysis, researchers can predict disease outbreaks and devise strategies to prevent or mitigate their spread, ultimately saving lives and resources.
3. **Drug Discovery and Development** - Pharmaceutical companies are increasingly employing machine learning techniques in the drug discovery process. Advanced models like deep learning can analyze molecular structures and identify potential new therapeutics more efficiently, significantly reducing the time and cost for drug development.

III. Sports Analytics

1. **Performance Analysis and Player Evaluation** - Data-driven insights have become vital in sports to understand player performance across various game situations. Using statistical models and machine learning, teams can analyze large volumes of historical game data to determine individual player strengths and weaknesses, driving better recruitment and coaching decisions.
2. **Injury Prevention and Rehabilitation** - Sports injury data can be analyzed using machine learning algorithms to predict the likelihood of injury for individual athletes based on historical data and in-game factors. These predictions can help coaches make informed decisions regarding player workload, adapting training programs, and implementing preventative measures.

IV. Financial Applications

1. **Stock Price Prediction** - By analyzing historical stock prices, using machine learning models like recurrent neural networks (RNN), financial institutions can predict future trends and make data-driven investment decisions.
2. **Credit Risk Assessment** - Banks and financial services providers can utilize statistical models and machine learning approaches to better assess the creditworthiness of borrowers by evaluating historical transaction data, spending patterns, and other relevant factors to make real-time loan decisions.

V. Climate Change and Environmental Applications

1. **Climate Modeling and Prediction** - By analyzing historical climate data and constructing machine

learning models, scientists can predict future weather patterns, including temperature, precipitation, and storm activity. These predictions help policymakers, businesses, and communities take appropriate action and adapt to climate change.

2. **Ecological Conservation** - Machine learning algorithms can be applied to study animal populations, habitats, and migration patterns, helping conservationists make data-driven decisions to protect ecosystems and preserve endangered species more effectively.

In conclusion, statistics, forecasting, and machine learning have become essential tools in tackling real-world challenges across diverse domains. By leveraging the power of data and implementing these models in industries ranging from business to healthcare, sports, finance, and the environment, we can make better-informed decisions, optimize resources, and uncover groundbreaking solutions that spark innovation and drive success.

Chapter 4.4: Integrating Statistics, Forecasting and Machine Learning into Daily Life

In this section, we will discuss how statistics, forecasting, and machine learning can be instrumental in our daily lives. From personal decision-making to professional industries, these methods have a broad range of applications that allows us to navigate the complexities of the world.

4.4.1 Personal Decision-Making

The techniques learned in statistics, forecasting, and machine learning can prove especially useful when making important decisions in our personal lives, such as purchasing a house, planning for retirement, or even getting an education. Below are a few examples of how these tools can be employed in personal decision-making.

Example 1 – House Purchase: When purchasing a house, various factors come into play such as the location, price, size, and accessibility. By utilizing statistical methods, potential buyers can compare similar homes in the area and evaluate whether the asking price is reasonable or not. Further, forecasting methods can help predict the future growth of the neighborhood, property taxes, and potential resale value. Machine learning algorithms can yield more accurate recommendations for houses based on the buyer's preferences.

Example 2 – Retirement Planning: Planning for retirement involves analyzing the performance of various investment strategies, estimating the required savings, and predicting how long the funds will last. Statistics allow us to make informed decisions about distribution of wealth, forecasting helps anticipate financial needs in the future, and machine learning techniques can optimize investments for long-term growth.

Example 3 – Education Choices: Selecting a college, major, or course of studies often involves comparing numerous options based on potential salaries, employment opportunities, and overall satisfaction levels. By leveraging statistical analysis, students can make data-driven decisions about their educational path. Forecasting future job markets can aid in selecting a field of study that will have better employment prospects, while machine learning tools can help students find schools that fit their unique profiles.

4.4.2 Professional Applications

In various industries, statistics, forecasting, and machine learning play an integral role in optimizing processes, reducing costs, and making data-driven decisions. This section will explore some specific examples of applications in professional environments.

Example 4 – Healthcare: Healthcare providers increasingly rely on statistics to make data-driven decisions regarding patient care. This may include analyzing clinical trial data to evaluate new treatments or forecasting the spread of infectious diseases. Machine learning algorithms can be used to enhance medical diagnostics or predict patient outcomes based on historical data.

Example 5 – Retail and Marketing: Retailers and marketers use statistical analyses to understand consumer behavior, assess campaign performance, and allocate resources. For example, A/B testing can help identify the most effective strategies for increasing conversions. Forecasting methods can predict seasonal trends or inventory needs, while machine learning tools can personalize marketing communications to individual customers, enhancing their overall experience.

Example 6 – Finance and Banking: Financial institutions employ statistical methods to manage risks, assess creditworthiness, and identify fraudulent activity. Forecasting models help predict economic trends, stock market movements or interest rates. Machine learning is increasingly employed to develop trading strategies or automate decision-making in the financial industry.

4.4.3 Society and Policy-Making

Governments and policymakers can leverage the power of statistics, forecasting, and machine learning to inform public policies, manage resources, and enhance the overall well-being of society. Some examples include:

Example 7 – Environmental Monitoring: Governments use statistical data to analyze environmental trends and quantify the impact of various initiatives. Forecasting models can help predict the future state of the environment, identify potential risks, and plan for sustainable development. Machine learning algorithms can be used to analyze satellite imagery for signs of deforestation, pollution, or other environmental concerns.

Example 8 – Urban Planning and Infrastructure: Cities and municipalities can utilize statistics to understand the needs of their communities, manage limited resources, and optimize infrastructure investments. Forecasting models can help anticipate population growth or traffic patterns, while machine learning tools can be used to optimize public transportation routes or develop more energy-efficient infrastructure.

Example 9 – Public Health: Public health organizations use statistical methods to track the spread of diseases, evaluate the effectiveness of preventative measures, and allocate resources for treatment. Forecasting models can project future healthcare needs, allowing governments to plan for adequate healthcare facilities and services. Machine learning can assist in identifying factors that contribute to disease spread or help develop targeted education campaigns.

Overall, the applications of statistics, forecasting, and machine learning are wide-ranging and have the potential to significantly improve our daily lives. Learning to integrate these methods into decision-making and problem-solving can lead to more well-informed choices and accurate predictions, ultimately benefiting individuals, businesses, and society as a whole.

Chapter 4: Applications of Data-Driven Decision Making: Demystifying the Techniques and Real-World Use Cases

In today's world, data-backed decision-making has become essential across various industries. Decision-makers are leveraging statistical methods, predictive analytics, and machine learning models to gain insights, forecast future trends, and optimize business operations. In this chapter, we will take a comprehensive look at specific real-world use cases and applications of these data-driven techniques in different sectors. But before we dive into that, let's recap some fundamental concepts that form the basis of these methods.

4.1 Recap: Statistics, Forecasting, and Machine Learning

4.1.1 Statistics

Statistics is the science that deals with the collection, analysis, interpretation, and presentation of data. It helps us understand patterns and trends in the data and make conclusions based on these observations. There are two primary branches of statistics:

1. Descriptive Statistics: Techniques to summarize and describe the features of a dataset, such as mean, mode, median, variance, and standard deviation.
2. Inferential Statistics: Techniques used to make generalizations and predictions about populations based on samples, using concepts like correlation, regression, hypothesis testing, and probability.

4.1.2 Forecasting

Forecasting uses data-driven techniques to predict future events, trends, or outcomes based on historical data. It is widely applicable in various domains, including finance, economics, meteorology, and transportation. Forecasting techniques can be broadly classified into:

1. Qualitative Methods: Such methods use expert judgment and subjective inputs to make forecasts, like the Delphi method or market research.
2. Quantitative Methods: These approaches rely on historical data and mathematical models to make predictions. Examples include time series analysis, moving averages, and exponential smoothing.

4.1.3 Machine Learning

Machine Learning (ML) is a subset of artificial intelligence that uses algorithms to learn from data, identify patterns, and make decisions or predictions without direct human intervention. ML techniques can be broadly divided into three categories:

1. Supervised Learning: Learning from labeled examples where the correct output is known, such as classification and regression. Examples include Linear Regression, Decision Trees, and Support Vector Machines.
2. Unsupervised Learning: Learning from unlabeled data to discover hidden patterns or structures, like clustering and dimensionality reduction. Examples include K-means clustering, PCA, and DBSCAN.
3. Reinforcement Learning: Learning from interacting with an environment, where an agent learns to make decisions by taking actions that maximize cumulative rewards or minimize penalties. Examples of algorithms include Q-learning and SARSA.

Now that we have a basic understanding of these concepts, let's explore their real-world applications in various domains.

4.2 Applications in Finance

4.2.1 Portfolio Optimization

Investment managers often use statistical models and machine learning algorithms to optimize their investment portfolios. They analyze historical data and correlations between the rates of return of various assets and apply optimization techniques like the Markowitz portfolio theory to maximize returns while minimizing risks.

4.2.2 Algorithmic Trading

Many trading firms use algorithms to perform high-frequency trading with the aid of statistical models and machine learning. They use time series analysis and predictive analytics to forecast market trends, identify arbitrage opportunities, and execute trading strategies with minimal human intervention.

4.3 Applications in Healthcare

4.3.1 Disease Prediction and Diagnosis

Machine learning algorithms have made it possible to predict and diagnose diseases with remarkable accuracy using medical data such as electronic health records, genomics data, and medical images. For example, deep learning models have been successful in detecting various medical conditions such as cancer, diabetes, and heart diseases based on these data sources.

4.3.2 Personalized Medicine

Advanced statistical models and machine learning techniques are helping healthcare professionals develop personalized treatments for patients. By analyzing factors like patient data, genetic information, and lifestyle habits, doctors can identify the best possible treatments tailored to the specific needs of individual patients.

4.4 Applications in Retail

4.4.1 Demand Forecasting and Inventory Management

Retailers use predictive analytics and machine learning models to forecast product demand, manage inventory, and optimize supply chain operations. Techniques such as time series analysis, regression, and clustering help retailers identify trends, seasonality, and customer preferences, ensuring that they stock the right products at the right time.

4.4.2 Customer Segmentation and Targeted Marketing

By leveraging customer data, retailers can identify distinct customer segments and tailor their marketing efforts. Machine learning algorithms like clustering and classification can help companies better understand their customers' preferences and buying behaviors, enabling targeted marketing campaigns and personalized offers to drive sales and customer loyalty.

4.5 Applications in Transportation

4.5.1 Traffic Prediction and Management

Cities and transportation agencies use historical data and predictive models to forecast traffic patterns, optimize transportation networks, and reduce congestion. Techniques such as time series analysis and machine learning models can help predict the impact of weather, special events, and road conditions on traffic flow, enabling better planning and management of transportation systems.

4.5.2 Autonomous Vehicles

Machine learning, particularly deep learning and reinforcement learning, plays a crucial role in developing advanced driver assistance systems (ADAS) and autonomous vehicles. The algorithms help vehicles perceive their environment, make decisions, and navigate safely by learning from vast amounts of data, such as images, Lidar, and radar signals.

4.6 Applications in Manufacturing

4.6.1 Quality Control and Defect Detection

Manufacturers increasingly employ machine learning techniques, such as image recognition and classification algorithms, to inspect products and detect defects automatically. This helps ensure consistent quality, reduces human inspection errors, and minimizes waste resulting from faulty products.

4.6.2 Predictive Maintenance

By analyzing sensor data and historical equipment failure data, machine learning algorithms can predict the likelihood of equipment failure and recommend optimal maintenance schedules. This proactive approach to maintenance reduces downtime, lowers maintenance costs, and improves overall equipment performance.

In conclusion, modern data-driven techniques such as statistics, forecasting, and machine learning have found numerous applications across various sectors, transforming how businesses operate and make decisions. By harnessing the power of data, decision-makers can gain valuable insights, identify trends, and make informed decisions to optimize operations, reduce costs, and drive growth.

Implementing Statistics, Forecasting, and Machine Learning in Real-Life Applications

In today's data-driven world, statistics, forecasting, and machine learning (ML) have proven to be invaluable tools for solving complex problems and improving the decision-making process across a wide range of fields, including business, finance, healthcare, and scientific research. Employing these techniques in real-life applications is not only beneficial but sometimes vital in the extraction of valuable insights from the ever-growing volumes of available data. This section discusses some steps on how to implement statistical techniques, make forecasts, and apply machine learning models in real-world applications.

Identifying the Problem

The first step in implementing any data analysis technique is to define the problem being addressed. It is essential to correctly identify the problem's objectives, scope, and potential impact. Below are some questions to help identify the problem:

- What are the goals of the analysis? Are you predicting future outcomes, seeking hidden patterns, or identifying anomalies?
- What type of data is available? Is it clean and complete, or does it need significant preprocessing?
- Who are the stakeholders involved? These could be managers, customers, or end-users.
- What is the specific domain or background knowledge that may help provide context for the analysis?

Data Acquisition and Preprocessing

After understanding the problem at hand, it is crucial to collect and preprocess the data. Data can come from a variety of sources, such as structured databases, APIs, web scraping, or manual input. Depending on the data's nature or format, it may require different preprocessing steps to prepare it for analysis, such as data cleaning, handling missing values, transforming data types, or normalization.

Choosing the Right Statistical Technique or Machine Learning Algorithm

Determining the right statistical technique or machine learning algorithm depends on the type of problem, the nature of the data, and the expected outcome. Here are some examples:

- Regression techniques, such as linear regression or support vector regression, can be used for numeric prediction problems, like forecasting sales or house prices.
- Classification algorithms, such as logistic regression or k-nearest neighbors, can be employed for predicting categorical outcomes, like customer churn, loan default, or medical diagnosis.
- Clustering techniques, such as k-means or hierarchical clustering, can be applied for unsupervised learning problems when the goal is to discover hidden patterns or grouping in data.
- Time series analysis techniques, like autoregressive integrated moving average (ARIMA), can be used for univariate time series forecasting problems.

Model Training, Evaluation, and Selection

Once the appropriate statistical or machine learning algorithm(s) are identified, it's time to train, evaluate, and select the best model(s). Here are some steps to follow:

1. **Split the dataset** into a training set for model training and a test set for evaluating the model's performance. Typically, a 7030 or 8020 train-test split ratio is frequently used.

2. **Fit the model(s)** to the training data. For machine learning algorithms, this step typically involves tuning hyperparameters and model optimization.
3. **Validate and evaluate the model(s)** using cross-validation and various performance metrics like accuracy, precision, recall, F1-score, or mean squared error.
4. **Select the best model(s)** based on performance metrics and domain-specific considerations, such as the trade-off between simplicity and complexity or interpretability and accuracy.

Model Deployment and Monitoring

After selecting the best-fitting model(s), it is essential to deploy the model(s) for real-world use. This step may involve:

- Integrating the model(s) into production systems, such as embedding machine learning models within applications or making them available through web services or APIs.
- Communicating the results of the analysis to stakeholders, like preparing reports or visualizations to explain the findings and their implications.
- Monitoring the model's performance and updating or retraining it when new data becomes available. This is important because the model's performance may degrade over time as the relevant data or problem characteristics change.

Final Takeaway

Implementing statistics, forecasting, and machine learning techniques in real-life applications may seem daunting at first glance, but breaking it down into the above steps can simplify the process. By identifying the problem, understanding the data, choosing the appropriate technique or algorithm, and deploying the model while continuously monitoring its performance, analysts and data scientists can significantly enhance decision-making and drive better insights in various real-world scenarios.

The Power of Integrating Statistics, Forecasting, and Machine Learning for Real-World Applications

In today's data-driven world, leveraging the power of statistics, forecasting, and machine learning can provide significant advantages and deeper insights into the complex problems we face on a daily basis. By applying these techniques, we can uncover hidden patterns, make more informed decisions, and develop strategies to optimize our actions for better results. This section will discuss how the integration of statistics, forecasting, and machine learning can be applied in real-world situations to arrive at beneficial solutions.

Making Data-Driven Decisions

Before we delve into the methodologies and applications of the subject, it is of paramount importance to acknowledge the pivotal role that data plays in enhancing the effectiveness of our decision-making process. Data permeates almost every aspect of our lives, whether it be in healthcare, finance, education, or any other field. Consequently, the ability to draw meaningful insights from data has become critical for decision-makers who aspire to make lasting impacts.

Using statistical analysis and machine learning techniques, we can rigorously examine data to uncover hidden patterns and relationships, derive empirical support for our hypotheses, and quantify the uncertainties associated with our decisions. As a result, businesses and organizations can become increasingly agile, basing their actions on data rather than intuition.

Forecasting with Statistical Techniques

Forecasting is the practice of making informed predictions and estimates about future events based on historical data, trends, and patterns. There are several statistical techniques that can be used for forecasting, such as time-series analysis, regression models, and exponential smoothing methods.

Time-series analysis is a popular method of forecasting that involves looking at data points collected over time to identify trends and patterns. By understanding these trends and patterns, we can extrapolate them to predict future behavior. Examples of time-series analysis include moving averages, autoregressive integrated moving average (ARIMA) models, and exponential smoothing state-space models.

Regression models, on the other hand, study the relationship between a dependent variable (i.e., the variable we want to predict) and one or more independent variables (i.e., features that help predict the dependent variable). These can include linear regression, logistic regression, and multiple regression, among others.

Machine Learning for Prediction and Optimization

Machine learning is a subset of artificial intelligence that enables computers to learn from data, usually for the purpose of making predictions or optimizing actions. In the context of real-world applications, machine learning can be classified into three major types: supervised learning, unsupervised learning, and reinforcement learning.

1. Supervised Learning: In supervised learning, we have access to a labeled dataset, where each data instance is associated with a target value or label. The goal is to learn a mapping from inputs to outputs based on this dataset. This can be used for regression tasks (predicting continuous values) or classification tasks (predicting discrete categories). Techniques used in supervised learning include linear regression, decision trees, support vector machines, and deep learning models.
2. Unsupervised Learning: In unsupervised learning, the dataset does not contain target labels, so the goal is to uncover patterns or hidden structure within the data itself. This can be particularly useful for tasks such as clustering, dimensionality reduction, or anomaly detection. Examples of unsupervised learning techniques include k-means clustering, hierarchical clustering, principal component analysis (PCA), and autoencoders.
3. Reinforcement Learning: Reinforcement learning is a type of machine learning where an agent learns to

make decisions by interacting with an environment. The agent receives feedback in the form of rewards or penalties and aims to maximize its cumulative rewards over time. This approach is especially helpful for dynamic decision-making or optimization problems, such as designing intelligent recommendation systems, optimizing manufacturing processes, or creating navigation strategies for autonomous vehicles.

Real-World Applications

The impact of integrating statistics, forecasting, and machine learning can be felt across a myriad of industries and sectors. Here are a few real-world examples:

- Healthcare: Predicting disease outbreaks, optimizing patient care plans, and estimating patient readmission risks are some ways these techniques are employed in healthcare settings.
- Finance: Many financial institutions and investment firms rely on advanced analytics to predict market trends, manage risk, and optimize investment portfolios.
- Retail: Major retailers use machine learning algorithms for better demand forecasting, price optimization, and personalized marketing campaigns.
- Manufacturing: Advanced analytics can streamline production processes by predicting machine failures, minimizing downtime, and simulating potential improvements via optimization techniques.
- Sports: Professional sports teams have started incorporating sophisticated data analysis methods to scout talent, develop game strategies, and improve player performance.

- Environment: Environmental researchers use statistical models to predict climate trends and study the ecological impact of human activities.

In conclusion, the integration of statistics, forecasting, and machine learning techniques in real-world settings offers unparalleled insights and capabilities that can greatly enhance how we understand and confront the challenges that lie ahead. By continually honing these methods and harnessing the power of data, we can drive innovation, solve complex problems, and ultimately create a better future.

2. Essential Statistics: Probability, Descriptive and Inferential Analysis

2. Essential Statistics: Probability, Descriptive and Inferential Analysis

In this section, we will introduce the fundamental concepts of probability, descriptive and inferential analysis, which are essential in the application of statistics, forecasting, and machine learning techniques for real-world problems. We will explore how these concepts lay the foundation for understanding, interpreting, and utilizing statistical measures in everyday life and various industries.

2.1 Probability

Probability is a measure of the likelihood that a particular outcome or event will occur in a given sample space. It usually ranges between 0 and 1, where 0 means the event is impossible, and 1 means the event is certain. In everyday language, we often use uncertainties like "probably" or "unlikely," which stem from the concept of probability..

Understanding probability forms the basis for the application of statistics, forecasting, and machine learning. In fields such as finance, sports, weather forecasting, and health sciences, it is valuable to determine the likelihood of an outcome, so decision-makers can make informed decisions.

Probability concepts:

- *Sample space:* It represents the set of all possible outcomes of a random experiment, usually denoted by the symbol `S`. For example, when flipping a coin, the sample space would be {Heads, Tails}.
- *Events:* Events are subsets of the sample space that describe specific outcomes of interest. An event occurs if any of its outcomes occurs in an experiment.
- *Probability rules:*
    - Rule 1: For any event A, `0 <= P(A) <= 1`
    - Rule 2: The sum of all events probabilities in a sample space should equal to 1.
    - Rule 3: If events A and B are mutually exclusive (meaning they cannot occur at the same time), then `P(A ∩ B) = 0` and `P(A ∪ B) = P(A) + P(B)`.

Probability distributions:

In many cases, applying probability to real-world problems can be approached using probability distributions. Probability distributions describe the probability of occurrence for different outcomes in an experiment. These distributions can be theoretically derived or empirically observed, and they come in two types: discrete and continuous probability distributions.

- *Discrete probability distributions:* These describe probabilities for discrete outcomes, such as flipping a coin, rolling a die, or counting the number of defective items from a production line. Common examples include the Binomial, Poisson, and Geometric distributions.
- *Continuous probability distributions:* These describe probabilities for continuous outcomes, such as measuring the height, weight, or blood pressure of individuals. Common examples include the Normal (Gaussian), Exponential, and Uniform distributions.

2.2 Descriptive Analysis

Descriptive analysis is the process of summarizing, organizing, and describing data to convey meaningful information effectively. It involves the calculation and presentation of various measures to help understand the properties, patterns, and features of a dataset. Descriptive analysis plays a crucial role in making sense of qualitative and quantitative data for decision making, performance evaluation, or visual examination.

Measures of center:

- *Mean:* The mean, or average, represents the sum of all data points divided by the total number of points, and it is a measure of the central tendency of a dataset. The mean can be influenced by extreme values, known as outliers and may not be an accurate representation of the center in skewed distributions.

- *Median:* The median is the middle value of an ordered dataset. If there is an odd number of data points, the median is the exact middle value, while for an even number of points, it is the average of the two middle values. The median is relatively immune to the effects of outliers and best used for skewed distributions.
- *Mode:* The mode represents the most frequently occurring value in a dataset. It is useful for categorical data and can also be applied to numeric data with repeated values.

Measures of dispersion:

- *Range:* The range represents the difference between the maximum and minimum values in a dataset. It gives an indication of the spread of data but is highly affected by outliers.
- *Interquartile range (IQR):* IQR is the range of values between the first quartile (25%) and the third quartile (75%) of an ordered dataset. It is a more robust measure of spread compared to the range due to its resilience to the effects of outliers.
- *Variance and standard deviation:* Variance measures the average squared distance of data points from the mean. It is helpful in assessing the dispersion of data values. The standard deviation is the square root of the variance, and it expresses dispersion in the same units as the original dataset. Both measures are sensitive to outliers and best used for symmetric distributions.
- *Coefficient of variation (CV):* The CV is the standard deviation divided by the mean, and it represents the relative variability in a dataset. It is useful for comparing the dispersion of two datasets with different means and units.

2.3 Inferential Analysis

Inferential analysis is the process of using a sample of data to make conclusions or generalize findings about a larger population. It forms the basis for hypothesis testing, confidence intervals, and model building techniques in various fields such as finance, medicine, social sciences, marketing, and engineering.

Inferential statistics concepts:

- *Population and sample:* A population represents the complete set of entities or measurements of interest, while a sample is a subset of the population that is selected for analyzing.
- *Parameter and statistic:* A parameter is a numerical summary of the population (e.g., mean or standard deviation), whereas a statistic is the corresponding numerical summary of a sample.
- *Sampling distribution:* The distribution of a statistic from multiple samples of a population is known as the sampling distribution. The Central Limit Theorem (CLT) states that the sampling distribution of the sample mean tends towards a normal distribution as the sample size increases, regardless of the shape of the population distribution.
- *Confidence intervals:* Confidence intervals provide an estimated range of values that is likely to contain the population parameter of interest. The interval is calculated based on the sample statistic, its standard error, and a specified confidence level (typically 90%, 95%, or 99%).
- *Hypothesis testing:* Hypothesis testing is a statistical procedure used to evaluate the validity of a claim or proposition about a population parameter based on sample data. It involves the formulation of a

null hypothesis (H0) and an alternative hypothesis (H1), followed by the computation of a test statistic, p-value, and a decision to accept or reject the null hypothesis.

In conclusion, probability, descriptive and inferential analysis are essential tools for applying statistics, forecasting, and machine learning techniques across various real-world scenarios. They offer valuable insights into data properties, patterns, relationships, and uncertainties, enabling informed decisions, accurate predictions, and robust models.

2.1 Probability: The Building Block of Statistical Analysis

Probability is the mathematical representation of the likelihood of an event occurring. In our fast-paced, data-driven world, understanding probability and its applications is essential for making informed decisions in various fields such as finance, healthcare, and sports, to name a few. We use probability in our everyday lives to analyze and forecast outcomes, develop strategies, and devise plans. Furthermore, probability plays an integral role in machine learning, where it is used to create and improve models to analyze data, recognize patterns, and predict future data points.

Basic Concepts

Before diving into the applications of probability, let's first familiarize ourselves with its basic concepts and terminologies:

- **Experiment**: An action or process that results in a set of possible outcomes.
- **Outcome**: The result of an experiment.
- **Sample Space**: The set of all possible outcomes of an experiment.
- **Event**: A subset of outcomes in the sample space.
- **Probability**: The measure of the likelihood that an event will occur.

The probability of an event occurring is represented as a value between 0 and 1, where 0 indicates that the event is impossible, and 1 signifies that the event is certain. To calculate the probability of an event, we can use the formula:

```
P(event) = (number of favorable outcomes) /
(total number of outcomes)
```

Applications of Probability in Real Life

Probability has numerous practical applications in various fields. Here, we discuss a few of them:

1. **Finance**: Investors and financial analysts use probability models to assess the risk and return of investment portfolios, predict stock prices, and forecast market trends. For example, they use historical data to analyze the probability of a stock reaching a certain price or a specific return on investment. Furthermore, financial institutions use probability distributions to manage risk, such as in determining loan eligibility, setting insurance premiums, and assessing credit risk.
2. **Healthcare**: Medical professionals apply probability to diagnose diseases, conduct clinical trials, and make treatment decisions. Probability is used to evaluate the effectiveness of medications, estimate disease prevalence, and assess the risk of

complications due to treatments. In addition, healthcare analysts use statistical models to predict patient outcomes and optimize hospital resources.

3. **Sports**: Teams and coaches leverage probability to analyze player performance, develop game strategies, and enhance decision-making. Sports analysts examine historical data to estimate the likelihood of specific events occurring, such as player performance in different weather conditions or the impact of a particular strategy on winning. Moreover, teams use predictive analytics to recruit the best players and maximize the likelihood of success for their franchise.
4. **Engineering and Quality Control**: Engineers rely on probability to design systems, predict equipment failure, and improve manufacturing processes. They utilize statistical techniques like Monte Carlo simulations to optimize performance and manage risk in engineering projects. In addition, companies use quality control methods like Six Sigma to identify and minimize defects in manufacturing processes based on probabilistic models.

Probability in Machine Learning and Forecasting

Machine learning is a subset of artificial intelligence, which uses statistical models to analyze data, recognize patterns, and make predictions. Probability plays an essential role in building and refining these models:

1. **Bayesian Inference**: A statistical approach based on Bayes' theorem, it combines prior knowledge (in the form of probabilities) with new data to update the probability of a hypothesis. Bayesian inference is used in various machine learning algorithms such as Naïve Bayes classifiers and Bayesian networks, which have

applications in natural language processing, spam filtering, and computer vision.

2. **Decision Trees and Random Forests**: These machine learning techniques rely on probability and entropy to make decisions based on input data. Decision trees divide the input data into branches based on specific criteria, whereas random forests use a combination of multiple decision trees to create a more accurate model.
3. **Neural Networks**: The use of probability in neural networks, such as deep learning algorithms, helps set the weights on the network connections and update them through training. Probabilistic models also contribute to assessing the uncertainty in the model's predictions.
4. **Time Series Forecasting**: Probability models like autoregressive integrated moving average (ARIMA) and state-space models are used to analyze time-series data, predict future values, and evaluate uncertainty in the forecasts. These models are applicable in various domains, such as stock market predictions, weather forecasting, and load forecasting.

In summary, probability is a fundamental building block of statistical analysis, with real-life applications across diverse fields. It is essential to understand and apply probability concepts to make informed decisions and effectively analyze data. Moreover, integrating probability into machine learning models helps enhance accuracy and handle uncertainty, equipping us with powerful tools for forecasting and decision-making.

2.1 Probability Theory: The Foundation of Statistical Analysis

Probability theory is the foundation of statistical analysis and it deals with the study of the likelihood of the occurrence of various events. It is a mathematical framework that enables us to make informed decisions and forecasts, mitigating the risks and uncertainties inherent in real-world scenarios. In this subsection, we will delve into the critical concepts of probability theory and why they are essential in statistical analysis.

2.1.1 Basics of Probability Theory

Probability theory originates from the field of mathematics and has strong ties to the principles of logic and rational reasoning. It is utilized to quantify uncertainties and is based on the following fundamental definitions:

- *Experiment*: An experiment in probability parlance is a process or an action that leads to one or several outcomes. These outcomes must be mutually exclusive, i.e., no two can occur simultaneously.
- *Sample Space*: It is the set of all possible outcomes of an experiment, usually denoted by the Greek letter Omega (Ω).
- *Event*: An event is a subset of the sample space. It is described as the specific outcome or a combination of outcomes that you are interested in observing in the experiment.

For instance, when we flip a coin, we can model it as an experiment with two possible outcomes: heads or tails. The sample space is then {Heads, Tails}, and each outcome individually is an event.

2.1.2 Probability Measures

The probability of an event is a measure of the likelihood that the event will occur, expressed as a number between 0 and 1, with 1 indicating the certainty of the event and 0, its impossibility. In the context of the coin toss example, the probability of getting a head is 0.5 and the probability of getting a tail is 0.5.

There are different methods for calculating probabilities:

1. *Empirical Probability*: It is determined by analyzing historical data or conducting experiments. The probability of an event is estimated by computing the ratio of the number of trials in which the event occurred to the total number of trials. Empirical probabilities are prone to biases and inconsistencies, especially in cases where prior information is lacking or sample sizes are small.
2. *Theoretical Probability*: It uses the principles and properties of probability theory to deduce the probabilities. Theoretical probabilities are based on analyzing the structure or the logic of the problem, without requiring any empirical observations.
3. *Subjective Probability*: It is an individual's personal estimation of the likelihood of an event, based on the individual's experience, knowledge, intuition, and emotions. Subjective probabilities are of great importance in the field of decision-making under uncertainty and can vary greatly between different individuals.

2.1.3 Probability Rules and Axioms

To reason coherently about probabilities, we need some fundamental rules and axioms that govern the relationships between different events and their probabilities. They are:

1. *Axiom of Non-Negativity*: For any event A, $P(A) \geq 0$. Probability values are always non-negative.
2. *Axiom of Unit Measure*: $P(S) = 1$, where S represents the entire sample space of all possible outcomes. The total sum of probabilities for all possible events must equal 1.
3. *Axiom of Finite Additivity*: For any two mutually exclusive events A and B, $P(A \cup B) = P(A) + P(B)$. The probability that either of the two events occurs is the sum of their probabilities.

Some crucial derived rules include:

- *Complement Rule*: The complement of an event A, denoted as A', represents the sample space's outcomes not contained in A. $P(A') = 1 - P(A)$.
- *Conditional Probability*: Given two events A and B, the conditional probability of A given that B has occurred, denoted $P(A|B)$, measures the degree to which one event's occurrence affects the other event's occurrence.
- *Independence*: Two events A and B are considered independent if the occurrence of one does not influence the other event's probability. In such cases, $P(A \cap B) = P(A) * P(B)$.

These rules and axioms provide the necessary background for performing statistical analyses involving probabilities, enabling us to understand interdependencies among variables and forecast possible outcomes.

2.1.4 Role of Probability Theory in Statistical Analysis

Probability theory is essential in statistical analysis due to its ability to address uncertainties and variability in the data comprehensively. Some ways it aids statistical analysis are:

1. *Descriptive Analysis:* Probability theory allows us to describe the behavior and properties of the data in terms of the likelihood of certain events or outcomes, utilizing probability distributions such as Gaussian or Poisson distributions.
2. *Inferential Analysis:* Probability theory lets us make inferences and generalizations about larger populations based on analyzing a sample. Techniques such as hypothesis testing and confidence intervals are rooted in probability theory.
3. *Modeling and Forecasting:* Probability theory forms the basis for predictive analysis using statistical and machine learning models. For instance, probabilistic graphical models such as Bayesian networks enable us to capture complex relationships and dependencies within the data.
4. *Decision Making Under Uncertainty:* Probability theory facilitates decision analysis by helping businesses quantify the potential risks and rewards associated with different actions, enabling them to make optimal choices.

In conclusion, probability theory is integral to understanding statistical analysis concepts and techniques. It serves as the underlying framework for dealing with uncertainty and variability in real-life scenarios, empowering us to make well-informed decisions, draw accurate inferences, and make accurate forecasts. As we continue our journey into the world of statistical analysis, forecasting and machine learning, the concepts, principles, and rules of probability will be our constant companions.

2.1 Essential Statistics: Probability, Descriptive, and Inferential Analysis

Let us dive deeper into the realm of Essential Statistics and explore the three critical components: Probability, Descriptive Analysis, and Inferential Analysis. We will elucidate the fundamental concepts, real-life applications, and their relevance to forecasting and machine learning techniques.

2.1.1 Probability

Probability provides the foundation for statistical analysis and helps quantify the likelihood of particular outcomes or events. In the context of forecasting and machine learning, it plays a pivotal role in determining the potential success of our models and techniques.

a. Key Concepts

- *Experiment*: Any action or process that generates well-defined outcomes. Examples include rolling a die, drawing a card from a deck, or launching a marketing campaign.
- *Sample Space*: The set of all possible outcomes for an experiment. For a six-sided die, the sample space would be {1, 2, 3, 4, 5, 6}.

- *Event*: A subset of the sample space representing a specific outcome or a group of outcomes. For instance, rolling an even number on a die is an event.
- *Probability*: A value between 0 and 1 that represents the likelihood of an event occurring. It is the ratio of the number of favorable outcomes to the total number of possible outcomes in the sample space.

Probability can be calculated using different methods, like classical probability, empirical probability, and subjective probability. Classical probability implies the absence of prior knowledge and equal likelihood for all outcomes, while empirical probability is derived from historical data or observed occurrences. Subjective probability, on the other hand, relies on experts' judgment or personal beliefs.

b. Real-life Applications

Probability is employed in various real-world scenarios, like risk assessment, medical diagnosis, weather forecasting, and finance. For example, in the finance sector, calculating the probability of investment returns allows professionals to create portfolios for clients that balance risk and reward optimally. Similarly, weather forecasters use probability models to predict the likelihood of rain or snow, enabling us to plan our day more efficiently.

c. Relevance to Forecasting and Machine Learning

In forecasting and machine learning, probability models enable more accurate predictions and assist in assessing the performance of our methods. For instance, in classification algorithms, the probability distribution helps determine the most likely class for a given input. Moreover, probability theory provides a foundation for advanced statistical techniques, like Bayesian statistics and Markov models, widely employed in machine learning.

2.1.2 Descriptive Analysis

Descriptive analysis aims to summarize, organize, and visualize the key features of a dataset, providing an invaluable starting point for a more thorough examination of the data.

a. Key Concepts

- *Measures of Central Tendency*: These metrics quantify the center of a dataset, including mean (arithmetic average), median (middle value), and mode (most frequent value). They provide insight into the typical or representative value of the data.
- *Measures of Dispersion or Variability*: These metrics assess the spread of data, including range (maximum-minimum), variance, and standard deviation, providing information about the diversity and heterogeneity of the dataset.
- *Measures of Distribution Shape*: These metrics describe the distribution of data in terms of symmetry (skewness) and peakedness (kurtosis), offering insights into the underlying patterns or trends.
- *Visualizations*: Graphical representations such as histograms, bar charts, scatterplots, and box plots are vital tools for illustrating the distribution and relationships within the data.

b. Real-life Applications

Descriptive analysis is employed in a wide range of fields, such as marketing, healthcare, sports, and finance. Retailers might use descriptive analysis to understand customer behavior patterns and purchasing trends, while healthcare professionals may use it to explore factors influencing patient outcomes. Descriptive statistics also form the foundation for data-driven storytelling in journalism and business intelligence.

c. Relevance to Forecasting and Machine Learning

Descriptive analysis is crucial in the initial phase of any forecasting or machine learning project, as it helps identify trends, anomalies, and relationships within the data that can inform subsequent model selection, feature engineering, and performance evaluation. Furthermore, descriptive statistics frequently serve as input features for machine learning algorithms.

2.1.3 Inferential Analysis

While descriptive analysis focuses on summarizing and illustrating the data, inferential analysis goes a step further by drawing conclusions and making predictions based on the dataset. At its core, inferential analysis encompasses techniques that allow generalization from a sample to a population.

a. Key Concepts

- *Estimation*: The process of approximating population parameters (e.g., mean, proportion) based on sample statistics. Estimates can be point estimates (single values) or interval estimates (range of values with a specified level of confidence).
- *Hypothesis Testing*: A procedure to evaluate claims or assumptions about population parameters

using sample data. It involves setting up a null hypothesis, formulating an alternative hypothesis, selecting an appropriate test statistic, computing the p-value, and making a decision based on the chosen significance level.

- *Regression Analysis*: A set of techniques used to model the relationship between a response (dependent) variable and one or more explanatory (independent) variables. Regression models, such as linear regression and logistic regression, allow predictions and estimation of the causal effect of specific factors on the response variable.
- *Non-parametric Tests*: Methods that do not rely on certain assumptions about the underlying population distribution, like the normality assumption. Non-parametric tests, like the Wilcoxonrank-sum test or Spearman's rank correlation, can be employed when parametric tests are not appropriate.

b. Real-life Applications

Inferential analysis has widespread use across various domains, like public policy, marketing, healthcare, and scientific research. For instance, drug trials use inferential techniques to determine the efficacy of new medications, while market researchers employ inferential analysis to gauge the impact of different advertising campaigns.

c. Relevance to Forecasting and Machine Learning

Inferential analysis underpins many forecasting techniques, such as time series analysis, and plays an integral part in evaluating and fine-tuning machine learning models. Hypothesis testing can be utilized to assess the significance of individual features or to compare the performance of multiple models, while regression analysis provides a means of quantifying feature importance and uncovering causal relationships in the data. Moreover, inferential concepts like sampling, confidence intervals, and error analysis are all essential for robust estimation and evaluation of forecasting and machine learning outcomes.

2.1 Probability: The Language of Uncertainty

Probability is a fundamental concept in statistics that quantifies the uncertainty associated with events or situations. It's a measure of how likely an event is to occur, and it plays a vital role in understanding and analyzing real-world phenomena. In this subsection, we'll discuss the basics of probability, its relation to randomness, and its application in statistical analysis.

2.1.1 Basic Concepts and Terminology

In probability theory, we deal with *experiments* and *events*. An experiment is a procedure that yields one or more outcomes, while an event is a specific outcome or set of outcomes of an experiment. Let's examine some examples:

- Flipping a coin: The experiment is flipping the coin, and the possible events are "heads" and "tails".
- Rolling a dice: The experiment is rolling the dice, and the possible events are "rolling a 1", "rolling a 2", and so on.

The probability of an event is expressed as a number between 0 and 1, where 0 means the event is impossible, and 1 means the event is certain. The probabilities of all possible events in an experiment always sum up to 1. Now let's define some concepts in formal terms:

- **Sample Space (S)**: The set of all possible outcomes of an experiment, e.g., S = {H, T} for flipping a coin.
- **Event (E)**: A subset of the sample space, e.g., E = {H} for the event "heads" in flipping a coin.
- **Probability (P)**: A function that assigns a number between 0 and 1 to each event in the sample space, satisfying the following axioms:

1. For any event E, 0 <= P(E) <= 1
2. P(S) = 1
3. If two events E and F are mutually exclusive (i.e., they cannot both occur simultaneously), then P(E ∪ F) = P(E) + P(F).

2.1.2 Randomness and Frequency Interpretation

The concept of a random event plays a crucial role in probability. Randomness refers to the unpredictability of an event, meaning that it is impossible to determine the exact outcome with certainty. However, the frequency interpretation of probability provides a way to understand and quantify the likelihood of random events.

In the frequency interpretation, the probability of an event is considered as the long-run relative frequency of its occurrence in a large number of trials. For example, if the probability of flipping heads on a coin is 0.5, then we expect that in a large number of tosses, half of them will result in heads. It is essential to note that the frequency interpretation does not guarantee the outcome of an individual trial; it merely gives a description of the long-run behavior of the experiment.

2.1.3 Conditional Probability and Independence

Conditional probability is a measure of the likelihood of an event occurring, given that another event has already occurred. The conditional probability of event E given that event F has occurred is denoted as P(E|F) and is defined as:

$$P(E|F) = P(E \cap F) / P(F), \text{ if } P(F) > 0.$$

Two events E and F are considered **independent** if the occurrence of one event does not affect the probability of the other event. Mathematically, two events are independent if $P(E|F) = P(E)$, or equivalently, $P(E \cap F) = P(E)P(F)$.

Independence is a crucial concept in statistical analysis as it simplifies the calculation of probabilities and allows us to make inferences about events without needing complete information about the underlying processes.

2.1.4 Bayes' Theorem

Bayes' theorem is a powerful result in probability theory that allows us to update our beliefs based on new evidence. In statistical terms, it helps us calculate the conditional probability of an event given the observed data. The theorem states that, for any events E and F:

P(E|F) = P(F|E) * P(E) / P(F), if P(F) > 0.

In practical applications, Bayes' theorem can be used in a wide range of fields, from medical diagnosis to spam filtering, and it forms the basis for Bayesian statistics, a branch of statistics that focuses on updating probabilities as new information becomes available.

2.1.5 Application: Statistical Modeling and Forecasting

Probability is at the core of statistical modeling and forecasting. By developing models that quantify the uncertainty associated with different events, we can make informed decisions and predictions based on the available data. Some applications include:

- **Risk assessment**: Analyzing the probabilities of adverse events in various industries, such as finance, insurance, and public health, allows organizations to manage risks and plan accordingly.
- **Quality control**: By using probability theory, companies can estimate the likelihood of defective products and implement strategies to improve manufacturing processes.
- **Signal processing**: In communication systems, probabilistic models help identify patterns in noisy signals and improve the accuracy of information transmission and reception.
- **Forecasting and prediction**: Probabilistic models are widely used in weather forecasting, sports

analytics, and economic projections to make predictions based on historical data.

In conclusion, probability is an indispensable tool in statistics and machine learning, allowing us to quantify uncertainty and make data-driven decisions in real-world situations. Understanding the principles of probability is crucial for effectively applying statistical methods and machine learning techniques to solve practical problems.

Analyzing and Predicting Customer Behavior

Introduction

A key aspect of running a successful business is understanding the customer. Knowing their preferences, spending habits, and how likely they are to purchase a product or service can be a game-changer when it comes to making strategic decisions. In the modern era, businesses have access to unprecedented amounts of data related to customer behavior. This data, when analyzed effectively, can provide insights that empower businesses to make informed decisions.

In this subsection, we will discuss the role of statistics, forecasting, and machine learning in analyzing and predicting customer behavior. You will learn about the different techniques and models used in these fields, as well as their real-life applications. We will start with a general overview of customer behavior analysis and then delve into specific methods and use-cases.

Customer Behavior Analysis

Customer behavior analysis is the process of examining the decisions and actions of customers regarding their interactions with products or services. This can involve tracking purchase histories, browsing behaviors on websites or apps, social media interactions, and more. Data collected from various touchpoints can be used to create a comprehensive picture of customers' preferences, which can help businesses improve their marketing strategies, product offerings, and overall customer experience.

There are several ways to analyze customer behavior, such as:

1. **Descriptive Analytics:** This approach focuses on understanding historical patterns in the data. Businesses can use descriptive analytics to summarize past customer behavior, which can help identify trends or seasonal patterns that inform decision-making.
2. **Predictive Analytics:** Predictive analytics involves using historical data to build models that can forecast future customer behavior. These models can help businesses anticipate customer needs or preferences, allowing them to proactively adapt their strategies accordingly.
3. **Prescriptive Analytics:** With prescriptive analytics, businesses can determine the best course of action by accounting for various constraints, costs, and potential outcomes. This approach helps businesses

evaluate different strategies and choose the one that will yield the best results.

Now let's take a closer look at the specific techniques used in forecasting and machine learning for analyzing customer behavior.

Statistical Forecasting Techniques for Customer Behavior

Statistical forecasting techniques involve the use of historical data to forecast future trends or patterns. Here are some commonly used methods:

1. **Moving Average:** This technique calculates the average value of a variable over a specified period of time. The moving average smooths out short-term fluctuations in the data, highlighting underlying trends. It is useful for detecting seasonal patterns or capturing overall trends in customer behavior.
2. **Exponential Smoothing:** Exponential smoothing is an extension of the moving average method but places more weight on the most recent data points. This makes it more responsive to recent changes in customer behavior and is useful for understanding shorter-term trends.
3. **Decomposition:** This technique breaks down the historical data into three components: trend, seasonality, and randomness. These components can be used to understand underlying patterns in customer behavior and inform forecasting models.
4. **Box-Jenkins (ARIMA) Model:** The Box-Jenkins model is used to describe time series data using autoregression (AR), integration (I), and moving average (MA) components. This versatile technique

can capture complex patterns in customer behavior and generate accurate forecasts.

Machine Learning Techniques for Customer Behavior Analysis

Machine learning techniques use algorithms that learn from historical data to predict or detect patterns in customer behavior. Some popular machine learning methods include:

1. **Decision Trees:** Decision trees are a type of algorithm that can classify or predict customer behavior based on a hierarchy of conditions or features. They are highly interpretable, which makes them useful for understanding the factors that drive customer decision-making.
2. **Random Forest:** Random forest is a collection of decision trees that work together to improve the accuracy of predictions. It is an efficient and accurate technique for predicting customer behavior and can handle large datasets with multiple features.
3. **Clustering:** Clustering is an unsupervised machine learning technique that groups customers based on similarities in their behavior or preferences. This can help businesses in segmentation, target marketing, and personalization efforts.
4. **Neural Networks:** Neural networks are a type of machine learning model inspired by the human brain. They can be used to predict customer behavior and preferences, but their structure can be complex and hard to interpret.

Real-Life Applications

Here are some real-life applications of how businesses use statistical forecasting and machine learning techniques to analyze customer behavior:

1. **Customer Segmentation:** Using clustering and other unsupervised learning techniques, businesses can group customers based on their preferences, behavior, demographics, and other characteristics. This helps in creating targeted marketing campaigns, improving customer experience, and creating personalized offers.
2. **Customer Churn Prediction:** Churn prediction models can help businesses identify customers who are likely to stop using their products or services. By understanding the factors that contribute to churn, businesses can take proactive steps to mitigate it, such as improving customer support or tailoring marketing efforts.
3. **Product Recommendations:** Collaborative filtering and other recommendation algorithms can be used to suggest products or services that are relevant to a specific customer, based on their preferences and past behavior. This can improve the overall customer experience and increase sales.
4. **Sales Forecasting:** By leveraging statistical models and machine learning algorithms, businesses can predict future sales volumes with more accuracy. Accurate sales forecasts enable better production planning, resource allocation, and pricing strategies.
5. **Marketing Campaign Optimization:** Businesses can use machine learning algorithms to optimize their marketing campaigns, determining the strategies that resonate best with their target audience. This can lead to higher returns on investment, increased customer engagement, and improved brand loyalty.

Conclusion

Understanding and predicting customer behavior is crucial if a business wants to thrive in today's competitive market. Statistical forecasting and machine learning techniques offer powerful ways to analyze, understand, and predict customer behavior, helping businesses make informed decisions to improve their products, services, marketing strategies, and overall customer experience.

As more and more data becomes available, it is essential for businesses to invest in the skills, tools, and knowledge necessary to effectively apply these techniques in real-life scenarios. By doing so, they will be better positioned to adapt to the rapidly changing landscape and stay ahead of the competition.

Combining Statistical Techniques, Forecasting Methods, and Machine Learning Models for Optimal Solutions

In real-world applications, it is often beneficial to integrate statistical techniques, forecasting methods, and machine learning models to develop robust and optimal solutions for various scenarios. This subsection will outline how these approaches can work together powerfully in practice, enhancing the effectiveness of each tool.

Data Exploration and Preparation

Before applying any statistical or predictive models, it is essential to explore and understand the underlying data, which involves:

1. **Data Cleaning and Pre-processing**: This phase includes handling missing values, removing duplicates, correcting inconsistencies, and detecting outliers. Using statistical techniques like median imputation, interquartile ranges, or z-scores can help address these issues effectively.
2. **Data Transformation**: Applying transformations, such as log transformations or Box-Cox transformations, can stabilize the variance and reduce the skewness of data, which ultimately enhances the performance of the predictive models.
3. **Feature Engineering**: Creating relevant features from raw data is essential for efficient machine learning models. Techniques like one-hot encoding, normalization, and dimensionality reduction using Principal Component Analysis (PCA) or other statistical methods can be applied to create effective features.

Descriptive and Inferential Statistics

Descriptive statistics serve as the foundation for data analysis by providing a summary of the data, while inferential statistics use sample data to make predictions about the population. These techniques can help identify critical patterns and trends within the data, which can, in turn, support the selection of appropriate forecasting methods or machine learning models. Examples of techniques to use include:

1. **Central Tendency and Dispersion Measures**: Mean, median, mode, variance, and standard

deviation can provide valuable information about the data distribution, allowing for better understanding and model selection.

2. **Hypothesis Testing**: Techniques like t-tests, chi-square tests, and ANOVA can help assess the statistical significance of observed patterns or differences between groups, which could influence the features chosen for the predictive models.
3. **Correlation and Regression Analysis**: Identifying relationships between variables, either linear or non-linear, can be vital for selecting the most suitable model and ensuring the validity of predictions.

Time Series Analysis and Forecasting

Time series data, which is a sequence of observations collected over time, often requires specialized techniques for analysis and forecasting, as it exhibits particular characteristics like seasonality, trends, and noise. Examples of widely used methods include:

1. **Exponential Smoothing**: An approach that applies different weights to past observations, with more recent observations receiving higher importance. Techniques like Simple Exponential Smoothing, Holt's Linear Trend method, and Holt-Winters Seasonal method can be used depending on the time series data's characteristics.
2. **ARIMA (AutoRegressive Integrated Moving Average)**: A popular statistical method that combines auto-regression, moving average, and differencing to model and forecast time series data.

3. **Prophet**: An open-source forecasting tool developed by Facebook, designed to handle the common features of time series data automatically.

Machine Learning Models

In addition to traditional statistics and forecasting techniques, machine learning algorithms can be used to make predictions based on complex patterns within the data. Examples of popular machine learning models include:

1. **Linear and Logistic Regression**: Simple yet powerful techniques used primarily for regression and classification tasks. They can be enhanced with regularization techniques like Lasso and Ridge regression for better performance.
2. **Decision Trees and Random Forests**: Non-linear models constructed using a set of decision rules that can handle both regression and classification tasks. Random forests improve on this technique by constructing multiple trees and aggregating their results.
3. **Neural Networks and Deep Learning**: Highly flexible models that can approximate complex functions and adapt to a wide range of data types, including images, text, and time series.

Model Evaluation and Selection

After developing multiple models using the aforementioned techniques, it is crucial to evaluate and select the one that provides the best performance for the task at hand. Measures like Root Mean Squared Error (RMSE), Mean Absolute Error (MAE), and R-squared can be used to compare models and choose the best-fitting one.

Moreover, cross-validation methods, such as k-fold cross-validation or time series cross-validation, can help estimate the performance of a model on unseen data by splitting the dataset and training the model on different subsets.

Conclusion

Integrating statistical techniques, forecasting methods, and machine learning models can significantly enhance the overall effectiveness of solving real-world problems. By understanding and preparing the data, selecting suitable techniques, and evaluating the performance of models, it is possible to derive optimal solutions adaptable to unique situations in various fields, such as finance, healthcare, and transportation, among others.

Real-World Applications of Statistics, Forecasting, and Machine Learning

In recent years, the growing ubiquity of data and the rapid advancement in technology have led to a significant increase in demand for individuals skilled in the areas of statistics, forecasting, and machine learning. These disciplines are crucial in a wide range of real-world applications, spanning various industries, and sectors. In this subsection, we will discuss several prominent examples of how these techniques are being applied in real-life settings, driving innovation, informing decision-making, and shaping our understanding of the world around us.

Healthcare

The application of statistics, forecasting, and machine learning in healthcare has revolutionized the industry and saved countless lives. These techniques play a vital role in various aspects of healthcare, such as diagnostics, treatment planning, and personalized medicine.

- **Diagnostics**: Machine learning algorithms, particularly deep learning models, have shown impressive results in diagnosing various illnesses like cancers, heart diseases, and neurodegenerative disorders based on medical imaging data. These algorithms can analyze complex patterns within the images to identify early signs of disease, leading to early interventions and improved patient outcomes.
- **Treatment Planning**: Another area where these techniques are making an impact is in the development of personalized treatment plans for patients. Machine learning algorithms can analyze vast amounts of medical data to ascertain an individual patient's response to different treatments. This allows healthcare professionals to create tailored treatment recommendations that are more likely to be effective and have fewer side effects.
- **Forecasting Epidemics**: The ability to predict the spread of infectious diseases is essential for effective public health management. Statistical models and machine learning techniques are extensively used to forecast epidemics, identify hotspots, and develop strategic intervention plans. This was particularly

evident during the COVID-19 pandemic when researchers from around the world utilized these methods to predict the disease's progression patterns and assess the effectiveness of various mitigation strategies.

Finance

The finance industry is another domain where statistics, forecasting, and machine learning have demonstrated significant promise. Financial institutions and investors rely heavily on these techniques to inform their decision-making processes and minimize risk exposure.

- **Credit Scoring**: Lending institutions use statistical models and machine learning algorithms to evaluate the creditworthiness of potential borrowers. Factors such as credit history, income level, and outstanding debts are fed into the model to produce a credit score that helps lenders determine the likelihood of default.
- **Portfolio Management**: Machine learning algorithms are commonly employed to optimize investment portfolios and manage risk. These models can analyze historical financial data and apply various forecasting techniques to predict the future performance of different assets. This informs investment strategies that seek to maximize returns while adhering to specified risk tolerance levels.
- **Algorithmic Trading**: High-frequency and algorithmic trading are increasingly dominating financial markets. These trading systems leverage statistics and machine learning to identify patterns in market data, inform trading decisions, and execute orders at lightning-fast speeds. The use of these techniques has transformed the dynamics of global

financial markets by improving liquidity and reducing transaction costs.

Marketing

One of the most rapidly evolving applications of statistics, forecasting, and machine learning is in the field of marketing. Businesses are leveraging these techniques to understand consumer behavior, inform marketing strategies, and optimize overall performance.

- **Customer Segmentation**: Machine learning algorithms are used to analyze vast amounts of demographic, behavioral, and transactional data to identify similarities among customers. These similarities are then used to group customers into segments, allowing marketers to design targeted advertising campaigns that resonate better with different audiences.
- **Sentiment Analysis**: Sentiment analysis, a subfield of natural language processing, is used to gauge public opinion on a particular product, service, or idea by analyzing text data, such as social media posts and product reviews. This information allows marketers to identify opportunities and address possible concerns before they escalate.
- **Demand Forecasting**: Accurate demand forecasting is crucial for effective inventory management and resource allocation. Statistical models and machine learning techniques enable businesses to predict future demand for products and services by analyzing historical sales data, economic trends, and other relevant factors. This allows companies to make more informed decisions and avoid potential pitfalls.

This is but a glimpse of the many real-world applications of statistics, forecasting, and machine learning. As data continues to grow at an exponential rate, and technologies advance further, the potential of these techniques in transforming industries and improving lives will likely only continue to expand. There has never been a better or more exciting time to dive into the world of data, algorithms, and probability.

Leveraging Statistics, Forecasting, and Machine Learning in Real-World Applications

In today's data-driven world, making evidence-based decisions is paramount. By leveraging the power of statistics, forecasting, and machine learning, individuals and organizations can gain actionable insights and make more informed choices. This section will explore several real-world applications of these techniques, highlighting their practicality and effectiveness in various industries and situations.

Sales and Demand Forecasting

One of the most common applications for statistics and forecasting is predicting future sales and demand for products or services. Retailers, manufacturers, and service providers alike can benefit from accurate forecasts to optimize inventory management, production planning, and resource allocation.

Methods such as time series analysis, regression models, and machine learning algorithms (e.g., ARIMA, exponential smoothing, and neural networks) can be employed to analyze historical data, identify patterns and trends, and generate forecasts. These techniques enable businesses to make data-driven decisions, reduce operational costs, and improve customer satisfaction by ensuring the availability of products and services.

Marketing and Customer Segmentation

Understanding customer behavior is critical for developing effective marketing strategies. By applying clustering algorithms, classification models, and other machine learning techniques, marketers can segment customers into groups with similar characteristics, preferences, and purchasing habits.

This targeted approach allows organizations to tailor their marketing messages, promotional offers, and product recommendations for each segment, resulting in higher conversion rates and increased customer loyalty. Additionally, advanced machine learning models can be used to analyze customer sentiment and track brand reputation on social media platforms, enabling businesses to make data-driven decisions on product development and public relations strategies.

Healthcare and Medical Research

Statistics, forecasting, and machine learning play crucial roles in the healthcare industry. From analyzing clinical trial data to predicting disease outbreaks, these techniques are pivotal in driving medical advancements and improving patient outcomes.

For example, machine learning algorithms can be used to predict disease progression and develop personalized treatment plans for patients with chronic conditions, such as diabetes or cancer. Furthermore, statistical analysis of electronic health records can reveal correlations between patient characteristics, treatments, and outcomes, enabling researchers to identify potential risk factors and develop targeted interventions.

Finance and Risk Management

In the finance sector, the use of statistics and machine learning is extensive. Investment firms employ predictive algorithms to forecast market trends and inform investment decisions, while banks and credit institutions use machine learning models to assess the creditworthiness of clients and predict the likelihood of loan default.

Risk management, in particular, relies heavily on statistical analysis and forecasting. For instance, Value at Risk (VaR) models are widely used to estimate potential losses in a given portfolio, enabling financial managers to make more informed decisions about asset allocation and risk mitigation strategies.

Manufacturing Quality Control and Predictive Maintenance

Ensuring product quality and maintaining equipment availability are critical factors for success in the manufacturing sector. By harnessing the power of statistics, forecasting, and machine learning, companies can optimize both aspects.

Statistical methods, such as control charts and hypothesis testing, can be used to monitor manufacturing processes in real-time, detect anomalies and deviations, and signal when corrective action is required. Machine learning algorithms can also be applied to predict equipment failure and estimate maintenance requirements based on sensor data, preventing costly shutdowns and increasing operational efficiency.

Transportation and Logistics Optimization

In transportation and logistics, sophisticated algorithms and forecasting techniques are key in reducing costs, improving service delivery, and optimizing operations. Flight-prediction models, for example, can provide guidance on optimal flight paths, taking into account factors such as weather conditions and air traffic.

Similarly, logistics companies employ routing algorithms and demand forecasting models to plan optimal delivery routes and ensure efficient utilization of resources. Recent developments in machine learning and artificial intelligence, such as autonomous vehicles and intelligent traffic management systems, promise even greater advancements in this domain.

In conclusion, the applications of statistics, forecasting, and machine learning are vast and varied, spanning a wide range of industries and use cases. By applying these techniques to real-world problems, businesses and organizations can unlock valuable insights, improve decision-making, and increase efficiency, ultimately leading to better outcomes and results.

Section: Applying Statistics, Forecasting and Machine Learning IRL

Subsection: Real-Life Use Cases and Practical Tips

In today's ever-evolving digital landscape, the application of statistics, forecasting, and machine learning proves essential in a wide range of real-life scenarios. From healthcare to finance, these proactive approaches have brought significant improvements to various sectors, empowering organizations to extract valuable insights from available data. This subsection aims to provide an overview of practical use cases for these technologies and offer some tips for their successful implementation.

1. Healthcare

Use case: Disease diagnosis & treatment

Machine learning techniques, particularly deep learning, have shown great promise in transforming the way medical professionals diagnose and treat various health conditions. For example, image recognition models have been successfully employed to identify tumors in medical scans, enabling better prediction and earlier intervention.

Practical tips:

- Collaborate with healthcare professionals to understand specific diagnostic and treatment needs.
- Ensure compliance with data protection regulations like HIPAA.
- Invest in high-quality training data and use cross-validation to assess model performance.

2. Finance

Use case: Fraud detection & risk management

Financial institutions often rely on advanced statistical models and machine learning algorithms to identify suspicious transactions and assess the risks associated with lending and investment decisions. By leveraging historical transaction data and other relevant information, these models can detect patterns that suggest fraudulent activity or potential credit risk.

Practical tips:

- Regularly update your models with new data to maintain effectiveness against evolving fraud strategies.
- Utilize ensemble methods to combine the strengths of various algorithms and improve overall performance.
- Understand the specific risks involved in different financial products, and adjust models accordingly.

3. Retail

Use case: Demand forecasting

Accurate demand forecasting plays a crucial role in ensuring efficient inventory management and distribution processes. By analyzing historical sales data, along with external factors like seasonal trends and competitor activities, statistical models and machine learning techniques can predict future demand, allowing retailers to optimize order quantities and allocate resources effectively.

Practical tips:

- Incorporate external factors such as holidays, competitor promotions, and product life cycles into your forecasting model.
- Regularly review your model's performance to identify opportunities for improvement.
- Use multiple forecasting techniques, such as time series analysis and machine learning algorithms, to increase accuracy.

4. Marketing

Use case: Customer segmentation & targeting

Companies can segment their customer base by analyzing data like demographics, purchase behavior, and engagement patterns with advanced statistical techniques and machine learning algorithms. This allows for better targeting of marketing campaigns, ensuring that promotional efforts resonate with the intended audience, resulting in improved customer satisfaction and retention.

Practical tips:

- Begin with a simple segmentation approach, such as clustering or decision trees, and gradually move to more advanced techniques.
- Regularly re-evaluate your customer segments to account for changes in consumer behavior and preferences.
- Integrate your segmentation insights into various aspects of your business, from product development to customer service.

5. Transportation

Use case: Traffic prediction & route optimization

Transportation organizations often use statistical models and machine learning techniques to analyze traffic patterns and predict congestion levels. Such forecasts can help reduce traffic jams, improve the efficiency of public transportation systems, and enhance route planning.

Practical tips:

- Incorporate real-time data, such as weather conditions and events, into your traffic prediction models.
- Use location-based data to improve route optimization algorithms.
- Collaborate with urban planning and transportation experts to understand changes in transportation infrastructure that may impact your models.

6. Manufacturing

Use case: Predictive maintenance

Combining sensor data with historical maintenance records and using machine learning algorithms, manufacturers can accurately predict equipment failures and other maintenance issues. This empowers them to schedule maintenance activities proactively, preventing costly downtime and ensuring optimal performance of the production line.

Practical tips:

- Carefully select features and sensors that deliver relevant data for predictive maintenance.
- Train your machine learning models on diverse sets of maintenance scenarios to ensure robust performance.
- Pay attention to the interpretability of your models, as this can help build trust among maintenance teams and facilitate adoption.

By understanding the real-life use cases of statistical models, forecasting, and machine learning techniques, and following the practical tips outlined in this subsection, professionals across various sectors can optimize processes, adapt to change, and navigate the complexities of today's digital landscape with greater confidence.

3. Time Series Analysis and Forecasting Techniques

3. Time Series Analysis and Forecasting Techniques

Time series analysis and forecasting are essential techniques used across various fields, including finance, economics, ecology, and meteorology. These techniques allow practitioners to analyze and predict trends and patterns in sequential data, making them invaluable tools for decision-making and risk management.

In this section, we will discuss popular time series analysis and forecasting methods, their applications in the real world, and the role of machine learning in these techniques.

3.1 Intro to Time Series Analysis

A time series is a sequence of data points indexed in time order. Time series analysis encompasses the methods used for extracting meaningful statistics and other characteristics from observed time series data.

The main goal of time series analysis is to understand the underlying structure and patterns within the data, which can then be used to make informed forecasts.

There are two main components to time series analysis:

1. *Trend analysis*: This involves examining the long-term movement or direction of the series as a whole.
2. *Seasonal analysis*: This involves discovering recurring patterns in the series—such as cyclical variations or periodic fluctuations—over a fixed time span (e.g., daily, weekly, monthly, or yearly).

Real-world applications of time series analysis include stock price prediction, sales forecasting, weather forecasting, and energy consumption estimation.

3.2 Time Series Forecasting Techniques

There are numerous techniques to choose from when performing time series forecasting. Here, we will explore some of the most popular approaches and their respective advantages and disadvantages.

1. *Autoregression (AR)*: The autoregressive model assumes that the current value of a time series depends linearly on its past values. The autoregression model helps describe the autocorrelation structure of the series and can be used for short-term forecasting.
2. *Moving Averages (MA)*: The moving average model is used to smooth out the series, reducing noise and identifying underlying trends. It involves calculating the mean of a rolling window in the series, which can help detect patterns and trends over time. It is a simple technique and might not capture complex patterns in time series data.
3. *Exponential Smoothing*: Exponential smoothing is a time series forecasting method that assigns exponentially decreasing weights to past observations. The main advantage of this technique is that it is more sensitive to recent changes in data patterns than simple moving average models.
4. *ARIMA (Autoregressive Integrated Moving Average)*: ARIMA is a class of linear models that combines the techniques of autoregression and moving averages. It is designed to handle stationary time series data and can be applied to univariate time series data. It requires careful tuning of parameters, which might be challenging for practitioners.
5. *Seasonal Decomposition of Time Series (STL)*: STL is a method that decomposes a time series into trend, seasonal, and residual components. It helps

identify and quantify underlying components, making it easier to build forecasting models based on the decomposed time series.

6. *Prophet*: Developed by Facebook, Prophet is an open-source time series forecasting library based on additive regression models. It's designed to handle time series data with seasonality, holidays, and other special events. It is especially useful for business time series data, providing an accurate and flexible forecasting solution.

3.3 Machine Learning for Time Series Forecasting

Machine learning models have become increasingly popular in time series forecasting due to their ability to learn complex patterns and non-linear dependencies in the data. Some common machine learning models used for time series forecasting include:

1. *Recurrent Neural Networks (RNNs)*: RNNs are a type of artificial neural network designed to process sequential data. They are particularly well-suited for time series forecasting, as they can learn patterns at different time scales and account for long-term dependencies in the data.
2. *Long Short-Term Memory (LSTM) Networks*: LSTM is a type of RNN architecture that addresses the challenges of capturing long-term dependencies in time series data. LSTM networks have been widely used in applications such as sales forecasting, stock price prediction, and weather forecasting.
3. *Convolutional Neural Networks (CNNs)*: Although primarily employed in image recognition tasks, CNNs have proven effective at time series forecasting, especially when dealing with multivariate time series data. By processing local temporal patterns, CNNs can

capture hierarchical features and dependencies in the time series data.

4. *Support Vector Machines (SVMs)*: SVMs are a class of discriminative classifiers widely used for their ability to handle high-dimensional data. They have also been applied to time series forecasting, where they can be combined with kernels and feature extraction techniques to predict future values.
5. *Ensemble Methods*: Ensemble methods combine multiple base models to improve the accuracy and robustness of time series forecasts. Examples of ensemble methods include bagging, boosting, and stacking, which blend the strengths of individual models to create a more powerful predictor.

In conclusion, time series analysis and forecasting techniques are essential tools for understanding and predicting trends and patterns in sequential data. Whether using traditional statistical methods or more advanced machine learning approaches, these techniques provide invaluable insights in various fields, driving intelligent decision-making and improving our ability to anticipate future events.

3. Time Series Analysis and Forecasting Techniques

Time Series Analysis is the study of data points, ordered sequentially either over time or space. In general, time series analysis focuses on analyzing the patterns and trends in the data to make meaningful interpretations, understand the driving force behind the observed behavior, and make accurate predictions and forecasts for future data points. Time-series analysis is used extensively in numerous fields, including economics, finance, medicine, meteorology, and social sciences.

In this section, we will dive into various techniques of Time Series Analysis and Forecasting, discussing their theory, use-cases, benefits, and limitations.

3.1 Components of Time Series Data

Before diving into various techniques, we need to understand the components of time-series data. The following four components are generally observed in time series data:

1. **Trend**: The overall progression of the time series data over time, either increasing or decreasing.
2. **Seasonality**: A repeating pattern or variation over fixed periods, usually due to the calendar or the season (e.g., monthly or quarterly fluctuations).
3. **Cyclical**: Fluctuations with no fixed period, which are caused by non-seasonal events such as business cycles or market conditions.
4. **Irregular noise**: Residual variations or fluctuations which cannot be attributed to any of the above components and are considered random.

3.2 Smoothing Techniques

Smoothing techniques in time series analysis are designed to remove noise and variation within the data, helping to identify the underlying trend, seasonality, and cyclical components.

- **Moving Average**: This method computes the average of data points within a specified window, effectively smoothing out short-term fluctuations and identifying the long-term trends.

- **Exponentially Weighted Moving Average**: Similar to the moving average, but assigns more weight to recent data points, thus giving a more accurate representation of the latest trends.
- **Seasonal Adjustment**: This technique applies corrections to the time series data considering seasonal components, aiming to discern the underlying trend and cyclical components more accurately.

3.3 Autoregressive Integrated Moving Average (ARIMA)

ARIMA is a popular statistical model for forecasting and understanding time-series data. It combines the components of AutoRegressive models (AR), Moving Average models (MA), and the concept of differencing to stationarize the data.

- **Autoregressive (AR)**: Predicts the value of a variable based on its previous values. Mathematically, it is the linear combination of previous data points, multiplied by specific coefficients.
- **Moving Average (MA)**: Uses a similar mathematical approach to predict values based on the previous errors or residuals in the data. The errors from the previous forecasts are used to adjust the current forecast.
- **Integrated (I)**: Represents the differencing order needed to make the data stationary. Stationarity is essential in most time-series analysis techniques, as it reduces the effects of trends and seasonality, allowing us to focus on the inherent pattern of the data.

ARIMA models are particularly useful when the data has a linear pattern, stationary, and has no missing values.

3.4 Seasonal Decomposition of Time Series (STL)

STL is a technique that decomposes a time series into three components: trend, seasonal, and residual (remainder). It uses smoothing methods such LOESS (Locally Estimated Scatterplot Smoothing) to estimate each component.

- **LOESS smoothing**: A non-parametric regression method that combines multiple linear models in a k-nearest-neighbor-based meta-model. It is particularly useful for analyzing non-linear patterns and creating accurate and smooth trend curves.

After decomposing the time series data using STL, we can analyze and forecast each component separately, providing a more accurate and comprehensive understanding of the underlying patterns and future behavior.

3.5 Long Short-Term Memory Network (LSTM)

LSTM is a type of recurrent neural network (RNN) designed to learn long-term dependencies and patterns in time-series data. This machine learning model is particularly useful for handling large datasets with complex patterns and non-linear relationships.

LSTMs work by maintaining a hidden state that evolves over time, as new data points are added. The model adjusts its weights and biases as it learns the sequence of data, allowing it to incorporate long-term dependencies into its predictions effectively.

LSTMs have found significant use in various applications, including speech recognition, natural language processing, and financial forecasting, due to their ability to capture intricate patterns and sequence dynamics.

3.6 Facebook Prophet

Prophet is an open-source time-series forecasting library developed by Facebook. It is built on top of the popular statistical programming language R and Python, making it easy to use and integrate with existing data-analysis pipelines.

Prophet uses an additive regression model to create forecasts by combining a piecewise linear or logistic growth curve trend, a yearly seasonal component, and a weekly seasonal component. It also has features to handle holidays and special events, providing more accurate forecasts for irregular time series.

Prophet's simplicity, flexibility, and robustness have made it popular among both beginners and experienced practitioners, allowing them to analyze and forecast a wide variety of time series data.

In conclusion, time series analysis and forecasting are essential tools for understanding data and predicting future trends. The techniques discussed in this section can be applied to various industries and use-cases, providing valuable insights and improving decision-making. By understanding the underlying principles and limitations of each method, we can more effectively apply these techniques in our work and further our understanding of the complex patterns and dynamics of real-world data.

3. Time Series Analysis and Forecasting Techniques

Time series analysis and forecasting techniques are critical components in numerous real-world applications, ranging from economics to weather prediction, sales forecasting, and even healthcare. This subsection will delve into various time series analysis and forecasting techniques used in real-life settings, as well as their importance and functionality.

3.1 Understanding Time Series Data

Before diving into the techniques, it is crucial to familiarize yourself with time series data. Time series data is a sequence of data points collected at consistent time intervals. For example, daily stock prices or monthly sales figures are time series data. Time series analysis aims to uncover hidden patterns and trends within the data, which can then be leveraged to forecast future values.

3.2 Techniques for Time Series Analysis

There are numerous techniques for time series analysis, each offering unique insights and forecasting capabilities. The following methods are widely used in real-life applications:

3.2.1 Autoregressive (AR) Model

An autoregressive model assumes that the current value of a time series can be estimated using a linear combination of previous values. This technique is often used in applications such as finance and economics, where historical trends are important in making predictions. The AR model can be used for short-term forecasts but has limitations when applied to longer-term predictions.

3.2.2 Moving Average (MA) Model

A moving average model calculates the average of data points within a specified window in the time series. By "smoothing" the data, moving averages can help to eliminate noise and reveal underlying trends. It is often employed to interpret time series in sales and finance, where revealing seasonal patterns and trends is crucial.

3.2.3 Autoregressive Integrated Moving Average (ARIMA) Model

ARIMA combines the benefits of both the AR and MA models. It includes differencing the time series to make it stationary—for example, removing seasonality and trends that may be present. This technique is versatile and can handle various time series data types, making it widely used for forecasting purposes.

3.2.4 Exponential Smoothing State Space Model (ES)

Exponential smoothing encompasses several forecasting techniques that assign different weights to past observations, typically decreasing the weight as the observation gets older. The simple exponential smoothing, double exponential smoothing (Holt's method), and triple exponential smoothing (Holt-

Winters method) are examples of exponential smoothing techniques. They are extensively employed in business, finance, and economics for accurate short-term forecasts.

3.2.5 Machine Learning Models

Machine learning techniques, such as Long Short-Term Memory (LSTM) and Gated Recurrent Unit (GRU) neural networks, can also be adopted for time series analysis and forecasting. These deep learning models have gained popularity in recent years due to their ability to model complex patterns and large datasets. They are frequently used in applications where heavy computational resources are available and high-precision forecasts are desired.

3.3 Forecasting Techniques in Action: Real-World Applications

3.3.1 Weather Forecasting

Weather forecasting heavily employs time series analysis to predict future meteorological conditions. Techniques such as AR models, exponential smoothing, and deep learning models help forecast temperatures, precipitation, and other weather variables by leveraging previous weather data.

3.3.2 Stock Market Prediction

In the finance sector, time series analysis techniques are essential for forecasting stock prices, exchange rates, and market trends. By using historical data to predict future values, traders and investors can make informed decisions to minimize risk and maximize returns.

3.3.3 Economic Forecasting

Economic indicators such as GDP, inflation, and employment rates are frequently modeled using time series analysis. By analyzing historical data and identifying trends, policymakers and economists can develop better strategies for economic growth and stability.

3.3.4 Healthcare

Time series analysis plays a crucial role in healthcare, helping forecast disease prevalence, patient admissions, and resources required in hospitals. In the context of disease prevention, time series models can aid in detecting potential outbreaks, enabling healthcare professionals to respond quickly and effectively.

3.3.5 Supply Chain Management and Demand Forecasting

Businesses use time series analysis to predict future demand for their products, allowing them to optimize inventory levels, manufacturing schedules, and marketing strategies. By employing techniques such as ARIMA and machine learning models, companies can make confident decisions based on accurate demand forecasts.

In conclusion, time series analysis and forecasting techniques are indispensable tools in a wide variety of real-world applications. Becoming proficient in these methods will enhance your skills in data analysis and predictive modeling, allowing you to unlock the hidden potential of time series data in various fields.

3. Time Series Analysis and Forecasting Techniques

Time series analysis is a statistical technique used to study and analyze a series of data points, collected over discrete and equally spaced time intervals. The primary objective of time series analysis is to extract meaningful insights, identify patterns, trends, and seasonality in the data, and forecast future data points based on historical patterns.

In this section, we will discuss the following time series analysis and forecasting techniques, widely used across industries and applications, including finance, economics, marketing, and quantitative analysis:

3.1 Autoregressive (AR) Models

An autoregressive (AR) model is a linear model that uses previous data points (lagged values) to forecast future values. The primary assumption in AR models is that the current value of the variable is linearly dependent on its previous values. Autoregressive models are commonly used in various fields, such as finance, economics, and engineering, for analyzing and forecasting time-series data.

The basic equation for an autoregressive model of order *p* (AR(p)) is defined as:

$Y_t = c + \phi_1Y_{t-1} + \phi_2Y_{t-2} + \dots + \phi_pY_{t-p} + \epsilon_t$

Where:

- Y_t is the value of the time series at time *t*
- *c* is the constant term
- $\phi_1, \phi_2, \dots, \phi_p$ are the model's parameters
- $Y_{t-1}, Y_{t-2}, \dots, Y_{t-p}$ are the previous values of the time series
- ϵ_t is the error term at time *t*

3.2 Moving Average (MA) Models

Moving average (MA) models are another popular linear forecasting technique used for time-series data. Instead of using previous observations like AR models, MA models use past error terms for forecasting future data points. MA models assume that the current value is a linear combination of previous error terms, which can be interpreted as "shocks" or "noise" in the time series data.

The basic equation for a moving average model of order *q* (MA(q)) is defined as:

$Y_t = \mu + \epsilon_t + \theta_1\epsilon_{t-1} + \theta_2\epsilon_{t-2} + \dots + \theta_q\epsilon_{t-q}$

Where:

- Y_t is the value of the time series at time *t*

- μ is the constant term (mean of the time series)
- $\theta_1, \theta_2, \dots, \theta_q$ are the model's parameters
- $\epsilon_{t-1}, \epsilon_{t-2}, \dots, \epsilon_{t-q}$ are the previous error terms
- ϵ_t is the error term at time t

3.3 Autoregressive Integrated Moving Average (ARIMA) Models

Autoregressive Integrated Moving Average (ARIMA) models combine both autoregressive (AR) and moving average (MA) components, and also take into account the differencing process to make the time series stationary (i.e., constant mean and variance over time). ARIMA models are particularly useful for forecasting non-stationary time series data with a well-defined trend and/or seasonality components.

The ARIMA model is defined by three parameters: p (order of the autoregressive term), d (degree of differencing), and q (order of the moving average term). An ARIMA(p, d, q) model can be expressed as:

$(1-\Sigma \phi_iL^i)(1-L)^d Y_t = \mu + (1+\Sigma \theta_jL^j)\epsilon_t$

Where:

- Y_t is the value of the time series at time t
- L is the lag operator (e.g., $L^1Y_t = Y_{t-1}$)
- ϕ_i are the autoregressive parameters
- θ_j are the moving average parameters
- d is the degree of differencing
- ϵ_t is the error term at time t

- μ is the constant term

3.4 Seasonal Decomposition of Time Series (STL)

Seasonal decomposition of time series (STL) is a technique used to separate time series data into multiple components, such as trend, seasonal, and residual components. STL is particularly useful for analyzing seasonality patterns in time series data and making adjustments to forecasts for seasonal effects.

The STL decomposition can be represented as:

$Y_t = T_t + S_t + R_t$

Where:

- Y_t is the value of the time series at time *t*
- T_t is the trend component at time *t*
- S_t is the seasonal component at time *t*
- R_t is the residual component at time *t*

3.5 Exponential Smoothing State Space Model (ETS)

Exponential smoothing state space models (ETS) are a family of forecasting models that extend upon the exponential smoothing techniques with state space modeling. ETS models can handle various types of time series patterns, such as additive or multiplicative trends and seasonalities. The primary advantage of using ETS models is their ability to produce accurate short-term forecasts with relatively lower computational complexity compared to other advanced techniques.

ETS models can be categorized into three main components:

- Level (denoted by *l*): The persistent or long-term value of the time series
- Trend (denoted by *b*): The slope or change in the level component over time
- Seasonal (denoted by *s*): The periodic or repeating pattern in the time series

The state space representation of an ETS model is given by:

$Y_t = l_{t-1} + \alpha \epsilon_t$ $l_t = l_{t-1} + b_{t-1} + \alpha \epsilon_t$ $b_t = b_{t-1} + \beta \epsilon_t$

Where:

- Y_t is the value of the time series at time *t*
- l_t is the level at time *t*
- b_t is the trend at time *t*
- s_t is the seasonal factor at time *t*
- α,β are the smoothing parameters
- ϵ_t is the error term at time *t*

3.6 Machine Learning and Deep Learning Techniques for Time Series Forecasting

Apart from the traditional time series models, various machine learning and deep learning techniques have gained popularity in recent years for solving complex time series forecasting problems. Some of these techniques include:

- **Support Vector Machines (SVM)**: SVM is a machine learning technique that can be used for time series forecasting by transforming the time series data into a higher-dimensional space using kernel functions and finding the optimal separation hyperplane.
- **Random Forests and Gradient Boosting Machines**: These ensemble techniques can be applied to time series forecasting problems by using sliding window or "rolling-origin" cross-validation strategies to train multiple decision trees or weak learners on different subsets of the time series data.
- **Recurrent Neural Networks (RNN)**: RNNs are a type of artificial neural networks specifically designed for handling sequence data, such as time series, by using feedback connections or "memory" units to store past information.
- **Long Short-Term Memory (LSTM) and Gated Recurrent Unit (GRU) Neural Networks**: Both LSTM and GRU models are advanced variations of RNNs, with improved memory units capable of learning long-term dependencies in time series data, making them suitable for complex forecasting problems.
- **Convolutional Neural Networks (CNN)**: CNNs are specialized neural networks originally designed for image analysis but can also be applied to time series forecasting problems by treating the time series data as a one-dimensional "image" and learning hierarchical representations using convolutional layers.

All these techniques, when applied appropriately, offer robust and accurate methods for time series analysis and forecasting. Selecting the right technique depends on the nature and complexity of the time series data, domain knowledge, and the specific requirements of the forecasting task at hand.

3. Time Series Analysis and Forecasting Techniques

Time series analysis involves the study of historical data to identify patterns and trends to predict future events. This type of analysis is critical in many business, economic, and scientific domains, as it helps guide decision making and understanding the temporal dynamics of various processes. In this section, we will discuss the following forecasting techniques:

- Autoregressive Integrated Moving Average (ARIMA) models
- Seasonal Decomposition of Time Series (STL) and Seasonal-Trend decomposition using LOESS (STL)
- Exponential smoothing state space models (ETS)
- Long Short-Term Memory (LSTM) models

3.1 Autoregressive Integrated Moving Average (ARIMA) models

The ARIMA model is a widely-used approach for time series forecasting. It combines autoregressive (AR) and moving average (MA) elements with differencing to make the time series stationary. In simple terms, stationary time series data does not have trends or seasonality, making it easier to analyze and predict. The model is defined by three parameters: p (order of the AR term), d (degree of differencing), and q (order of the MA term).

Selecting the optimal parameters for the ARIMA model can be done using grid search, with the goal of minimizing a metric such as the Akaike Information

Criterion (AIC) or the Bayesian Information Criterion (BIC). Once the parameters are chosen, the model can be fit to the historical data and used to forecast future observations. However, ARIMA struggles when dealing with irregular, high-frequency, or seasonal data.

3.2 Seasonal Decomposition of Time Series (STL) and Seasonal-Trend decomposition using LOESS (STL)

Seasonal decomposition techniques, such as STL, are used to break down a time series into its constituent components—seasonal, trend, and residual. This decomposition allows us to understand the underlying patterns and behaviors in the data, such as how the trend and seasonality change over time. STL is an acronym for Seasonal and Trend decomposition using Loess, a non-parametric method for fitting a smooth curve to data.

The STL method is highly customizable and robust, allowing for the analysis of data with missing or contaminated observations. Additionally, STL can be combined with other forecasting methods, such as ARIMA or ETS, to account for seasonality, which may not be captured by these models.

3.3 Exponential smoothing state space models (ETS)

Exponential smoothing state space models, sometimes called the `Holt-Winters method`, are a family of time series forecasting techniques that generalize various forms of exponential smoothing.

These models can account for trends and seasonality, as well as generate point forecasts, prediction intervals, and smoothing. ETS distinguishes itself from ARIMA by being able to handle time series with irregular patterns and high-frequency data.

There are three main components of ETS models: error (E), trend (T), and seasonality (S). The choice of these components is determined by the data and the desired forecasting properties. For example, a model with additive errors, additive trends, and no seasonality would be denoted as ETS(A, A, N). Selecting the optimal model parameters can be done using various criteria, such as minimizing the AIC or BIC.

3.4 Long Short-Term Memory (LSTM) models

Long Short-Term Memory (LSTM) is a type of Recurrent Neural Network (RNN) architecture specifically designed to handle time series data by capturing long-term dependencies. LSTMs have been successful in predicting complex patterns and non-linear relationships, making them an excellent choice for time series forecasting tasks.

LSTMs consist of multiple layers, where each layer has several memory cells. These cells have input, output, and forget gates which help control and maintain the flow of information through the network. This design helps mitigate the vanishing gradient problem, which is common in traditional RNNs.

Training an LSTM model involves splitting the time series data into sequences and providing these sequences as inputs to the model. The model is then trained to predict one or more steps ahead in the time series. Hyperparameter optimization, for example, the number of layers, number of cells per layer, learning rate, and dropout rate, is an essential step in LSTM model development.

Conclusion

Time series analysis and forecasting play a crucial role in various real-life applications. Understanding and implementing the appropriate techniques can provide valuable insights and assist in making informed decisions. The techniques discussed in this section—ARIMA, STL, ETS, and LSTM—offer an exciting array of options for analysts and practitioners looking to harness the power of time series analysis. The choice of method depends on the nature of the data, the desired forecasting properties, and, of course, the requisite computational resources.

Integrating Statistics, Forecasting, and Machine Learning into Decision Making

In our increasingly data-driven world, it is essential for individuals and organizations to not only understand and work with data but also leverage it in making informed decisions. This is where the integration of statistics, forecasting, and machine learning comes into play. The combined implementation of these approaches helps refine decision-making and ultimately leads to more precise outcomes. In this subsection, we will discuss some practical steps and best practices for incorporating these techniques into your real-life decision-making process.

1. Defining the Problem

Before diving into the data analysis, it is crucial first to identify the problem that needs solving or the question you're trying to answer. By establishing a clear objective, you can tailor your statistical approach and machine learning models to achieve the desired results. To define the problem:

- Clearly outline the question or issue at hand,
- Determine the variables and factors that can impact the outcome, and
- Define the analytical approach, whether it be descriptive, predictive, or prescriptive.

2. Assembling Your Data

After determining the questions that need answering, gather the data you will need to conduct your analysis. Data may come from different sources such as structured databases, unstructured text, or even online sources like social media platforms. Make sure that the data are reliable and relevant to the problem at hand. Cleaning and preprocessing the data, including organizing, de-duplication, missing value handling, and normalization, are essential steps to ensure accurate and robust results.

3. Selecting the Right Method

Depending on your problem, different statistical and machine learning methods may be more suitable than others. A good rule of thumb is to start with traditional statistical techniques like hypothesis testing, regression, or time series analysis. If these methods do not yield satisfactory results or the problem is complex, machine learning algorithms such as decision trees, neural networks, or ensemble methods can be employed. To choose the right method:

- Understand the assumptions and limitations of the methods you'll use,
- Start with simple models and build complexity if required, and
- Perform thorough model validation to compare the accuracy and reliability of your models.

4. Implementing Models and Interpreting Results

Once you've chosen your analysis methods, the next step is to build your models and generate forecasts or predictions. It's essential to be cautious about overfitting, which can happen when a model is too complicated or trained too heavily on the given data. In real-life situations, it's better to opt for a simpler, more generalized model than an overly complex one. Interpreting the results of your analysis involves:

- Evaluating the significance and relevance of your outputs,
- Understanding how your results relate to the problem at hand, and
- Communicating findings and insights to stakeholders using visualizations and clear language.

5. Translating Insights into Action

After interpreting your results, take the time to consider how they can translate into actionable recommendations. It's essential to consider the real-world implications of your findings, as they can help guide decision-makers on a path to better problem-solving. To transform insights into action:

- Clearly outline the steps you believe should be taken based on your findings,
- Quantify your recommendations if possible (e.g., forecasted increase in revenue), and
- Be prepared to revise your models and adjust your recommendations based on new data and evolving conditions.

6. Monitor and Update Your Models

As more data becomes available and situations change over time, regularly reevaluate and update your models to maintain accuracy and relevance. This step ensures a continued refining of your decision-making process by adapting to changing environments and incorporating new information. To stay up-to-date:

- Set benchmarks and performance metrics for your analysis,
- Regularly gather feedback from end-users and decision-makers, and
- Make adjustments and improvements to your models based on new data, methodologies, or domain knowledge.

In conclusion, integrating statistics, forecasting, and machine learning into real-life decision-making involves identifying the problem, gathering relevant data, selecting appropriate methods, assessing model results, and translating insights into actionable recommendations. By following these best practices and continuously monitoring and updating models, individuals and organizations can make data-driven decisions that lead to enhanced outcomes and success.

Leveraging Big Data: Extracting Insights and Patterns

In today's fast-paced world, companies and organizations generate an immense amount of data daily. This data is a goldmine, containing information and patterns that can carry significant potential for managing businesses, making predictions, and influencing decision-making. This is where statistics, forecasting, and machine learning play a crucial role that cannot be underestimated.

In this section, we will discuss how to leverage big data to extract insights and patterns and use them effectively in real-life situations.

1. Exploratory Data Analysis (EDA)

The first step in the process of extracting patterns from data is **Exploratory Data Analysis (EDA)**. It involves visually and quantitatively exploring data to understand its main characteristics and identify initial patterns, trends, and relationships. This step allows us to:

- Investigate the data's variability and consistency
- Identify anomalies and outliers
- Identify correlations between variables

- Formulate hypotheses for further analysis

Tools and Techniques

Several tools and techniques can help us during the EDA process, including:

1. *Descriptive statistics*: Measures of central tendency (mean, median, and mode) and variability (range, variance, and standard deviation) can be employed to summarize data and describe its distribution.
2. *Visualizations*: Various plots such as bar charts, histograms, scatterplots, and boxplots can reveal the underlying structure of the data, relationships between variables, and possible outliers.
3. *Correlation analysis*: Identify the possible correlation between variables using measures such as Pearson's correlation coefficient or Spearman's rank correlation coefficient.

2. Data Preprocessing

Data preprocessing is a crucial step that ensures the quality of data being fed into the modeling process. Big data often comes in raw, unprocessed, and noisy form; hence, data preprocessing techniques are essential to clean, transform, and prepare data to be used effectively in predictive modeling and machine learning tasks. Some common data preprocessing tasks include:

1. *Data Cleaning*: Address and manage missing data, duplicate records, and outliers.

2. *Feature Engineering*: Creation of new features from existing data that may improve model accuracy.
3. *Feature Scaling*: Normalize or standardize features to be within the same range or distribution.
4. *Feature Selection*: Identify the most relevant features that contribute to the prediction.

3. Choosing the Right Model

After preparing the data, it is essential to select the most suitable model(s) for your specific problem. This requires knowledge of various methods, understanding the problem domain, and an awareness of the trade-offs associated with each algorithm. Some key aspects to consider when choosing a model include:

1. *Model complexity*: The balance between model complexity and model interpretability should be considered. Complex models, such as deep learning or ensemble methods, may produce better predictions but be harder to explain or interpret.
2. *Model assumptions*: Ensure that the assumptions made by the model align with your data and that they hold true.
3. *Metrics*: Use appropriate evaluation metrics that match your problem domain and goals, such as accuracy, F1 score, or mean squared error.

4. Model Validation and Evaluation

Once you have chosen and trained your model, it is important to validate its performance and evaluate its accuracy. This process will help you understand the model's robustness in the face of new data and verify that it generalizes well beyond the training dataset.

1. *Cross-Validation*: Split your dataset into multiple training and validation sets to learn how well your model generalizes to unseen data.
2. *Hyperparameter Tuning*: Iterate through different hyperparameter configurations to identify the best-performing model.
3. *Model performance visualization*: Utilize tools such as learning curves, confusion matrices, or ROC curves to evaluate model performance visually and quantitatively.

5. Model Deployment and Monitoring

It is essential to deploy and integrate your trained model into a real-life situation to effectively utilize its insights and predictions. This could involve incorporating the model into various applications, services, or platforms. It is vital to monitor your model continuously, as a model's performance may deteriorate with time due to changes in the data distribution, known as *concept drift*.

1. *Model Deployment*: Deploy your model on production systems or integrate it with APIs.
2. *Model Monitoring*: Regularly evaluate your model's performance via metrics and user feedback.
3. *Maintenance and Updating*: Continuously update and train your model on new data as required.

Conclusion

Understanding how to effectively apply statistics, forecasting, and machine learning in real-life situations is vital in unlocking the vast potential hidden within big data. By mastering exploratory data analysis, data preprocessing, model selection, validation, and deployment, you enhance your ability to generate accurate, robust predictions that can guide and drive decision-making across various domains.

Demystifying the Myths Surrounding Statistics, Forecasting, and Machine Learning for Real-Life Applications

In our everyday lives, we encounter numerous practical problems that can potentially be solved using statistical techniques, forecasting methods, and machine learning algorithms. However, it is important to first clear up some misconceptions that may hinder the understanding and effective application of these powerful concepts.

Myth 1: You need to have a specialized degree or be a 'math person' to understand and apply statistics, forecasting, and machine learning

While it is true that a strong foundation in mathematics and statistics can give you an edge while learning and applying these concepts, it is by no means a prerequisite. Many real-life problems can be broken down into simpler components and tackled using basic statistical techniques or simple forecast models. There are plenty of resources, including books, online courses, and tutorials, that allow those from different backgrounds to grasp the foundations of these fields effectively.

Moreover, we live in an era where programming languages like Python and R, as well as user-friendly software packages and libraries, are available for solving complex statistical and machine learning problems. These tools make it easier for non-experts to implement, fine-tune, and visualize predictions from their data.

Myth 2: Complex models and algorithms guarantee better results

Although advances in machine learning have led to the development of powerful and complex algorithms, it does not necessarily mean that more complicated models always yield better results. In fact, for many real-life problems, applying traditional statistical methods or simple models can yield equally accurate or even more interpretable results.

Highly complex models can sometimes lead to overfitting, where the model captures the noise in the data instead of the underlying pattern. This can result in poor prediction accuracy, making the model unsuitable for deployment in real-world applications. It is crucial to first understand the nature of the problem and the data before choosing an appropriate model or algorithm.

Myth 3: You need vast amounts of data for machine learning and forecasting models to be effective

While it is true that some machine learning algorithms, such as deep learning, require large amounts of data, there are many techniques that can work effectively with smaller datasets. Techniques like cross-validation, bootstrapping, and Bayesian methods can help improve model accuracy even when data is scarce.

Similarly, in the case of forecasting, domain knowledge and feature engineering can often compensate for limited data. Understanding seasonal patterns, cyclical behavior, and trend changes can significantly aid the forecasting process.

Moreover, transfer learning, a technique in which a model is pre-trained on large datasets and then fine-tuned using small amounts of domain-specific data, can greatly outperform models trained from scratch with limited data.

Applying Statistics, Forecasting, and Machine Learning to Solve Real-Life Problems

To illustrate the practical applications of statistics, forecasting, and machine learning, let's consider some example scenarios that can be tackled using these techniques.

1. **Business Decision Making**

In the business world, data-driven decision-making is often crucial to stay competitive. Sales data can be analyzed to identify market trends, customer preferences, and seasonal fluctuations. Forecasting models can then be used to estimate future demand, optimize inventory levels, and allocate resources. Machine learning can be deployed to segment customers for targeted marketing campaigns, predict customer churn, and identify potential sources of revenue growth.

2. **Healthcare**

Quantitative methodologies play a significant role in advancing healthcare. Statistical analyses are widely used in clinical trials, epidemiology, and healthcare operations. Forecasting models can be used to predict disease outbreaks, patient admission rates, and medical staff requirements. Machine learning techniques can be applied to early diagnosis, personalized medicine, and identifying patterns in disease progression.

3. **Finance and Economics**

The finance sector relies heavily on statistical techniques, forecasting methods, and machine learning algorithms for portfolio optimization, risk management, stock predictions, and economic forecasts. Data-driven insights can guide investment strategies, and machine learning can be employed to detect fraud or create accurate credit risk models.

By debunking the myths surrounding statistics, forecasting, and machine learning, we can better understand how these techniques can be employed to tackle real-world problems. Armed with the right tools and understanding, individuals from diverse backgrounds can leverage these powerful methodologies to improve decision making and drive meaningful outcomes in various domains.

Leveraging Probability, Modeling Uncertainty and Influencing Decisions

In this subsection, we'll focus on understanding the importance of effectively utilizing probability, uncertainty modeling, and persuading decision-making processes in real-life settings. In practice, when working with statistics or machine learning models, we often encounter uncertainties that require a rigorous approach for interpretation, communication and, ultimately, guiding action.

Understanding Probabilities and Real-life Applications

Probability is a crucial concept that allows us to measure the likelihood of an event occurring. Probability theory can help us model uncertainty and make informed decisions in various real-life situations. Let's consider some common examples:

1. **Finance**: Assessing the risk of investment portfolios, predicting stock prices, and estimating the probability of defaulting loans.

2. **Healthcare**: Predicting the likelihood of disease outbreaks, analyzing the success rate of various treatments, and determining prescription medication efficacy.
3. **Manufacturing**: Forecasting machine failures, improving production processes and supply chain efficiency, and determining quality control parameters.
4. **Sports**: Analyzing team or athlete performance, predicting match outcomes, and setting odds for betting markets.

In each of these cases, probability assists us in making decisions by quantifying the uncertainty involved in the problem at hand.

Modeling Uncertainty

Effectively modeling uncertainty is a key aspect of working with data, as real-world data usually contains a degree of ambiguity. To improve decision-making, we should be aware of various sources of uncertainty and the corresponding techniques to handle them. Some common sources of uncertainty include:

1. **Measurement errors**: Data might contain inaccuracies stemming from the limitations of measuring devices, subjective interpretations, or faulty data recording.
2. **Sampling uncertainties**: Surveys or studies often involve a limited number of samples, extrapolating conclusions about the entire population can introduce uncertainty.
3. **Model inaccuracies**: The assumptions and simplifications we make while building statistical or machine learning models can lead to inaccuracies in the predictions.

To tackle the uncertainties associated with these situations, we can leverage methods such as:

- **Bayesian statistics**: This approach allows us to update our beliefs (in the form of probability distributions) as we gather more evidence (data). When working with limited or noisy data, Bayesian methods can provide a robust framework for handling uncertainty.
- **Confidence intervals**: These provide an estimated range of values within which the true parameter value is likely to fall. Confidence intervals can help us quantify the uncertainty surrounding sample-based estimates.
- **Monte Carlo simulations**: This technique involves simulating a large number of possible scenarios and calculating the corresponding outcomes. It's especially useful for modeling complex, multi-variable systems where analytical solutions are difficult to compute.

Influencing Decisions

As data scientists or analysts, we must effectively communicate our findings and persuade stakeholders to take appropriate actions based on our analyses. Here are some tips for communicating uncertainties and influencing decisions:

1. **Visualization**: Properly expressing uncertainty through visualizations (e.g., error bars, confidence bands, or probability density plots) can help decision-makers grasp the key findings more intuitively.
2. **Narrative**: Frame your results in a compelling narrative that highlights the main insights and their implications for the stakeholder's objective.

3. **Simplify**: Present the key takeaways in an easy-to-understand manner, avoiding overwhelming technical jargon. Emphasize how the results will impact stakeholders' specific concerns.
4. **Acknowledge limitations**: Be transparent about the limitations of your analysis and assumptions made. This openness fosters trust among stakeholders and encourages a more accurate interpretation of the findings.

In summary, applying statistics, forecasting, and machine learning in real-life settings requires that we effectively understand, model, and communicate uncertainties. By leveraging probability, accounting for various sources of uncertainty, and influencing decision-making through effective communication, we can turn the inherent complexity of real-world problems into well-informed, actionable insights.

Real-World Applications of Statistics, Forecasting, and Machine Learning

In today's data-driven world, understanding how to apply statistics, forecasting, and machine learning effectively can make a difference in various contexts, from industry to everyday life. These methods have a wide range of applications, from targeted advertising and fraud detection to energy management and climate modeling. In this section, we will explore several prominent and practical uses of these techniques.

1. Finance and Economics

Statistics, forecasting, and machine learning are integral to finance and economics, where predicting future trends and managing risk are essential.

- **Stock Market Predictions**: Machine learning algorithms, such as deep learning and neural networks, can process large amounts of financial data to analyze patterns and make predictions about stock prices. Investors use these predictions to make informed decisions and maximize returns.
- **Credit Scoring and Default Prediction**: Banks and financial institutions need to assess the creditworthiness of their clients. They use machine learning and statistical models to analyze a person's financial history, including outstanding debts, payment history, and income, to predict the likelihood of default.
- **Risk Management**: The finance sector must identify and manage potential risks to minimize losses. Machine learning and statistical models help identify patterns in market data and predict potential threats, allowing for better decision-making and risk mitigation.

2. Healthcare

The healthcare industry benefits from applying advanced analytical techniques to improve patient care and disease diagnosis.

- **Diagnosis**: Machine learning algorithms can analyze medical images (such as X-rays, MRIs, and CT scans) and identify patterns that indicate specific diseases. This enables doctors to diagnose ailments more accurately and quickly.
- **Drug Development**: Pharmaceutical companies face the challenge of quickly and accurately determining which compounds are most effective

against disease. Analyzing complex biological data with machine learning accelerates drug discovery and reduces the time and resources needed for clinical trials.

- **Genetics and Genomics**: Advanced statistical and machine learning techniques help researchers understand the relationship between genetic variations and the expression of diseases, paving the way for personalized medicine and therapies.

3. Sports Analytics

Sports organizations are increasingly relying on data to make informed decisions about player performance, strategy, and team management.

- **Performance Analysis**: Coaches and management can use machine learning algorithms to extract insights from player performance data (such as plays, stats, and movement patterns) to assess strengths, weaknesses, and areas for improvement.
- **Injury Prevention**: By analyzing historical injury data, clubs can identify common patterns and factors that contribute to injuries, enabling them to develop prevention strategies and minimize risk.
- **Game Strategy**: Advanced statistical models can help teams study their opponents and create more effective game strategies.

4. Marketing and Advertising

Businesses use data-driven marketing strategies to target customers more effectively and improve the efficiency of their advertising campaigns.

- **Customer Segmentation**: Machine learning techniques help businesses identify customer segments based on behavior, preferences, and demographics. This enables them to target marketing campaigns more accurately and deliver improved results.
- **Product Recommendations**: Online retailers can analyze massive datasets on customer behavior to identify buying patterns, preferences, and trends. Machine learning algorithms are then used to provide personalized product recommendations to customers, increasing sales and customer satisfaction.
- **Sentiment Analysis**: Machine learning models can process text data from social media, customer reviews, and other sources to understand customer sentiment regarding a brand, product, or service. Brands can use these insights to improve their offerings, address customer concerns, and launch targeted marketing campaigns.

5. Environment and Energy Management

Accurate forecasting of climate, weather, and energy consumption is crucial for environmental conservation and resource management.

- **Climate Modeling**: Scientists use sophisticated statistical models and machine learning algorithms to analyze vast volumes of climate data, allowing them to make projections about future climate trends, sea level rises, and extreme weather events.
- **Weather Forecasting**: Accurate weather forecasts have significant implications for industries like agriculture, aviation, and energy management. Machine learning models help improve the accuracy of

these forecasts by analyzing complex meteorological data.

- **Energy Consumption Forecasting**: Utility companies can use machine learning and statistical modeling to estimate future energy demand, allowing them to optimize energy production, reduce waste, and manage resources efficiently.

In conclusion, statistics, forecasting, and machine learning techniques have a wide range of real-world applications across various industries. By harnessing the power of data and implementing these methods, organizations can make informed decisions to improve decision-making, optimize operations, and drive innovation.

4. Regression Models and Predictive Analytics

4.1 Regression Models and Predictive Analytics

Regression models are one of the most widely used techniques in the realm of predictive analytics. These models are used to understand relationships between variables and make predictions about future values of a target variable based on the current values of one or more input variables. In this section, we'll learn about various types of regression models, how they work, and how they can be used in forecasting and machine learning applications.

4.1.1 Simple Linear Regression

Simple linear regression is a statistical method that models the relationship between two variables by fitting a linear equation to the observed data. This is done by adjusting the slope and intercept of the line so that the sum of the squared differences between the observed values and the corresponding predicted values is minimized. The resulting line can then be used to predict the value of the target variable for any given value of the input variable.

A simple linear regression model can be represented as follows:

$$ y = \beta_0 + \beta_1 \times x $$

where:

- y represents the dependent variable (i.e., the variable we want to predict)
- x represents the independent variable (i.e., the variable used to make predictions)
- β_0 is the intercept (i.e., the value of y when x is zero)
- β_1 is the slope (i.e., the strength and direction of the relationship between x and y)

Once the model has been fit to the data, the coefficients (β_0 and β_1) can be used to make predictions for new values of x. Simple linear regression models are often used in forecasting applications, where the goal is to make predictions for future values based on historical data.

4.1.2 Multiple Linear Regression

While simple linear regression models the relationship between two variables, multiple linear regression extends this concept to model the relationship between one dependent variable and multiple independent variables. Like in simple linear regression, the goal is to find the best-fit linear equation that minimizes the sum of the squared differences between the observed values and the corresponding predicted values. The resulting model can be used to predict the value of the target variable based on any combination of input variable values.

A multiple linear regression can be represented as follows:

$$ y = \beta_0 + \beta_1 \times x_1 + \beta_2 \times x_2 + ... + \beta_n \times x_n $$

where:

- $x_1, x_2, ..., x_n$ represent the independent variables
- β_0 is the intercept, and $\beta_1, \beta_2, ..., \beta_n$ represent the coefficients for each independent variable

Multiple linear regression models are commonly used in machine learning to make predictions with many input features. They can also be used as a baseline model to compare more advanced techniques, such as neural networks or decision trees.

4.1.3 Logistic Regression

Logistic regression is a variation of linear regression that is used to model the probability of a categorical outcome, typically in the form of binary classification problems (e.g., yes/no or 0/1). It is particularly useful in situations where the relationship between the independent and dependent variables is not linear, or where the variance of the residuals is not constant.

A logistic regression model can be represented as follows:

$$ \hat{p}(x) = \frac{e^{\beta_0 + \beta_1 \times x}}{1 + e^{\beta_0 + \beta_1 \times x}} $$

where:

- $\hat{p}(x)$ is the estimated probability of the target variable being equal to 1 (typically a success or positive outcome)
- The other variables and coefficients are similar to the ones used in linear regression

Once the model has been fit to the data, the coefficients can be used to estimate the probability of the target variable being equal to 1 for any given value of the input variables. These probabilities can then be thresholded to make binary predictions.

Logistic regression models are widely used in machine learning for binary classification tasks or in cases where the target variable is a probability.

4.1.4 Polynomial Regression

Polynomial regression is a type of regression analysis that models the relationship between the dependent and independent variables as an nth-degree polynomial. Polynomial regression can be used to fit more complex, non-linear relationships between variables, and it can be considered as an extension of multiple linear regression.

A polynomial regression model with a single independent variable can be represented as follows:

$$ y = \beta_0 + \beta_1x + \beta_2x^2 + ... + \beta_nx^n $$

Polynomial regression models are particularly useful in cases where the relationship between the variables is not linear or where there are strong interactions between the independent variables. However, these models can also be prone to overfitting, especially when the degree of the polynomial is large.

4.1.5 Regularized Regression Models

Regularized regression models, such as Ridge Regression and Lasso Regression, are extensions of linear regression models that introduce a penalty term to the loss function. This penalty term helps to control the complexity of the model and prevent overfitting by shrinking the coefficients towards zero. Regularized regression models are especially useful when dealing with a large number of correlated input variables, as they can help to reduce multicollinearity and improve model stability.

Conclusion

In summary, regression models are a fundamental technique in forecasting and machine learning, allowing us to model and predict the relationships between variables. These models encompass a wide array of techniques, from simple linear regression to more complex models like logistic regression and regularized regression models. Understanding each type of regression model and its applications in real-life scenarios is essential for making informed decisions when building predictive models and forecasts.

4.1 Regression Models and Predictive Analytics

4.1.1 Introduction to Regression Models

Regression models are powerful statistical tools used to estimate the relationship between one or more independent variables (predictors) and a dependent variable (response) while taking into account the variability in the data. In other words, regression models help in understanding the underlying associations and trends between variables by identifying a direct relationship which can be translated into a mathematical equation to predict or explain the behavior of the response variable.

There are different types of regression models, including linear regression, logistic regression, and multiple regression, among others, each with specific applications depending on the nature of the variables involved, data distribution, and desired outcome.

4.1.2 Linear Regression

Linear regression is a statistical method that seeks to model the linear relationship between one or more independent variables and a continuous dependent variable. The method estimates the coefficients of the independent variables, which can be interpreted as the amount by which the dependent variable changes for each unit change in the independent variable(s), everything else being held constant.

The primary goal of linear regression is to minimize the sum of the squared differences between the observed values and the predicted values. This is referred to as the residual sum of squares (RSS), which can be represented mathematically as:

$$ RSS = \sum_{i=1}^n (Y_i - \hat{Y}_i)^2, $$

where:

- n is the number of observations,
- Y_i is the observed values of the dependent variable, and
- $\hat{Y}_i$ is the predicted values of the dependent variable.

Linear regression has several applications in real life, such as predicting sales, estimating house prices, and determining the relationship between GDP growth and unemployment rate.

4.1.3 Logistic Regression

Logistic regression is similar to linear regression but is used when the dependent variable is binary or categorical in nature. The model estimates the probabilities of each outcome by applying the logistic function to the linear regression equation, represented as:

$$ \text{logit}(p) = \text{ln}\left(\frac{p}{1-p}\right) = \beta_0 + \beta_1 X_1 + \cdots + \beta_n X_n, $$

where:

- p is the probability of the event of interest (success) occurring,
- X_i are the independent variables, and
- β_i are the coefficients to be estimated (similar to linear regression).

The logistic regression model can be extended to handle multiple categorical outcomes (multinomial logistic regression) and ordered categorical outcomes (ordinal logistic regression). Logistic regression is widely used in medical research, marketing, and social sciences research for purposes like predicting customer churn or analyzing the likelihood of a patient developing a specific disease based on certain attributes.

4.1.4 Multiple Regression

Multiple regression extends the idea of linear and logistic regression by including several independent variables to better explain the variability in the dependent variable. This can be particularly useful when working with complex systems where a single variable cannot explain the changes in the dependent variable.

In multiple linear regression, the equation becomes:

$$ Y = \beta_0 + \beta_1 X_1 + \beta_2 X_2 + \cdots + \beta_n X_n + \epsilon, $$

where:

- Y is the dependent variable,
- X_i are the independent variables, and
- β_i are the coefficients to be estimated.

Similarly, multiple logistic regression models multiple independent variables' influence on a binary or categorical dependent variable.

In addition to the benefits of taking into account more than one independent variable, multiple regression also allows for the analysis of interactions between variables, potential confounding effects, and the identification of the most important predictors for a given outcome.

4.1.5 Applications in Forecasting and Machine Learning

Regression models play an essential role in predictive analytics by providing a mathematical framework to estimate or forecast the value of a dependent variable based on one or more independent variables. In machine learning, regression models, especially linear regression, are often used as a baseline to compare the performance of more complex models like decision trees, support vector machines, and deep learning algorithms.

Moreover, regression models can be integrated with other techniques like time series analysis, ensemble learning, and regularization methods to enhance their predictive performance and enable better generalization to unseen data.

4.1.6 Key Takeaways for Regression Models

1. Regression models are robust tools for estimating the relationship between variables, providing a mathematical equation to predict or explain the

behavior of dependent variables based on independent variables.

2. Linear regression, logistic regression, and multiple regression are widely used regression models, each with specific applications depending on the nature of the variables involved, data distribution, and desired outcome.

3. Regression models play a vital role in predictive analytics, and they can be utilized for a wide range of forecasting and machine learning applications in various fields like economics, marketing, medicine, and social sciences.

Title: 4. Regression Models and Predictive Analytics

4.1 Introduction to Regression Models

Regression models are statistical tools used to understand the relationship between a dependent variable and one or more independent variables. They are primarily used for predictive analytics, forecasting, and casual inference. Regression models are widely used in various fields, such as finance, healthcare, sports, and social sciences.

4.2 Linear Regression

Linear regression is the most basic and widely used regression model. It establishes a linear relationship between the dependent variable (Y) and the independent variable(s) (X). The equation for a simple linear regression (one independent variable) is:

$$Y = \alpha + \beta X + \epsilon$$

Where:

- Y is the dependent variable
- X is the independent variable
- α is the intercept (value of Y when X=0)
- β is the slope (change in Y for a unit change in X)
- ε is the error term (difference between the predicted and actual values of Y)

In multiple linear regression, the equation expands to include multiple independent variables *(X1, X2, ..., Xn)*:

$$Y = \alpha + \beta_1 X_1 + \beta_2 X_2 + ... + \beta_n X_n + \epsilon$$

4.3 Model Evaluation and Assumptions

Evaluating the performance of a regression model involves checking its accuracy and adherence to the underlying assumptions. Key metrics for model evaluation include:

1. **R-squared (R^2):** A measure of how well the model explains the variation in the dependent variable. R-squared ranges between 0 and 1, with higher values indicating better model fit.
2. **Adjusted R-squared:** Similar to R-squared but adjusts for the number of independent variables in the model. This metric allows for better model comparisons.
3. **Mean Squared Error (MSE):** A measure of the average squared difference between the predicted and actual values of the dependent variable. Lower MSE values indicate better model performance.

4. **Mean Absolute Error (MAE):** A measure of the average absolute difference between the predicted and actual values of the dependent variable. Lower MAE values indicate better model performance.

Linear regression models are based on several assumptions:

1. **Linearity:** There is a linear relationship between the dependent and independent variables.
2. **Independence:** The observations are independent of each other.
3. **Constant Variance:** The variance of the error term is constant for all values of the independent variables.
4. **Normality:** The error term follows a normal distribution.

If these assumptions are violated, the model's predictions might be unreliable. To check for these assumptions, residual analysis and diagnostic tests can be performed.

4.4 Regularization in Regression Models

Overfitting is a common problem in machine learning, where the model performs well on the training data but poorly on new, unseen data. Regularization techniques can help address this issue by adding a penalty term to the regression equation, which prevents the model from fitting the noise in the data.

Two popular regularization techniques in regression models are Lasso (L1) and Ridge (L2) regression. Lasso regression adds an L1 penalty term, which is the sum of the absolute values of the regression coefficients, to the cost function. Ridge regression adds an L2 penalty term, which is the sum of the squares of the regression coefficients, to the cost function.

These techniques can help reduce the model's complexity, prevent overfitting, and improve generalization to unseen data.

4.5 Non-linear Regression Models

In real-world scenarios, the relationship between the dependent and independent variables might not always be linear. Non-linear regression models can help capture these non-linearities and improve prediction accuracy. Some commonly used non-linear regression models include:

1. **Polynomial Regression:** The model introduces higher-order terms of the independent variable(s) to capture non-linear relationships.
2. **Logistic Regression:** A generalized linear model used for binary classification tasks. It models the probability of the dependent variable being either 0 or 1.
3. **Generalized Additive Models (GAMs):** These models use smooth functions to model non-linear relationships between the dependent and independent variables.
4. **Neural Networks:** These are powerful models capable of capturing complex non-linear relationships in datasets with a large number of features.

4.6 Conclusion

Regression models and predictive analytics play a crucial role in various real-life applications, from sales forecasting to medical diagnostics. Understanding the underlying concepts and techniques is essential for effective application and interpretation of findings.

When working with regression models, it is essential to ensure the model meets the assumptions and performs well on the given data. Consider using regularization techniques to prevent overfitting and explore non-linear regression models when linear relationships aren't evident in the data.

4. Regression Models and Predictive Analytics

4.1 Introduction

In this section, we will delve into one of the most widely used techniques in both statistics and machine learning: regression models. A regression model is a type of statistical model that attempts to predict the relationship between a dependent (target) variable and one or more independent (predictor) variables. While there are various types of regression models, they all serve one essential purpose: to understand and forecast the behavior of a phenomenon by analyzing the impact of certain factors on the response variable.

Predictive analytics is a branch of data analytics that utilizes statistical models and machine learning techniques to make predictions and forecasts on future events based on historical data. Regression models play a crucial role in predictive analytics, allowing stakeholders to make informed decisions and take appropriate actions in various real-life scenarios, such as risk management, financial forecasting, customer targeting, and health care.

In this section, we will explore different types of regression models, their assumptions, and how they can be applied in various industry domains. Furthermore, we will discuss evaluation metrics, model validation techniques, and best practices to optimize and tune regression models to achieve the highest possible predictive performance.

4.2 Linear Regression Models

Linear regression is probably the most well-known and widely used regression model. It assumes that the relationship between the dependent variable and the predictors is linear. In its simplest form, a linear regression model with one predictor variable can be represented as:

$$y = \alpha + \beta x + \varepsilon$$

where:

- y is the dependent variable,
- α is the intercept of the model (value of y when $x=0$),
- β is the coefficient (slope) of the predictor variable x, and
- ε is the error term, representing model residuals (difference between the observed and predicted values).

When dealing with multiple predictor variables, the equation takes the following form:

$$y = \alpha + \beta 1x1 + \beta 2x2 + ... + \beta nxn + \varepsilon$$

There are various algorithms to estimate the parameters, such as Ordinary Least Squares (OLS), Gradient Descent, and others. Linear regression models are easy to interpret and often serve as the starting point for more sophisticated models.

4.3 Non-Linear and Generalized Regression Models

While linear regression models can be quite useful, they often do not capture the complexity and non-linear relationships in real-world data. Thus, we have non-linear and generalized regression models that can address these limitations. Some examples are:

1. **Polynomial Regression**: Involves adding higher-degree terms of predictor variables, thereby capturing non-linear relationships.
2. **Generalized Linear Models (GLMs)**: A family of models that allow dependent variables to follow various distributions other than the normal distribution (e.g., Poisson or binomial), while maintaining a linear relationship in a certain function space (e.g., logistic regression for binary classification).
3. **Decision Trees and Random Forests**: Non-linear, hierarchical models that can adapt to complex data patterns and capture interactions among predictor variables.
4. **Support Vector Machines (SVM)**: A versatile algorithm that can be adapted for regression applications (e.g., Support Vector Regression) by minimizing a specific loss function.
5. **Artificial Neural Networks (ANN)**: A family of models inspired by biological neural networks, which can learn complex non-linear relationships between

predictors and the dependent variable using a combination of artificial neurons and layers.

4.4 Model Evaluation and Validation

Selecting the best regression model for a particular problem is not a straightforward task. In addition to the choice of model, there are numerous factors such as feature selection, model assumptions, and hyperparameter tuning that can significantly affect the model's performance. Therefore, it is essential to evaluate and validate the predictive performance of the regression model.

In this context, evaluation metrics and model validation techniques are two key aspects to consider. The most common evaluation metrics for regression models are:

1. **Mean Squared Error (MSE)**: Measures the average squared difference between the predicted and actual values.
2. **Root Mean Squared Error (RMSE)**: The square root of MSE, which represents the average deviation (in the same unit as the dependent variable).
3. **Mean Absolute Error (MAE)**: The average of the absolute differences between predicted and actual values.
4. **R-Squared (Coefficient of Determination)**: Represents the proportion of the variance in the dependent variable explained by the predictor variables.

To validate the model's performance, cross-validation techniques are often employed, such as:

1. **K-Fold Cross-Validation**: Partitioning the dataset into k equal-sized subsamples, training the model on

k-1 folds, and validating on the remaining fold. This process is repeated k times, and the average performance is calculated.

2. **Leave-One-Out (LOO) Cross-Validation**: A special case of K-Fold where k equals the number of data points, providing a less biased estimate of the model's performance.
3. **Bootstrapping**: Resampling with replacement from the original dataset, training, and validating the model on each resampled dataset, providing a more robust estimation of model performance and uncertainty.

4.5 Applications and Use Cases

Regression models and predictive analytics can be applied to a wide range of industry domains and use cases. Some examples include:

1. **Finance**: Forecasting stock prices, credit risk assessment, customer lifetime value, and portfolio optimization.
2. **Healthcare**: Predicting patient outcomes, disease progression, and identifying risk factors for various medical conditions.
3. **Marketing**: Customer segmentation, targeting, and predicting the effectiveness of marketing campaigns.
4. **Sports**: Performance analysis and prediction of teams or individual athletes.
5. **Supply Chain and Logistics**: Demand forecasting, inventory optimization, and transportation planning.

In conclusion, regression models and predictive analytics are essential tools for analyzing real-world data and making informed decisions. By understanding the underlying theory and applying best practices, practitioners can leverage these techniques to drive substantial value and find solutions to contemporary challenges faced by various industry sectors.

4. Regression Models and Predictive Analytics

4.1 Introduction to Regression Models

Regression analysis is a powerful statistical and machine learning technique used to understand relationships among variables and allows us to make predictions about future events based on the observed historical data. In a nutshell, regression analysis helps us to uncover patterns, trends and relationships within the data, which enables us to make informed decisions.

There are many types of regression models, but the most widely used ones are linear regression, logistic regression, and multiple regression. Each of these models has its own strengths and limitations, and their applicability depends on the type of data being analyzed, as well as on the objectives of the analysis. In this subsection, we will focus on the concepts and applications of these regression models, and how they can be employed effectively in real-life scenarios.

4.2 Linear Regression

Linear regression is an approach to model the relationship between a dependent variable (often denoted as 'y') and one or more independent variables (often denoted as 'x'). This relationship is described by the equation:

$$y = a + bx + \varepsilon$$

where 'a' is the intercept (the value of 'y' when 'x' is 0), 'b' is the slope (the rate at which 'y' changes as 'x' increases), and 'ε' is the error term (the difference between the predicted and actual values of 'y'). The goal of linear regression is to determine the best-fitting line (i.e., the line with the smallest error) that can be used to predict 'y' based on 'x'.

In real-life applications, linear regression can be used for a wide range of purposes, such as predicting the sales of a product based on its price and advertising expenses, estimating the energy consumption of a building based on the outside temperature and occupancy rates, and predicting the income of individuals based on their education level and experience.

4.2.1 Assumptions of Linear Regression

For linear regression to produce accurate and reliable results, a number of assumptions have to be met. Some of the key assumptions include:

1. Linearity: The relationship between the independent and dependent variables must be linear.
2. Independence: The observations (rows of data) should be independent of each other.
3. Homoscedasticity: The variance of the error terms should be constant across all levels of the independent variables.
4. Normality: The error terms (residuals) should be normally distributed.

If these assumptions are not met, linear regression may not be the best modeling technique, and alternative methods (e.g., non-linear regression, transformations of variables) should be considered.

4.3 Logistic Regression

While linear regression is used when the dependent variable is continuous, logistic regression is used when the dependent variable is binary (i.e., it takes on only two possible values, such as 0 or 1, success or failure, yes or no). The main goal of logistic regression is to estimate the probability that an event occurs, given a set of predictor variables.

The logistic regression model takes the form of the logistic function, which is an S-shaped curve that maps the relationship between the independent and dependent variables, and it is bounded between 0 and 1. The logistic function is given by:

```
P(y=1) = 1/(1 + e^-(a + bx))
```

where 'P(y=1)' represents the probability of the event occurring, and 'e' is the base of the natural logarithm.

Logistic regression has numerous real-life applications, including medical diagnosis (predicting the presence or absence of a disease based on patient characteristics), credit scoring (determining the likelihood of a borrower defaulting on a loan based on their credit history), and customer churn analysis (identifying the probability of a customer leaving a service based on their usage patterns).

4.4 Multiple Regression

In many real-life situations, there are multiple independent variables that can influence the dependent variable. Multiple regression is an extension of linear and logistic regression models, which allows us to incorporate multiple predictor variables into the regression equation. The multiple linear regression model has the form:

```
y = a + b1x1 + b2x2 + ... + bnxn + ε
```

where 'x1, x2, ..., xn' are the independent variables, and 'b1, b2, ..., bn' are the corresponding regression coefficients.

Multiple regression enables us to extract more insights from the data and obtain better predictions by considering the interactive effects of multiple variables. Some real-life applications of multiple regression include house price prediction (based on factors such as location, size, and amenities), financial forecasting (based on economic indicators, company-specific variables, and market conditions), and climate change analysis (based on CO2 emissions, solar radiation, and human activities).

4.5 Model Evaluation and Selection

After fitting a regression model to the data, it is crucial to evaluate its performance and goodness-of-fit to ensure the accuracy and reliability of the predictions. One popular metric for model evaluation is the coefficient of determination (R-squared), which represents the proportion of the variance in the dependent variable that can be explained by the independent variables. Other common metrics include the root mean squared error (RMSE), mean absolute error (MAE), and the Akaike information criterion (AIC).

In addition to evaluating the performance of a single model, it is often necessary to compare and select the best model among several competing models. In this context, techniques like cross-validation, stepwise selection, and regularization (ridge, LASSO, and elastic net) can be employed to find the optimal combination of predictor variables and model parameters.

4.6 Conclusion

Regression models and predictive analytics have a broad range of real-life applications across various domains, including business, finance, healthcare, and environmental sciences, among others. By understanding and applying these techniques effectively, professionals can harness the power of data to make better-informed decisions and drive innovation in their respective fields. Mastering these models and their underlying assumptions, as well as the best practices for model evaluation and selection, is an essential skill for statisticians, data scientists, and machine learning practitioners.

Real-World Applications of Statistics, Forecasting, and Machine Learning

In a world that is increasingly data-driven, it is essential for businesses, researchers, and policymakers to harness the power of data analytics to gain insights, make informed decisions, and predict future trends. In this section, we'll explore a wide variety of real-world applications of statistics, forecasting, and machine learning, highlighting how these techniques can be applied in various disciplines and industries.

Business and Finance

Businesses from various sectors extensively utilize statistics, forecasting, and machine learning to optimize their operations, monitor key performance indicators (KPIs), and gain competitive advantages. Specific applications in this domain include:

1. **Sales forecasting**: Companies can use historical sales data and external factors such as holidays, economic indicators, and promotions to predict future sale patterns. Accurate forecasts can help businesses optimize supply chain management, allocate resources efficiently, and reduce costs.
2. **Customer segmentation**: Customer data, including demographics, purchasing behavior, and preferences, can be analyzed to group customers into market segments. With this information, businesses can design targeted marketing campaigns, develop specialized products or services, and enhance customer relationships.
3. **Fraud detection**: Machine learning algorithms can identify irregularities in financial transactions by analyzing patterns in spending behavior. Banks and credit card companies can use these insights to quickly flag and prevent fraudulent activities, protecting both themselves and their customers.
4. **Stock market predictions**: Quantitative analysts or "quants" use statistical models and machine

learning algorithms to forecast stock prices, identify investment opportunities, and manage financial risk.

Healthcare and Medicine

Statistics, forecasting, and machine learning play a vital role in improving patient care, optimizing treatment plans, and advancing medical research. Some specific applications include:

1. **Disease prediction and risk assessment**: By analyzing genetic data, lifestyle factors, and environmental conditions, healthcare providers can evaluate a patient's risk of developing certain diseases and recommend preventative measures.
2. **Personalized medicine**: Data analysis can identify patterns in a patient's medical history and response to treatments, allowing doctors to tailor therapies and medications on an individual basis, potentially increasing their effectiveness and reducing side effects.
3. **Drug development**: Machine learning algorithms can analyze large datasets of molecular structures and predict their pharmacological properties, assisting in the drug discovery process and helping to identify new therapeutic targets.
4. **Epidemiology**: Forecasting models can predict the spread of infectious diseases, assisting in the allocation of public health resources and informing public policy. For instance, during the COVID-19 pandemic, statistical models were crucial in predicting the spread of the virus and guiding the implementation of containment measures.

Government and Public Policy

Public institutions rely on data analysis to shape policy, allocate resources, and assess the effectiveness of programs. Key applications include:

1. **Population forecasting**: Governments use demographic data to predict population growth and estimate future needs for infrastructure, healthcare, education, and other public services.
2. **Criminal justice**: Data-driven models can help identify high-crime areas and inform law enforcement strategies. Additionally, machine learning can assist in predicting recidivism rates and identifying effective rehabilitation programs.
3. **Environmental monitoring**: Analyzing data from remote sensing technologies, climate models, and other sources can help predict natural disasters, monitor pollution, and assess the impact of environmental policies.
4. **Elections and polling**: Political campaigns and media organizations use polling data to estimate voter sentiment, creating statistical models to forecast election outcomes and informing political strategy.

Education

Educators and administrators can leverage data analytics to improve teaching methods, assess student performance, and optimize school management. Some applications include:

1. **Curriculum development**: By analyzing students' test scores and learning styles, educators can identify areas where students struggle and adapt curricular materials to better meet their needs.
2. **Predicting student performance**: Machine learning algorithms can help predict which students

are likely to struggle or excel in specific subjects, allowing educators to provide targeted interventions, additional support, or opportunities for advanced coursework.

3. **Resource allocation**: Education institutions can use data on enrollment, demographics, and community needs to allocate resources such as teachers, funding, and facilities strategically.

Manufacturing and Logistics

The efficient operation of manufacturing plants and supply chains relies heavily on the analysis of production data and optimization of processes. Key applications include:

1. **Quality assurance**: Manufacturers can use statistical process control to identify issues in production lines, helping to reduce defects and maintain high levels of product quality.
2. **Predictive maintenance**: Machine learning algorithms can analyze data from equipment sensors to predict when a machine is likely to fail, allowing maintenance to be scheduled proactively and minimizing downtime.
3. **Supply chain optimization**: By analyzing demand forecasts and production schedules, businesses can optimize their supply chain operations, reducing inventory costs, and improving customer satisfaction.

The applications of statistics, forecasting, and machine learning across various disciplines and industries outlined in this section illustrate the power and flexibility of these methods. By leveraging these data-driven techniques, businesses, governments, and other organizations can make better-informed decisions, optimize resource allocation, and ultimately achieve significant gains in efficiency and effectiveness.

Real-World Applications of Statistics, Forecasting and Machine Learning

In today's data-driven world, the knowledge of statistics, forecasting, and machine learning has become essential for making well-informed decisions, whether it is in business, research, or other domains. This section will explore various real-world applications of these techniques, showcasing how they can improve decision-making, uncover hidden patterns and predict future events more accurately.

Healthcare

In healthcare, the proper use of these techniques can lead to improved patient outcomes, early detection of diseases, and personalized treatment plans. For example:

- *Disease prediction*: Leveraging machine learning algorithms, healthcare professionals can analyze vast amounts of historical patient data to predict diseases and identify risk factors. This can lead to early detection and improved prevention strategies.
- *Personalized medicine*: Machine learning can help create individualized treatment plans by analyzing a

patient's unique genetic and molecular profile, alongside their medical history and lifestyle factors.

- *Drug development*: Machine learning and advanced statistical techniques are being used to analyze complex biological data, accelerating the drug discovery process, and enabling more targeted and effective therapies.

Finance and Economics

From risk management to investment strategies and consumer behavior analysis, the finance industry heavily relies on statistics, forecasting, and machine learning methods. Some applications include:

- *Credit scoring*: Banks and other financial institutions use machine learning models to predict the likelihood of customers defaulting on loans, enabling them to make better credit decisions.
- *Algorithmic trading*: Machine learning algorithms are used to analyze real-time market data, identify trading opportunities, and execute trades automatically, optimizing portfolio performance.
- *Fraud detection*: Financial institutions employ machine learning and pattern recognition techniques to identify and flag suspicious activities, enhancing cybersecurity and preventing financial fraud.

Retail and Marketing

The retail and marketing sectors can leverage these techniques to predict customer preferences, optimize pricing, and improve supply chain efficiency. Key applications in these areas are:

- *Product recommendation*: Machine learning algorithms examine user preferences, past browsing, and purchase behavior to generate personalized product recommendations, improving customer experience and driving sales.
- *Demand forecasting*: By using statistical models and machine learning techniques, retailers can predict future sales patterns and craft effective marketing strategies, ensuring that the right products are available at the right time.
- *Dynamic pricing*: Advanced algorithms can determine optimal pricing strategies based on factors such as supply, demand, and competition, maximizing revenue and profitability.

Transportation and Logistics

Optimizing transportation and logistics operations can result in reduced costs, increased efficiency, and enhanced customer satisfaction. Some instances where statistics, forecasting, and machine learning can be utilized include:

- *Route optimization*: Machine learning models can identify patterns in traffic data, allowing transportation and logistics companies to optimize routes and reduce travel times.
- *Predictive maintenance*: By analyzing historical data on vehicle performance and component failures, machine learning models can predict when maintenance will be required, reducing downtime and maintenance costs.
- *Delivery time prediction*: Efficient delivery time forecasts can be achieved by leveraging machine learning algorithms, considering factors such as traffic,

weather, and historical delivery times. This improves customer satisfaction and operational efficiency.

Environmental Science and Sustainability

Tackling environmental challenges and fostering sustainability also benefit from the use of statistical models and machine learning techniques. For instance:

- *Climate modeling*: Advanced statistical techniques are used to analyze environmental data, predict future climate trends, and inform policy decisions on climate change mitigation and adaptation strategies.
- *Natural resource management*: Machine learning can be employed to detect patterns in resource consumption and optimize resource allocation, promoting sustainable practices.
- *Renewable energy*: Forecasting algorithms can predict renewable energy production, such as solar and wind power, helping grid operators balance supply and demand effectively.

These examples illustrate the wide-ranging and transformative impact of statistics, forecasting, and machine learning across various industries. By investing in these techniques, organizations can improve decision-making, enhance efficiency, and drive innovation in the real world.

In the following chapters, readers will gain a deeper understanding of the theory and practical applications behind these techniques, empowering them to employ them effectively in their own industries and domains.

Real-World Applications of Statistics, Forecasting, and Machine Learning

The concepts of statistics, forecasting, and machine learning might appear abstract or highly technical, but they have numerous practical applications in our daily lives. From businesses using these tools to make informed decisions to researchers leveraging them to drive scientific discoveries, their value in tackling real-world challenges cannot be understated. This section will explore various areas where these three methodologies are applied, demonstrating how they work together to enhance our understanding of the world and improve our decision-making processes.

Business and Finance

One of the most important functions of statistics, forecasting, and machine learning in the business world is in aiding decision-making processes and market analyses. In finance, stocks, currencies, and other asset prices are analyzed using these techniques, with a focus on identifying patterns, predicting trends, and managing risks.

- **Sales Forecasting**: Companies rely on statistical models and machine learning to predict future sales volumes, allowing them to efficiently allocate resources, manage inventory, and plan marketing campaigns. Techniques such as time series analysis, regression models, and neural networks are applied to historical sales data to generate accurate forecasts.

- **Customer Analytics**: Businesses gather a wealth of data about their customers, including demographics, purchase history, and online behavior. Advanced machine learning algorithms such as clustering and classification can help businesses identify customer segments, tailor marketing campaigns, and enhance product offerings.
- **Credit Scoring**: Banks and lending institutions use statistical models and machine learning to predict the likelihood that a borrower will default on their loan. Factors such as credit history, income level, and other demographic information are taken into account to generate a credit score, which is then used to determine loan eligibility and interest rates.

Healthcare and Medicine

Statistics, forecasting, and machine learning have become essential tools in healthcare, where they play a critical role in improving patient outcomes and optimizing healthcare delivery.

- **Disease Prevention and Control**: Epidemiologists use statistical methods and mathematical modeling techniques to study the patterns and spread of infectious diseases, identify risk factors for specific diseases, and evaluate prevention strategies. Both forecasting and machine learning have proven invaluable in predicting and responding to outbreaks and pandemics.
- **Drug Discovery**: The development of new drugs is a costly and time-consuming process. Machine learning and statistical methods are used to accelerate this process by predicting potential drug candidates, optimizing existing compounds, and identifying potential side effects and interactions.

- **Medical Imaging**: Machine learning algorithms, particularly deep learning methods, have made significant advances in image recognition and analysis in recent years. This has been particularly useful in the medical field, where these techniques are employed in the automated detection and classification of tumors and other medical conditions using medical imaging data such as X-rays, MRIs, and CT scans.

Climate and Weather Forecasting

Accurate climate and weather forecasting is crucial for various industries, such as agriculture, transportation, and construction. It also plays a significant role in disaster planning and mitigation efforts. Modern weather forecasting relies on a blend of statistics, forecasting techniques, and machine learning algorithms.

- **Numerical Weather Prediction**: Weather forecasting relies heavily on numerical weather prediction (NWP) models, which involve simulating the Earth's atmosphere, oceans, and land surface using mathematical equations. These models generate a massive volume of data, which is then analyzed using statistical and machine learning techniques to make short-term and long-term weather predictions.
- **Climate Change Modeling**: Forecasting potential future climate changes relies on complex models that incorporate numerous factors, such as greenhouse gas emissions, land use changes, and solar radiation. These models generate large amounts of data, which need to be carefully analyzed using statistical and machine learning techniques in order to understand the potential impacts of climate change and determine effective mitigation strategies.

Sports and Entertainment

The sports and entertainment industries have also embraced the use of statistics, forecasting, and machine learning to analyze performance data, predict outcomes, and inform decision-making.

- **Sports Analytics**: Professional sports teams routinely collect and analyze a vast amount of performance data, allowing them to gain valuable insights into the strengths and weaknesses of their players and opposition. Advanced statistical methods and machine learning algorithms may be used to develop strategies, evaluate players, and identify talent.
- **Box Office Prediction**: Movie studios, distributors, and theaters use forecasting techniques and machine learning to predict box office revenues for upcoming films. By analyzing historical box office data, marketing expenditures, and social media trends, they can make more informed decisions about which movies to produce, distribute, and promote.

In conclusion, statistics, forecasting, and machine learning are indispensable tools in real-world applications across numerous industries. They allow us to analyze complex data, generate accurate predictions, and ultimately make better decisions. With the rapid advancement of these techniques and technologies, their impact and relevance are only set to grow.

Real-World Applications of Statistics, Forecasting, and Machine Learning

In the contemporary world, various fields actively integrate statistics, forecasting, and machine learning techniques in their decision-making processes. These methods are applied in diverse domains, from finance, marketing, economics, and medicine, to environmental sciences and even sports. In this section, we will explore some common real-world applications of these pervasive tools.

Finance and Stock Market

Stock markets and finance are one of the most significant areas where the application of statistics, forecasting, and machine learning technologies is indispensable. Portfolio managers, investors, and financial analysts work relentlessly on determining the optimum investment strategies, future price trends, risk assessment, and asset allocation to maximize returns and minimize risks.

- *Risk Assessment*: Financial experts use statistical analysis to assess historical returns, measure and monitor financial risk using various risk metrics, and calculate value-at-risk (VaR) measurements or expected shortfall to determine exposure.
- *Algorithmic Trading*: Machine learning algorithms, including deep learning and reinforcement learning models, are used to analyze historical and real-time market data, understand patterns, and make trade

decisions in the high-speed, competitive environment of the stock market.

- *Credit Scoring and Loan Assessment*: Financial institutions use data analytics to evaluate clients' creditworthiness by analyzing their financial history, income, and demographic information, resulting in better risk management and lending decisions.

Healthcare and Medicine

Healthcare systems worldwide are increasingly leveraging statistical analysis, machine learning, and forecasting techniques to improve diagnosis, treatment planning, and patient outcomes.

- *Diagnosis and Treatment*: Advanced analytical techniques, such as logistic regression and support vector machines, aid in the efficient detection and classification of diseases, such as cancer and cardiovascular conditions, by examining medical images or electronic health records.
- *Drug Discovery and Development*: Machine learning algorithms, including deep neural networks, facilitate the identification of potential therapeutic targets, drug discovery, and personalized medicine efforts by exploring massive amounts of biomedical data.
- *Epidemiology*: Forecasting models, including time-series analysis and agent-based models, play a critical role in predicting the spread of infectious diseases and understanding the impact of various intervention strategies on population health.

Marketing and Sales

Data-driven marketing has emerged as a strategic pillar for organizations to enhance customer engagement, build brand loyalty, and drive revenue.

- *Customer Segmentation*: Data clustering and classification techniques, such as k-means clustering and decision trees, help identify and group customers based on their demographics, purchase behavior, and preferences, enabling the development of targeted and effective sales and marketing campaigns.
- *Recommendation Systems*: Machine learning algorithms, such as collaborative filtering and matrix factorization, are often used to build recommendation engines that predict consumer preferences and direct them to appropriate products and services.
- *Sales Forecasting*: Time-series analysis and machine learning models, such as ARIMA and LSTM, are employed to forecast sales, understand market trends, and facilitate better demand planning and inventory management.

Environmental Sciences

Researchers in environmental sciences use statistical methodologies and machine learning algorithms to study, predict and address various environmental problems, ultimately contributing to sustainable development.

- *Climate Forecasting*: Climate scientists adopt statistical techniques, such as principle component analysis, and machine learning methods, including artificial neural networks, to analyze and forecast climate patterns to better understand and manage the consequences of climate change.

- *Pollution Monitoring and Control*: Environmental scientists leverage data analytics to monitor air and water quality, identify pollution sources, and develop policies to mitigate pollution and maintain ecological balance.

Sports Analytics

Sports teams use data analytics for devising winning strategies, scouting and player performance analysis.

- *Player Performance Analysis*: Athletes and sports teams adopt analytics techniques, such as regression models and cluster analysis, for evaluating player performance, identifying strengths and weaknesses, measuring success factors, and optimizing training and game preparation.
- *Injury Prediction and Prevention*: Machine learning models, including logistic regression and decision trees, are increasingly used to assess athletes' risk of injury by examining historical injury data and individual training load, biomechanics, and physiological factors.

These real-world applications represent only a small fraction of the ways that statistics, forecasting, and machine learning are being utilized to improve various aspects of modern life. The opportunities to apply these methodologies to solve problems and make better-informed decisions across multiple domains continue to grow as data becomes more abundant and technology more advanced.

Real-Life Applications of Statistics, Forecasting, and Machine Learning

In this section, we will dive into various real-life examples and case studies where statistics, forecasting, and machine learning have played a pivotal role in transforming industries, shaping decisions, and solving problems. As we explore these applications, you will gain an understanding of how these methods can be implemented to bring about meaningful changes and improvements in various sectors.

Healthcare

The healthcare industry has been revolutionized by the implementation of statistics, forecasting, and machine learning techniques. From early diagnosis of diseases to personalized medicine, these methods have improved both patient care and overall efficiency.

- **Disease prediction and prevention**: Machine learning methods, especially classification algorithms, are used to predict the likelihood of patients developing certain medical conditions, such as diabetes, cancer, and heart diseases. By identifying high-risk individuals, doctors can intervene at an earlier stage and prescribe preventive measures.
- **Medical imaging**: Pattern recognition and deep learning algorithms have been extensively used for automatic feature extraction from medical images, such as MRI, CT scans, and X-rays. This aids doctors in identifying and diagnosing diseases more accurately and quickly.
- **Drug development**: Machine learning is also employed in the discovery and development of new drugs. By analyzing massive amounts of data, algorithms can identify potential therapeutic

compounds, predict their effectiveness, and suggest optimal treatment plans.

Finance

The finance sector is another area where statistics, forecasting, and machine learning techniques have been widely embraced.

- **Stock market predictions**: Time-series analysis, a statistical forecasting method, is often used in predicting stock prices, market trends, and currency exchange rates. Based on historical data, these predictions can inform trading decisions and investment strategies.
- **Credit risk assessment**: Machine learning models, such as classification algorithms, help financial institutions assess the credit risk associated with loan applicants. By analyzing applicants' credit history, income, and other variables, these models can predict the likelihood of default.
- **Fraud detection**: Fraudulent activities, such as credit card fraud and insider trading, can be detected using machine learning techniques like anomaly detection. By identifying unusual patterns in large datasets, these methods can flag suspicious transactions for further investigation.

Retail and E-commerce

The retail and e-commerce industries have greatly benefited from the application of statistics, forecasting, and machine learning methods.

- **Demand forecasting**: Accurate demand forecasting is crucial for optimal inventory management, which minimizes costs and prevents stockouts. Time-series analysis and machine learning methods are employed to better predict customer demand for a product, taking into account seasonal trends and other influencing factors.
- **Customer segmentation**: Machine learning techniques, particularly clustering algorithms, are used to group customers with similar buying behaviors, preferences, and demographics. This information allows businesses to tailor their marketing efforts and offer personalized recommendations, which result in higher customer satisfaction and loyalty.
- **Dynamic pricing**: Machine learning algorithms can analyze various factors such as competitor pricing, demand, and historical sales data to calculate the optimal price for a product. This dynamic pricing strategy helps retailers and e-commerce businesses maximize their profits.

Transportation and Logistics

Effective integration of statistics, forecasting, and machine learning techniques has significantly improved the efficiency and effectiveness of transportation and logistics systems.

- **Route optimization**: Machine learning models, particularly reinforcement learning algorithms, can optimize vehicle routing, factoring in real-time traffic data, road conditions, and delivery deadlines. This saves both time and fuel, lowering costs and environmental impact.
- **Demand prediction**: Public transportation providers use time-series analysis and machine

learning models to predict ridership demand. This allows them to alter routes, schedules, and capacity to cater to fluctuating passenger loads, improving overall efficiency.

- **Autonomous vehicles**: Machine learning plays a central role in developing autonomous vehicles. It enables vehicles to make decisions and learn from their environment using data from sensors, cameras, and GPS.

The examples presented in this section represent only a fraction of possibilities when it comes to applying statistics, forecasting, and machine learning in real-life situations. As technology continues to advance, more industries will adopt these data-driven methodologies to address complex problems, optimize processes, and deliver better results.

5. Machine Learning Fundamentals: Classification, Clustering, and Recommendation

5.1 Machine Learning Fundamentals: Classification, Clustering, and Recommendation

Machine learning is a method of data analysis that automates analytical model building. It is a branch of artificial intelligence that uses algorithms to iteratively learn from the data and improve the predictions over time. The goal of machine learning is to explore data patterns, make accurate predictions, and improve decision-making capabilities. Machine learning can be categorized, based on the tasks, into three primary areas: classification, clustering, and recommendation systems. In this section, we'll dive deep into these three areas, discuss their real-world applications, and learn how they can add value to different industries.

5.1.1 Classification

Definition & Application

Classification is a supervised learning technique that deals with the problem of categorizing data points into one of several discrete classes. The goal of classification is to build a model that can predict the class of a new, unseen data point based on the data that it has already studied.

Some common applications of classification include:

1. Email filtering: An email provider can use machine learning classification algorithms to filter spam or categorize emails into different labels such as Primary, Social, or Promotions.
2. Fraud detection: Classification can be applied to identify fraudulent financial transactions by analyzing different patterns and abnormal behavior.
3. Medical diagnosis: Machine learning models can be used to predict diseases based on the analysis of patient's medical records and test results, such as diagnosing cancer from X-ray images or ECG signals.
4. Sentiment analysis: Classification can be used to identify the sentiment (positive, negative or neutral) of a given text or customer review.

Types of Classification Algorithms

There are several classification algorithms available, but some popular ones include:

1. Logistic Regression
2. Naïve Bayes Classifier
3. k-Nearest Neighbors (k-NN)
4. Decision Trees
5. Random Forests
6. Support Vector Machines (SVM)

Each algorithm has its strengths and weaknesses, thus making it essential to choose the best-fitting approach based on specific problem requirements and the available data.

5.1.2 Clustering

Definition & Application

Clustering is an unsupervised learning technique that involves grouping similar data points together based on their features. Unlike classification, no predefined labels are available, and the algorithm learns the patterns and structures within the data itself to derive clusters.

Some applications of clustering include:

1. Customer segmentation: Businesses can use clustering techniques to segment their customers based on their behavior, demographics, and preferences, enabling targeted marketing campaigns and personalized service offerings.

2. Anomaly detection: Clustering can be used to identify unusual patterns or outliers within the dataset that may indicate errors or potential fraud.
3. Document grouping: Clustering algorithms can help categorize documents into groups based on their topics, allowing for simplified content management or search engine results.
4. Image segmentation: Clustering can be employed to help identify distinct regions or objects within an image, thus aiding in image recognition tasks.

Types of Clustering Algorithms

Some commonly used clustering algorithms include:

1. k-Means Clustering
2. Hierarchical Clustering
3. Density-Based Spatial Clustering of Applications with Noise (DBSCAN)
4. Gaussian Mixture Models (GMM)

Different algorithms work best for particular datasets or problems, so understanding each method's underlying assumptions and characteristics is crucial to achieve good results.

5.1.3 Recommendation Systems

Definition & Application

Recommendation systems are models that predict users' preferences and make personalized product or service suggestions. They are essential for e-commerce platforms, streaming services, and other businesses that deal with a variety of products and rely on user engagement to generate revenue.

Some application areas include:

1. Product recommendations: Recommending items such as books, movies, or online products that a user may like based on their previous browsing history, purchases, or preferences.
2. Content personalization: Tailoring content on the web page or application to a user's specific interests and preferences.
3. Ad targeting: Recommending the most effective ads to users based on demographic data and browsing behavior.
4. Job recommendations: Connecting job seekers to potential job opportunities based on their skills and work history.

Types of Recommendation Systems

There are two primary types of recommendation systems:

1. Collaborative filtering: This approach is based on the assumption that users who have interacted with or liked similar items in the past will likely have similar preferences in the future. Collaborative filtering can be further divided into user-based and item-based methods.
2. Content-based filtering: This approach relies on the features of the items themselves and uses the similarity between those features to recommend items. For example, a content-based movie recommender might consider factors such as genres, actor lists, and plot keywords to suggest similar movies.

Often, a hybrid approach that combines collaborative and content-based filtering techniques is employed to improve recommendation accuracy and reduce data sparsity issues.

In conclusion, machine learning plays a pivotal role in the field of data analysis and decision-making. The fundamental techniques of classification, clustering, and recommendation systems allow businesses and organizations to make the most out of their data, discover hidden patterns, and devise actionable insights that ultimately lead to improved performance and user satisfaction. Understanding these core techniques and their real-life applications helps data enthusiasts and professionals build better models and develop more efficient solutions to address various challenges in the rapidly evolving world of technology.

5.1 Applying Classification, Clustering, and Recommendation in Real-World Situations

In this section, we will discuss how the fundamental techniques of machine learning - classification, clustering, and recommendation - can be applied to real-world situations. We will take a look at specific examples from various industries to get an understanding of how these techniques are leveraged to drive insights, automate tasks, and create value for organizations.

5.1.1 Classification in Action

Classification is the process of assigning a category to a data point or object based on its properties. This supervised learning technique is commonly used in many real-world applications, such as:

- **Spam Detection**: Email service providers like Google and Microsoft use machine learning algorithms to classify emails as spam or non-spam. Features like sender information, subject line, and email content are used to train the algorithm and identify patterns indicative of spam emails.
- **Medical Diagnosis**: Machine learning models can be trained on patient medical records and symptoms to predict the probabilities of various diseases. For example, classifying whether a tumor is malignant or benign based on factors like size, shape, and density can aid in the early detection and treatment of cancer.
- **Image Recognition**: Social media platforms like Facebook and Instagram use classification algorithms to identify and tag faces or objects in photos. This technology can also be extended to applications like autonomous vehicles, where object detection and classification are crucial for safe navigation.
- **Credit Risk Assessment**: Banks and financial institutions use classification models to evaluate the creditworthiness of potential borrowers, based on their credit history, income, and other relevant information. This aids in deciding whether to approve or reject loan applications.

5.1.2 Clustering in Action

Clustering is an unsupervised learning technique used to group similar data points or objects based on their properties. Some real-world applications of clustering are:

- **Customer Segmentation**: Retailers and eCommerce companies use clustering algorithms to group customers with similar purchasing habits, preferences, and demographics. This helps businesses target their marketing efforts and develop personalized promotions and recommendations.
- **Fraud Detection**: Clustering can be used to identify outliers or unusual patterns within large datasets, which may signal fraudulent activities. For example, banks use clustering algorithms to detect abnormal transaction data that could indicate credit card fraud or money laundering.
- **News Article Clustering**: Online news portals and aggregators use clustering algorithms to group similar news articles together, allowing users to explore a topic in-depth or discover related content.
- **Genomic Data Analysis**: Clustering is used in bioinformatics to group genes with similar patterns of expression, which can provide insights into gene functions, cellular pathways, and possible therapeutic targets.

5.1.3 Recommendation in Action

Recommendation systems are widely used to suggest items, products, or content based on users' historical behavior, preferences, and interests. Some popular applications of recommendation systems include:

- **E-commerce Product Recommendations**: Online retailers like Amazon and eBay use recommendation systems to suggest products that users might be interested in, based on their browsing history, past purchases, and other user behavior data.
- **Movie and TV Show Recommendations**: Streaming platforms like Netflix and Hulu leverage

recommendation algorithms to suggest movies and TV shows that users may enjoy, based on their viewing history, content ratings, and user-generated playlists.

- **Music Recommendation**: Music streaming services like Spotify and Pandora use recommendation systems to generate playlists or suggest songs for users based on their listening habits, favorite artists, and song preferences.
- **Job Recommendations**: Job portals and professional networking sites like LinkedIn use recommendation algorithms to suggest relevant job opportunities to users based on their skills, job history, and preferred industries.

In conclusion, machine learning techniques like classification, clustering, and recommendation have far-reaching implications and applications across various industries. By understanding their real-world implementations, we can grasp the potential impact of these techniques and harness them effectively to derive insights, create value, and solve complex problems.

5.1 Classification, Clustering, and Recommendation: Key Concepts and Real-World Applications

When applying machine learning techniques in real-world scenarios, it's vital to understand the basics of classification, clustering, and recommendation, as these concepts are widely used across various industries. In this subsection, we will delve deeper into these fundamentals and explore how they can be applied to real-life problems.

5.1.1 Classification

The primary goal of classification is to predict a discrete label for an input data point based on its features. This type of machine learning is referred to as *supervised learning* because during the model training phase, the target output is known and provided to the algorithm together with the input features. There are numerous applications of classification, including:

- **Spam detection**: Email service providers can employ classification algorithms to determine whether an email is spam or not, based on features such as the sender's IP address, subject line, and email contents.
- **Credit risk assessment**: Banks and financial institutions can use classification models to decide whether to approve or reject a loan application, based on the applicant's credit history, income, and other relevant information.
- **Medical diagnosis**: Doctors can leverage classification techniques to predict the likelihood of patients having a specific disease based on their symptoms and medical history.

Some popular classification algorithms include Logistic Regression, Decision Trees, and Support Vector Machines.

5.1.2 Clustering

Clustering is a type of *unsupervised learning* that involves grouping together similar data points, without using any known target outputs. The goal is to find the natural structure within the data by identifying clusters such that the data points within each cluster are as similar as possible, while the clusters themselves are as different as possible from each other. Some practical applications of clustering include:

- **Customer segmentation**: Businesses can use clustering algorithms to group their customers into different segments based on their shopping behavior, preferences, or demographics. This information can be utilized to develop targeted marketing campaigns or to personalize user experiences.
- **Image segmentation**: In computer vision, clustering can be applied to partition an image into distinct regions, helping identify objects or patterns within the image.
- **Anomaly detection**: Clustering techniques can be used to detect unusual occurrences in various domains, such as network security (e.g., identifying unusual network traffic that may indicate a cyber attack) or fraud detection (e.g., spotting unusual spending patterns on credit cards).

Common clustering algorithms include K-Means, Hierarchical Clustering, and DBSCAN.

5.1.3 Recommendation

Recommendation systems are a specific type of machine learning that aims to predict user preferences and suggest items or actions that users may be interested in. These systems are essential in fields where there is a vast and ever-changing selection of items (e.g., movies, books, news articles) or an overwhelming amount of data (e.g., social networks, e-commerce platforms). Some real-world applications of recommendation systems include:

- **Online shopping**: E-commerce businesses can utilize recommendation algorithms to suggest products that a customer is likely to be interested in, based on their browsing history or items they have previously purchased.
- **Entertainment**: Streaming platforms like Netflix or Spotify employ recommendation systems to suggest content (such as movies, TV shows, or songs) that a user may like, based on their viewing or listening history and the preferences of similar users.
- **News and information**: Websites or apps that provide news articles or information can use recommendation techniques to curate content tailored to a user's interests, based on their reading habits and the preferences of users with similar profiles.

Recommendation algorithms can be broadly categorized into two types: *content-based filtering* and *collaborative filtering*. Content-based filtering is based on the features of the items and the user's preferences, whereas collaborative filtering is based on the past behavior or preferences of other users who have similar tastes.

In summary, classification, clustering, and recommendation are fundamental techniques in machine learning that are widely used across various industries to tackle real-world problems. Understanding these concepts allows domain experts and data scientists to select appropriate algorithms and tailor them to specific tasks, ultimately leveraging machine learning to make better decisions, provide personalized experiences, or automate complex processes.

5.1 Applying Classification, Clustering, and Recommendation Techniques in Real-Life Scenarios

In this subsection, we will focus on real-life applications of three fundamental machine learning techniques: classification, clustering, and recommendation. We will examine practical examples from various domains, such as finance, healthcare, social media, and e-commerce, to elucidate how machine learning helps solve complex problems and bring value to businesses and individuals alike.

5.1.1 Classification in Real Life

Classification is a supervised learning technique in which a model learns from a labeled dataset to predict the class or category of new, previously unseen data points. Some real-life applications of classification are:

1. **Spam detection**: Email service providers use classification algorithms to identify and filter out spam emails. The algorithms learn from a labeled dataset containing both spam and non-spam emails to predict whether an incoming email is spam.
2. **Fraud detection**: Financial institutions and credit card companies use classification systems to detect fraudulent transactions. The model learns from historical transaction data and predicts, based on various factors such as transaction amount, location or user behavior, whether a new transaction is likely to be fraudulent or not.
3. **Medical diagnosis**: In healthcare, classification algorithms can help diagnose diseases based on

patients' symptoms or medical test results. For example, an algorithm can analyze lab test results, vital signs, and other relevant data to predict whether a patient has a particular illness or condition.

4. **Image recognition**: Classification techniques are widely used in image recognition tasks, such as facial recognition, object detection, and handwriting recognition. For instance, an algorithm can learn from a labeled dataset of images to recognize human faces in new, unknown images.
5. **Customer segmentation**: Businesses can use classification models to categorize their customers into different segments based on purchasing behavior, demographic information, or preferences. This allows companies to create personalized marketing campaigns and offer targeted promotions or services to specific customer groups.

5.1.2 Clustering in Real Life

Clustering is an unsupervised learning technique used to group data points based on their similarity or proximity without knowing the explicit categories in advance. Some examples of real-life applications of clustering are:

1. **Market segmentation**: Clustering algorithms can be employed to analyze customer data (e.g., demographics, preferences, purchase history) and identify groups or segments with similar characteristics. This helps marketing teams to design targeted advertising and promotions for different customer segments.
2. **Anomaly detection**: Clustering techniques can be used to detect anomalies or outliers by identifying data points that significantly differ from the other clusters.

This can be applied in various domains, such as preventing fraud in finance, identifying malfunctioning machines in manufacturing, or detecting unusual user behavior in cybersecurity.

3. **Social network analysis**: In social media platforms, clustering algorithms can be used to identify communities or groups of users based on their relationships, interactions, or shared interests.
4. **Document clustering**: Clustering techniques can be applied to group documents or articles with similar content, themes, or writing styles, facilitating better organization and retrieval of information from large text datasets.
5. **Bioinformatics**: Clustering is widely applied in bioinformatics research for tasks such as gene expression analysis, protein structure prediction, and biological network analysis. For example, clustering can be employed to group genes with similar expression patterns under specific conditions, which may indicate similar functionality or co-regulation.

5.1.3 Recommendation in Real Life

Recommendation systems use machine learning algorithms to suggest relevant items or content to users based on their preferences, past behavior, or the behavior of other similar users. Some practical examples of recommendation systems are:

1. **Movie and music recommendation**: Online streaming services such as Netflix and Spotify use recommender systems to suggest movies, TV shows, or songs to users based on their viewing or listening history and preferences.
2. **Product recommendation**: E-commerce websites like Amazon and eBay employ

recommendation systems to suggest items or products to customers based on their browsing history, past purchases, and the preferences of similar users.

3. **Content personalization**: News websites, forums, and social media platforms use recommender systems to tailor content to individual users, taking into account their interactions, interests, and preferences. This helps to ensure that users see the most relevant content and spend more time on the platform.
4. **Social connection recommendations**: Social networking platforms like LinkedIn and Facebook use recommendation algorithms to suggest potential connections or friends to users based on their existing network and shared interests.
5. **Job matching**: Job search websites and career portals can use recommendation systems to suggest suitable jobs to users based on their skills, work experience, location, and the preferences of similar job seekers.

In conclusion, classification, clustering, and recommendation techniques are core machine learning methods that can be leveraged to solve a wide range of real-world problems. By understanding the concepts and applications of these techniques, businesses and individuals can exploit the power of machine learning to make better decisions, streamline processes, and deliver personalized experiences to users.

5.3. Applying Statistics, Forecasting, and Machine Learning IRL (In Real Life)

After acquiring a comprehensive understanding of the fundamental concepts of classification, clustering, and recommendation, it is essential to dive into real-world applications that incorporate these techniques. In this section, we will explore the various domains, use-cases, and examples where statistics, forecasting, and machine-learning algorithms can be applied to solve real-life problems.

5.3.1. Business and Finance

Machine learning techniques play a vital role in supporting businesses and financial organizations in making informed decisions. Examples of applications within this domain include

- Credit scoring: By using classification models, banks and financial institutions can assess the creditworthiness of applicants or discriminate between potential good and bad borrowers based on historical data.
- Fraud detection: Machine learning models can be trained to recognize and flag suspicious transactions by analyzing patterns and correlations in large volumes of financial transaction data.
- Algorithmic trading: Forecasting models can predict stock prices and other financial variables of interest that enable organizations to make trading decisions on buying or selling stocks.
- Customer churn prediction: Recommendation systems can predict customer behavior and allow businesses to retain valuable customers by offering personalized incentives or promotions.
- Market segmentation: Clustering models help businesses identify groups of customers with similar

preferences, characteristics, or demographics that enable tailored marketing strategies.

5. &___second_completion<|im_sep|>3.2. Healthcare

Machine learning has been transforming the healthcare industry with its potential to analyze complex data and provide valuable insights. Some of the most prominent applications in this domain include:

- Disease diagnosis: Classification models assist in diagnosing various diseases or medical conditions by analyzing the patient's medical history, imaging data, and other test results.
- Drug discovery: Machine learning algorithms help biotechnology and pharmaceutical companies identify potential drug candidates by predicting their effectiveness, toxicity, and potential side-effects based on the chemical structures and known biological target interactions.
- Patient monitoring: Forecasting models can predict the likelihood of critical events, such as heart attacks, stroke, or diabetes, allowing for early intervention and better management of chronic conditions.
- Personalized medicine: Recommendation systems allow physicians to identify optimal treatment plans for patients based on their genetic makeup, medical history, and lifestyle factors, thus increasing the effectiveness of therapies while minimizing side effects.

- Genomic analysis: Clustering analysis can identify patterns and relationships within complex genomic data, allowing for targeted research and therapies.

5.3.3. E-commerce and Retail

The e-commerce industry has significantly benefited from the use of machine learning in its daily operations, enhancing customer experience and increasing profitability. Some of the key applications include:

- Personalized product recommendations: Recommendation systems analyze customers' browsing behavior, purchase history, and preferences to suggest relevant products or services.
- Demand forecasting: Sales forecasting models enable retailers to estimate future sales, allowing them to manage inventory better, optimize pricing strategies, and identify marketing opportunities.
- Sentiment analysis: Classification models can discern customer sentiment and opinions on products or brands by parsing through social media, online reviews, and other textual data sources.
- Anomaly detection: Fraudulent activities and other irregularities can be detected and mitigated using advanced pattern recognition and anomaly detection techniques.
- Dynamic pricing: Machine learning models can predict and set optimal pricing based on various factors, such as competitor pricing, demand fluctuations, and seasonality, allowing for maximizing revenue.

5.3.4. Manufacturing and Production

Machine learning has significantly impacted the manufacturing and production industry by optimizing processes and increasing efficiency. Some relevant applications include:

- Quality control: Image analysis and classification algorithms can automatically identify defects in products, thus reducing the need for manual inspections and mitigating the risk of human error.
- Predictive maintenance: Forecasting models can predict equipment failure and identify maintenance needs, allowing organizations to schedule timely repairs and minimize downtime.
- Supply chain management: Machine learning techniques can optimize logistic operations by accurately predicting demand, identifying bottlenecks in the supply chain, and enhancing supplier relationship management.
- Robot automation: Machine learning algorithms can control robotic arms and other automation equipment to optimize production processes, minimize human intervention, and increase overall efficiency.

5.3.5. Energy and Environmental Management

Machine learning can contribute significantly to managing and conserving environmental resources and renewable energy sources. Some major applications include:

- Energy consumption forecasting: Machine learning models can predict energy consumption trends and assist organizations in optimizing their energy usage.

- Renewable energy production: Advanced forecasting models can predict renewable energy outputs, such as solar power and wind energy, allowing for better integration with traditional power grids.
- Disaster prediction and management: Classification and clustering algorithms can analyze satellite images, climate data, and geographic information to predict natural disasters and help in efficient resource allocation during emergency response efforts.
- Climate change modeling: Machine learning techniques can help scientists analyze complex environmental data and better understand climate change patterns, thus enabling data-driven policy decisions in mitigating global warming.
- Pollution control: Machine learning models can track and predict pollution levels, helping policymakers devise strategies to reduce emissions and improve air quality.

To conclude, machine learning's pervasive nature transcends various industries and domains. Incorporating classification, clustering, and recommendation techniques can unlock the potential of data-driven decision-making and facilitate the optimization of processes, improved interaction with customers, and effective use of resources. Leveraging these concepts and tools in real-world scenarios can propel organizations to untapped heights, providing a competitive edge in a rapidly evolving global landscape.

Forecasting and Machine Learning In Real Life: From Business to Social Impact

In this section, we will delve into how statistical models, forecasting, and machine learning are applied in our daily lives, offering real-life examples from business, science, sports, and social impact. As we will see, these tools have the power to improve decision-making, drive economic growth, and transform the lives of millions around the world. The applications are vast, spanning from predicting consumer behavior to managing natural disasters, and they will only continue to grow in importance as we strive to build a better future.

Predicting Consumer Behavior in Retail

Retail businesses thrive on their ability to predict consumer behavior, optimize store layouts, and deliver the right products at the right time. In this realm, forecasting models and machine learning algorithms play a vital role in ensuring the success of these endeavors. For example, Walmart, one of the largest retailers in the world, has been using machine learning algorithms to optimize its inventory management and understand customer behavior patterns. By analyzing massive amounts of historical data, such as past sales and external factors like weather and holidays, Walmart can predict store traffic, product demands, and coordinate its supply chain accordingly. These models have proved invaluable in keeping store shelves stocked with items that customers need the most.

Finance and Investment Management

In financial markets, traders and investors are always on the lookout for ways to minimize risk and maximize returns. They rely heavily on statistical models and machine learning techniques to predict trends, identify opportunities, and develop trading strategies. Quantitative traders use algorithms to execute trades in the blink of an eye, responding to fluctuations in the market before most humans can even perceive them. In recent years, robo-advisors have emerged as an attractive option for individual investors, providing personalized investment management services using algorithms based on factors like risk tolerance, investment goals, and time horizon. These AI-driven tools can help individuals make informed decisions about their investments, even without any prior knowledge of finance.

Sports Analytics and Performance Prediction

The world of sports has seen a significant shift towards the use of data analytics and machine learning to predict outcomes and improve performance. Moneyball, a popular book and movie, portrayed how statistical analysis – particularly the concept of 'sabermetrics' – transformed the way baseball teams scout and evaluate players. Football clubs like Liverpool FC are using data analytics to improve recruitment, scouting, and strategy, contributing to their on-pitch success. In basketball, player-tracking technologies and spatial-temporal analysis allow teams to analyze and optimize player movements, shot selection, and defensive tactics. These techniques help teams gain a competitive edge, enhancing their chances of winning games and championships.

Healthcare and Personalized Medicine

Healthcare is another area where machine learning and statistics can have a profound impact on people's lives. In recent years, predictive analytics have become increasingly critical in detecting and diagnosing diseases, understanding patient outcomes, and guiding treatment plans. Algorithms can now examine medical records, lab results, and genomic data to identify patterns that may indicate illness, help guide treatment options or develop personalized medicine programs. For example, DeepMind's AlphaFold was able to predict protein structures, a breakthrough that can help our understanding of diseases and aid in drug discovery.

Natural Disaster Mitigation and Management

Natural disasters, such as hurricanes, earthquakes, and floods, can have devastating consequences for communities around the world. Predicting and preparing for these events is crucial to minimize their impact on lives and property. Statistical models, forecasting tools, and machine learning algorithms can help government agencies, meteorologists, and emergency responders understand the likelihood of natural disasters and prioritize resources accordingly. For example, IBM's Deep Thunder project combines data from multiple sources, such as weather stations and satellites, to create hyperlocal weather forecasts that can predict where a storm may hit, and how severe it may be. This information can be crucial in activating emergency response plans and ensuring aid reaches areas that need it the most.

Climate Change and Sustainable Development

As the world grapples with the effects of climate change, we need data-driven, evidence-based policies to address this pressing issue. Researchers use statistical models and machine learning algorithms to analyze climate data, project future scenarios, and evaluate the effectiveness of policy measures. For instance, tools like Global Forest Watch use satellite imagery to detect deforestation and land-use change across the planet. Climate models can project how temperature and precipitation patterns may change in the coming decades, helping policymakers evaluate the feasibility of proposed carbon-reduction strategies or assess the need for infrastructure investments that can withstand severe weather events attributed to climate change.

Conclusion

From predicting consumer purchases to understanding the changing climate, applying statistics, forecasting, and machine learning has proven to be a valuable tool in various real-world settings. These methods have not only transformed business practices but also enabled meaningful, life-saving advancements in social initiatives. As our 21st-century world becomes increasingly data-driven, the role of these methodologies will only become more significant; harnessing their predictive power will be essential for building a better tomorrow.

Real-World Implementation of Statistical Techniques, Forecasting Models, and Machine Learning Algorithms

In this subsection, we will discuss the practicality and importance of statistical techniques, forecasting models, and machine learning algorithms. We will delve into some real-world examples and explore how these powerful tools can impact various industries, improve decision-making processes, and enhance our understanding of complex patterns and behaviors in vast amounts of data.

Business

Businesses across all sectors rely on statistical analysis, forecasting models, and machine learning to make better decisions and predict outcomes. Examples include:

- **Market research:** Applying statistical techniques to survey data helps businesses understand their audience, develop effective marketing strategies, and optimize their product offerings.
- **Sales forecasting:** Time-series forecasting models can predict future sales based on historical data. This information is crucial for inventory management, resource allocation, and financial planning.
- **Customer segmentation:** Machine learning algorithms can analyze massive amounts of customer data to identify patterns and segment customers into different groups based on their behavior, preferences, or demographics.
- **Credit risk assessment:** Financial institutions use statistical and machine learning models to assess the creditworthiness of customers, reducing the risk of lending to individuals or businesses with a high probability of default.

Health Care

The health care industry benefits from the application of these tools in several ways:

- **Disease diagnosis and treatment:** Machine learning algorithms can analyze vast amounts of patient data, including medical images and electronic health records, to predict disease outcomes or recommend personalized treatments.
- **Drug discovery:** Researchers use statistical models and machine learning techniques to analyze

genomic data and identify potential drug targets, accelerating the drug development process.

- **Epidemiological studies:** Tracking and predicting disease outbreaks requires sophisticated statistical and forecasting models that can analyze various factors, such as geospatial data, population movement, socioeconomic indicators, and more.

Environment and Climate

Environmental and climate scientists use these powerful tools to improve our understanding of natural processes and the consequences of human activities:

- **Weather forecasting:** Meteorologists rely on statistics, numerical weather prediction models, and machine learning to predict short-term and long-term weather patterns with ever-increasing accuracy.
- **Climate change research:** Understanding the complex, interacting variables that contribute to global climate change involves the use of sophisticated statistical techniques and machine learning algorithms. These tools help scientists better understand past trends and make more accurate predictions about future climate scenarios.
- **Resource management:** Conservationists and policymakers rely on statistical analysis and forecasting models to assess the effectiveness of environmental policies and make informed decisions about the sustainable use of natural resources.

Transportation

The transportation industry is leveraging statistical techniques, forecasting models, and machine learning to improve efficiency and safety:

- **Traffic prediction:** Forecasting models can predict traffic patterns based on historical data, enabling city planners to optimize transportation infrastructure and reduce congestion.
- **Route optimization:** Machine learning algorithms can analyze geospatial data to identify the most efficient routes for transportation and logistics companies, reducing fuel consumption and cutting delivery times.
- **Autonomous vehicles:** The development of self-driving cars relies heavily on machine learning algorithms that can analyze massive amounts of data from cameras, LiDAR systems, and other sensors to enable safe and efficient driving.

Conclusion

The real-world applications of statistical techniques, forecasting models, and machine learning algorithms are vast, impacting virtually every industry and aspect of human life. In today's data-driven world, these powerful tools play an increasingly critical role in shaping our understanding of complex systems and making better-informed decisions.

By harnessing these techniques and adapting them to specific industries or applications, individuals and organizations can unveil patterns, trends, and insights that can lead to improved decision-making and long-term success. Whether it's predicting customer demand, diagnosing diseases, or mitigating climate change, statistical methods, forecasting models, and machine learning are playing an ever-growing role in our ability to navigate the challenges and opportunities of an increasingly complex world.

Real-world Applications of Statistics, Forecasting, and Machine Learning

In this subsection, we will delve into the practical applications of statistics, forecasting, and machine learning in various industries and sectors. These techniques greatly impact the way we analyze and make data-driven decisions in our everyday lives. From healthcare to finance, transportation to marketing, statistics, forecasting, and machine learning have revolutionized various fields, enabling us to make better predictions and draw valuable insight from the abundance of data we generate.

Healthcare

Statistics, forecasting, and machine learning play a crucial role in the healthcare industry. They help in the following ways:

1. **Predicting Disease Outbreaks**: Machine learning algorithms and forecasting models can be employed to predict the occurrence and spread of infectious diseases based on historical data, human mobility, and other relevant factors. This leads to better disease prevention and response strategies, as seen in the COVID-19 pandemic.
2. **Medical Imaging and Diagnostics**: Machine learning models, such as convolutional neural networks, are used to identify patterns and anomalies in medical imaging data (X-ray, CT scans, MRI, etc.).

This helps doctors to diagnose and treat various health conditions with higher precision and accuracy.

3. **Personalized Medicine**: With the help of statistics and machine learning, researchers can identify correlations between patients' genetic data, their response to medications, and treatment outcomes. This data-driven approach paves the way for personalized medicine, allowing doctors to tailor treatments to individual patients.
4. **Drug Discovery and Development**: Machine learning algorithms help pharmaceutical companies sift through vast amounts of data to identify promising drug candidates and make informed decisions about their potential efficacy and safety. This accelerates the drug discovery and development process, thus bringing life-saving drugs to market faster.

Finance and Banking

In the finance and banking sectors, statistical methods, forecasting models, and machine learning algorithms are employed in various ways:

1. **Fraud Detection**: Machine learning models are extensively used to detect and prevent fraudulent activities by analyzing patterns in large-scale transaction data. These predictive models help banks in identifying suspicious transactions and taking prompt remedial measures.
2. **Credit Scoring**: Banks and financial institutions use statistics and machine learning to assess the creditworthiness of customers based on their financial history, employment status, and other factors. This helps in making better lending decisions and minimizing risks associated with bad loans.

3. **Algorithmic Trading**: Investment firms use statistical models and machine learning algorithms to process and analyze large volumes of financial data to identify trends, patterns, and investment opportunities. These models help traders make better decisions, maximize gains, and minimize risk exposure.
4. **Portfolio Management and Optimization**: Advanced machine learning models such as reinforcement learning are used to construct optimal investment portfolios by considering factors such as expected returns, risk tolerance, and market conditions. This data-driven approach helps in effective resource allocation and long-term investment strategies.

Transportation and Logistics

In the transportation and logistics sectors, statistics, forecasting, and machine learning techniques are employed in the following ways:

1. **Demand Forecasting**: Machine learning models are utilized to forecast the demand for transportation services based on historical data, demographic patterns, socio-economic trends, etc. This enables transportation companies to optimize their fleet management, route planning, scheduling, and resource allocation.
2. **Supply Chain Optimization**: Statistical models are used to analyze and optimize various aspects of supply chain management, such as inventory management, vendor selection, risk mitigation, and logistic planning. By leveraging data analytics, companies can improve the efficiency of their operations, reduce costs, and make informed business decisions.

3. **Traffic Management**: Traffic data analysis, along with machine learning algorithms, can help in optimizing traffic flow, predicting congestion patterns, and recommending effective measures such as dynamic traffic signals, road capacity expansion, and public transportation improvements.

Marketing and Advertisement

In the marketing and advertising fields, statistics, forecasting, and machine learning can be applied in the following ways:

1. **Customer Segmentation and Targeting**: Machine learning models can analyze large-scale customer data to identify distinct customer segments based on their demographics, preferences, and behaviors. This helps marketers target their campaigns, promotions, and offers more effectively and maximize return on investment.
2. **Sentiment Analysis**: By processing and analyzing large volumes of social media data, machine learning algorithms can determine the sentiments and opinions of consumers about a particular product, service, or brand. This insight enables companies to gauge overall public perception, make data-driven marketing decisions, and improve their products and services.
3. **Market Forecasting**: Machine learning models and statistical techniques are used to forecast market trends, customer behavior, and demand patterns for various products and services. This helps businesses stay ahead of the competition, identify new opportunities, and make better strategic decisions.

To sum up, statistics, forecasting, and machine learning techniques greatly impact our everyday lives by enabling us to make better predictions, find patterns in large-scale data, and make informed decisions. The application of these techniques is continuously evolving, and as we generate more data in this digital era, their significance will only grow in the future.

Predicting the Stock Market using Time Series Analysis and Machine Learning

In the world of finance, the stock market plays a significant role, and its efficient forecasting can contribute significantly to the growth of investors' wealth. However, accurately predicting the stock market is an inherently complex task due to factors such as economic indicators, political climate, and investor sentiments. In this subsection, we will delve into different statistical techniques, time series analysis, and machine learning models that can be employed for forecasting stock prices.

Data Collection and Preprocessing

The first step in any analytical process is gathering historical stock data from financial sources such as Yahoo Finance, Google Finance, or specialized APIs like Alpha Vantage and Quandl. The collected data generally includes information on a stock's opening price, closing price, daily high, daily low, and trading volume.

Before proceeding with model building, the data should be preprocessed to:

1. Clean missing or inconsistent data, which may arise from corporate actions like stock splits and dividends.
2. Convert daily prices into more relevant time frames such as weekly, monthly, or quarterly data.
3. Transform raw data into meaningful features like moving averages or logarithmic returns.

Time Series Analysis

Time series analysis enables the understanding of temporal patterns in the data and estimation of future values. Some popular methods include:

1. **Autoregressive Integrated Moving Average (ARIMA):** This model captures relationships between an observation and a specified number of lagged observations. It has three main parameters:
   - *p* (autoregressive term): The number of lag variables included in the model.
   - *d* (integrated term): The number of times the raw observations have been differenced to achieve stationarity.
   - *q* (moving average term): The number of lagged forecast errors in the prediction equation.
2. **Exponential Smoothing State Space Model (ETS):** This model uses exponential smoothing techniques that give more weight to recent observations than older ones. Three main components include:
   - Level: The average value in the series.
   - Trend: The direction in which the series is moving.

○ Seasonality: The repeating patterns within the same period.

3. **Prophet:** Developed by Facebook, Prophet is a forecasting tool that can handle time series with missing values, outliers, and multiple seasonalities. It adapts to the user's choice and automatically selects the best model.

Machine Learning Models

Machine learning techniques can also be used for stock market prediction, with popular models including:

1. **Linear Regression:** By modeling the relationship between the dependent variable (stock price) and one or more independent variables (features), this model predicts future values through a linear function.
2. **Support Vector Machine (SVM):** SVM is a powerful algorithm designed for classification and regression, fitting a curve or surface to separate the data points with the largest possible margin.
3. **Random Forest:** This ensemble learning method constructs multiple decision trees and combines their output to improve the accuracy and stability of predictions.
4. **Recurrent Neural Networks (RNN), especially Long Short-Term Memory (LSTM) and Gated Recurrent Unit (GRU):** RNNs are specifically designed to model sequential data, capturing the temporal dependencies in the stock market data effectively. LSTM and GRU are improved RNN structures that can handle long-term dependencies.

Evaluation Metrics

The accuracy of the prediction model is determined by comparing its results with the actual stock prices. Common evaluation metrics include:

1. Mean Absolute Error (MAE): The average of the absolute differences between predictions and actual values.
2. Mean Squared Error (MSE): The average of squared differences between predictions and actual values.
3. Root Mean Squared Error (RMSE): The square root of MSE.
4. Mean Absolute Percentage Error (MAPE): The average of the absolute percentage differences between predictions and actual values.

Final Notes

While advanced statistical and machine learning techniques can offer insightful predictions, it is essential to remember the inherent unpredictability of the stock market. Factors like abrupt political events, economic crises, or natural disasters cannot be fully captured by models. Therefore, prediction models should be treated as a supplementary tool in the decision-making process.

When creating a robust prediction model, the following best practices can be considered:

- Use a diverse set of features to capture multiple aspects of stock behavior.
- Regularly retrain the model to adapt to changes in market dynamics.
- Employ ensemble learning techniques to combine the strengths of different models.

With these methods, investors can better understand the stock market and improve their decision-making process in the realm of finance.

Incorporating Statistical Models, Forecasting, and Machine Learning into Real-World Applications

In today's data-driven world, the power of statistical models, forecasting, and machine learning has become an essential part of solving complex problems and making informed decisions. These quantitative tools facilitate the analysis and interpretation of massive amounts of data, and allow researchers, analysts, and business executives to make better, more accurate, and more efficient decisions. In this section, we will discuss how to incorporate statistical models, forecasting, and machine learning into real-world applications.

Identifying the Problem

The first step to applying these methodologies effectively is to identify and define the problem you want to solve. A clear understanding of the issue at hand will help you choose the most appropriate approach to implement.

1. Is it a classification problem where you want to predict categories, such as emails being spam or not?
2. Is it a regression problem where you want to predict continuous variables, such as house prices or stock market trends?

3. Are you trying to discover hidden patterns or groups in your data, which might be suitable for clustering techniques?
4. Are you looking to forecast future patterns based on historical data, such as weather forecasts or monthly sales predictions?

Once you have identified the problem, you can determine which statistical techniques, machine learning algorithms, or forecasting methods will be most suitable for your objective.

Data Collection and Preparation

The next critical step in the process is collecting and preparing the data to be used in your analysis. This data can be obtained from various sources, such as company records, governmental databases, or consumer surveys. The quality of your data will have a significant impact on the accuracy and reliability of your models and predictions.

- Data Cleaning: Remove or correct any errors, inconsistencies, or outliers in the data, as these can lead to biased or inaccurate results.
- Data Transformation: Ensure that the data is in a format that can be easily processed and understood by the statistical and machine learning techniques you will be using. This step may involve scaling, normalization, or encoding of categorical variables.
- Feature Engineering: Identify and create new features that may provide additional insights or improve the performance of your models. This step can involve domain-specific knowledge or techniques such as dimensionality reduction.

Model Selection and Evaluation

Once your data is ready, you can start building and evaluating models. A combination of statistical and machine learning techniques may be employed depending on the specific problem and dataset. It is crucial to select models that are appropriate for your data and can handle the complexities of the problem at hand.

- Model Selection: Choose the most suitable model(s) or algorithm(s) for your specific problem. It is important to consider factors such as interpretability, complexity, and computational resources when selecting your models.
- Training and Validation: Divide your data into training and validation sets, and train your models using the training data. The validation data can be used to evaluate the performance of the models and fine-tune the parameters.
- Model Evaluation: Use performance metrics such as accuracy, precision, recall, F1-score, or mean squared error to assess the effectiveness of your models in solving the problem. It is also essential to consider the trade-offs between complexity, interpretability, and performance when selecting the final model.

Model Deployment and Monitoring

After you have selected the best model, you can deploy it in a real-world context, such as a production system or a decision-making tool. Regularly monitor the performance of your model as new data becomes available, and be prepared to update or retrain the model if necessary.

- Deployment: Implement your model in an appropriate environment, such as a cloud-based server or an on-premise solution, depending on the specific requirements of your application.
- Monitoring: Regularly review the performance of your model using real-world data, and keep track of any discrepancies or issues that may arise. This step will help you ensure that your model remains accurate and reliable over time.
- Model Updates: When necessary, retrain or refine your model using new data or improved techniques. This step will help you stay ahead of any changes in the underlying patterns or trends of your data, ensuring that your model remains relevant and effective.

In conclusion, incorporating statistical models, forecasting, and machine learning into real-world applications requires a systematic approach that includes problem identification, data collection and preparation, model selection and evaluation, and model deployment and monitoring. By following these steps and ensuring that your models are accurate and reliable, you can successfully harness the power of statistics, forecasting, and machine learning to solve complex problems and make better, more informed decisions.

6. Implementing Machine Learning Algorithms: Decision Trees, Neural

Networks, and Support Vector Machines

6. Implementing Machine Learning Algorithms: Decision Trees, Neural Networks, and Support Vector Machines

Machine learning has opened up numerous possibilities for solving complex problems that were once deemed impossible. From predicting customer behavior to diagnosing medical conditions and interpreting natural language, machine learning has provided us with innovative approaches to tackle a variety of challenges. In this section, we will discuss three popular machine learning algorithms: Decision Trees, Neural Networks, and Support Vector Machines. We will explore their applications in real-world scenarios and guide you through the steps involved in implementing them.

6.1 Decision Trees

A decision tree is a flowchart-like structure, comprising nodes and branches, where each internal node denotes a test on an attribute, each branch corresponds to the outcome of the test, and each leaf node holds a class label. The primary goal of using a Decision Tree is to create a training model that can determine the class variable by learning simple and complex decision rules.

Applications of Decision Trees:

1. Customer Relationship Management (CRM): Decision trees can be applied to understand customer behavior, segment them based on their preferences, and create targeted marketing strategies.
2. Healthcare: Decision trees can aid medical professionals in diagnosing diseases by analyzing patient history and medical records.
3. Finance: Financial analysts can utilize decision trees for credit scoring, risk assessment, and fraud detection.

Steps in Implementing Decision Trees:

1. Select a dataset and divide it into training and testing sets.
2. Determine the suitable attribute selection method, such as Information Gain, Gain Ratio, or Gini Index.
3. Create the decision tree based on the selected method.
4. Prune the tree to avoid overfitting, if necessary.
5. Train the algorithm using the training dataset.
6. Validate and fine-tune the model using the testing dataset.
7. Deploy the decision tree model for making predictions or decisions.

6.2 Neural Networks

A neural network is a computing model that takes inspiration from the human brain's biological neural network. It consists of interconnected nodes or neurons, which correspond to the neurons in the brain. These nodes process the incoming data and adapt their connections, known as weights, to improve prediction and pattern recognition.

Applications of Neural Networks:

1. Image and Speech Recognition: Neural networks have been employed in tasks such as facial recognition, object identification, and speech-to-text conversion.
2. Natural Language Processing: Neural networks have significantly improved translation accuracy and sentiment analysis in text data.
3. Game Playing: Neural networks have enabled programmers and researchers to develop sophisticated algorithms, like AlphaGo, that can conquer complex games like Go and Chess.

Steps in Implementing Neural Networks:

1. Choose an appropriate dataset and normalize/standardize the input features.
2. Define the structure of the neural network, including the number of hidden layers and neurons in each layer.
3. Initialize the weights and biases in the network.
4. Determine a suitable activation function for the neurons, such as ReLU, Sigmoid, or Tanh.
5. Select an appropriate loss function, such as Mean Squared Error (for regression tasks) or Cross-Entropy Loss (for classification tasks).
6. Implement a learning algorithm, like Gradient Descent or Adam, to train the model and update the weights and biases.
7. Validate the model by testing it on unseen data and assess its performance using relevant metrics like accuracy, precision, or recall.

8. Deploy the neural network model for making predictions or decision-making.

6.3 Support Vector Machines

Support Vector Machines (SVMs) are supervised learning models that are particularly useful for classification and regression tasks. The core idea behind SVM is to find the optimal hyperplane, which maximizes the margin between two classes. In a higher-dimensional space, the hyperplane is called the decision boundary, separating the data points into different classes.

Applications of Support Vector Machines:

1. Text Classification: SVM has been successful in email spam filtering, news articles classification, and sentiment analysis.
2. Image Classification: SVM algorithms excel at recognizing handwritten digits and categorizing images based on their content.
3. Bioinformatics: SVMs have been employed in protein recognition, finding non-coding RNA genes, and identifying remote homologs.

Steps in Implementing Support Vector Machines:

1. Prepare the dataset, divide it into training and testing sets, and normalize/standardize the input features.
2. Choose the appropriate kernel function, such as Linear, Polynomial, or Radial Basis Function (RBF).
3. Define the parameters for the chosen kernel function (e.g., degree and coefficient for polynomial, and gamma for RBF).

4. Determine the regularization parameter (C) to avoid overfitting or underfitting.
5. Train the SVM model using the training dataset.
6. Fine-tune the model parameters and validate the performance using the testing dataset by evaluating it with metrics like accuracy, F1-score, or confusion matrix.
7. Deploy the SVM model for decision-making and prediction tasks.

In conclusion, Decision Trees, Neural Networks, and Support Vector Machines offer powerful capabilities for tackling complex tasks and have found widespread applications across various domains. By understanding the principles behind these algorithms and following the steps involved in implementing them, you can harness the power of machine learning and significantly enhance your problem-solving abilities.

6. Implementing Machine Learning Algorithms: Decision Trees, Neural Networks, and Support Vector Machines

In this section, we shall discuss some of the most popular and widely used machine learning algorithms, such as Decision Trees, Neural Networks, and Support Vector Machines. Each of these algorithms has its unique properties, strengths, and limitations. Understanding their characteristics and implementation is crucial in order to apply them effectively in real-world applications. So let's dive right in!

6.1 Decision Trees

A decision tree is a hierarchical data structure that uses a tree-like model to represent decisions and their possible consequences. In this model, each internal node represents a feature or attribute, each branch represents a decision rule or split, and each leaf node represents an outcome or decision class.

6.1.1 Why Use Decision Trees?

Decision Trees are commonly used for both classification and regression tasks because they have the following advantages:

- Easy to understand and interpret: The model can be visualized and understood by non-experts, which makes it an attractive option for many applications.
- Requires minimal data preprocessing: Unlike most other algorithms, decision trees do not require scaling or normalization of input features.
- Handles categorical features naturally: Unlike many other methods, decision trees can handle categorical data directly without the need for one-hot encoding.
- Robust to outliers and missing values: Decision trees can handle missing and noisy data gracefully by using surrogate splits or imputation methods.

6.1.2 Building a Decision Tree

The process of building a decision tree primarily involves recursively partitioning the dataset based on a feature that minimizes a cost function or impurity measure. The most commonly used impurity measures are:

- Gini Index: Represents the probability of a randomly chosen sample being incorrectly classified.
- Entropy: Represents the information content or the level of disorder in the data.

Once the tree is built using a stopping criterion such as maximum tree depth, minimum node samples, or minimum impurity decrease, it can be used to make predictions for new data instances.

6.1.3 Implementing Decision Trees

Several popular libraries in Python, such as scikit-learn and XGBoost, offer Decision Tree implementations. Here is a simple example using scikit-learn's `DecisionTreeClassifier`:

```
from sklearn.datasets import load_iris
from sklearn.model_selection import train_test_split
from sklearn.tree import DecisionTreeClassifier
from sklearn.metrics import classification_report

# Load iris dataset
iris = load_iris()
X, y = iris.data, iris.target

# Split the dataset into train and test sets
X_train, X_test, y_train, y_test = train_test_split(X, y,
test_size=0.3, random_state=42)

# Train a Decision Tree classifier
dt_classifier = DecisionTreeClassifier(max_depth=3,
random_state=42)
dt_classifier.fit(X_train, y_train)

# Evaluate the model
```

```
y_pred = dt_classifier.predict(X_test)
print(classification_report(y_test, y_pred))
```

6.2 Neural Networks

A neural network is a computational model inspired by the structure and functioning of the biological nervous system. It consists of interconnected nodes or neurons that are organized in layers. Each neuron receives input from multiple sources, processes the information, and passes the result to connected neurons in the next layer. The neurons are trained to capture complex patterns and relationships in the input data.

6.2.1 Why Use Neural Networks?

Neural Networks have gained popularity due to their ability to:

- Model complex, non-linear functions: Neural networks are universal function approximators, meaning they can model virtually any relationship between inputs and outputs.
- Learn hierarchical feature representations: As layers in a network increase, the network learns increasingly higher-level feature representations.
- Scale to large datasets: Neural networks can be trained efficiently on large datasets using parallel computing architectures like GPUs.

6.2.2 Types of Neural Networks

Some commonly used types of neural networks include:

- Feedforward Neural Networks (FNNs): Information flows from input to output layers, passing through one or more hidden layers. These are the simplest form of neural networks.
- Convolutional Neural Networks (CNNs): Designed specifically for grid-like data, such as images or audio signals, CNNs use convolution and pooling layers to learn spatial hierarchies of features.
- Recurrent Neural Networks (RNNs): Developed for sequence data, RNNs maintain a hidden state that gets updated at each step of the sequence.
- Long Short-Term Memory (LSTM) Networks: A type of RNN that is capable of capturing long-term dependencies in sequence data.

6.3 Support Vector Machines

Support Vector Machines (SVMs) are a set of supervised learning methods primarily used for classification and regression tasks. They aim to find a hyperplane that best separates data instances into different classes, ensuring that the margin between classes is maximized.

6.3.1 Why Use SVM?

SVMs have gained popularity due to their ability to:

- Provide high accuracy and generalization performance: SVMs are designed to maximize the margin between classes, which results in a better generalization performance.
- Handle high dimensional data: SVMs can work effectively with high-dimensional data spaces.

- Adapt to different types of data: SVMs can be used for linearly separable as well as non-linearly separable data by using appropriate kernel functions.

6.3.2 Implementing SVM

Several popular libraries in Python, such as scikit-learn, offer SVM implementations. Here is a simple example using scikit-learn's `SVC` (Support Vector Classification):

```
from sklearn.datasets import load_iris
from sklearn.model_selection import train_test_split
from sklearn.svm import SVC
from sklearn.metrics import classification_report

# Load iris dataset
iris = load_iris()
X, y = iris.data, iris.target

# Split the dataset into train and test sets
X_train, X_test, y_train, y_test = train_test_split(X, y,
test_size=0.3, random_state=42)

# Train an SVM classifier
svm_classifier = SVC(kernel='linear', random_state=42)
svm_classifier.fit(X_train, y_train)

# Evaluate the model
y_pred = svm_classifier.predict(X_test)
print(classification_report(y_test, y_pred))
```

In conclusion, understanding and properly implementing these machine learning algorithms

(Decision Trees, Neural Networks, SVMs) is of paramount importance in tackling real-world tasks. To get the most out of these techniques, it is necessary to apply domain knowledge, preprocess data effectively, and fine-tune the algorithms' hyperparameters. With practice, one can excel in using these powerful tools and unlock their full potential in research and industry applications.

6. Implementing Machine Learning Algorithms: Decision Trees, Neural Networks, and Support Vector Machines

Before we dig deep into the technical details of Decision Trees, Neural Networks, and Support Vector Machines, it is essential to understand that these algorithms are just various approaches to solving real-world problems. These algorithms, when applied effectively to real-world data sets, help in making future decisions, enable organizations to optimize their investments, and make life better in several other ways.

6.1 Decision Trees

Decision Trees are a type of flowchart that enable users to make optimized decisions based on specific conditions by evaluating all possible outcomes. This method is incredibly suitable for business, finance, and healthcare industries, where multiple factors need to be considered before making decisions.

6.1.1 Applications of Decision Trees

- **Medical Diagnosis:** Decision trees have been successfully applied in the field of medical diagnosis. Medical practitioners can use decision trees to predict the likelihood of a particular disease based on the patient's diagnostic test results and demographic information.
- **Credit Scoring:** Financial institutions can use decision trees to prioritize high-risk customers who request credit. By analyzing historical data, they can categorize new customers based on their credit score, income, and other demographic information.
- **Predictive Analytics in Marketing:** Companies can use decision trees to predict customer behavior and create targeted marketing campaigns. Decision trees analyze existing customer data to predict how various customer segments will respond to different marketing techniques, resulting in a more personalized and better-yield approach.
- **Supply Chain Management:** Operations managers can use decision trees to optimize their supply chain by selecting the best suppliers, identifying potential bottleneck areas, and determining the ideal transportation method for shipping goods.

6.2 Neural Networks

Neural Networks are a mathematical model of the human nervous system. They consist of interconnected artificial neurons that can be trained to learn non-linear patterns in large datasets. They are typically used in situations where the relationship between inputs and outputs is complex or poorly understood.

6.2.1 Applications of Neural Networks

- **Speech recognition:** Neural networks have been used to develop robust speech recognition systems. With deep learning techniques, neural networks accurately process user commands and convert them into text with minimal error rates.
- **Image processing and computer vision:** In recent years, Convolutional Neural Networks (CNNs) have revolutionized the field of computer vision by creating state-of-the-art algorithms for image classification, object detection, and image generation.
- **Natural Language Processing (NLP):** Neural networks have become the backbone of many NLP applications, including sentiment analysis, language translation, and question answering systems. Powerful models like BERT and GPT-3 have made it possible to understand and generate human-like context with deep learning approaches.
- **Fraud detection:** Neural networks can be an effective tool to identify potential fraud cases in dynamic environments like finance, where patterns are constantly changing. They can learn from historical data and create robust models that can detect anomalies and alert the necessary authorities.

6.3 Support Vector Machines

Support Vector Machines (SVM) is a supervised learning algorithm that is widely applied to perform classification, regression, and outlier detection. SVM primarily focuses on constructing the best decision boundary that separates different classes effectively, with a maximum margin.

6.3.1 Applications of Support Vector Machines

- **Text categorization:** SVMs have been proven effective in categorizing large volumes of textual data, such as precisely determining whether an email is spam or not. The algorithm's efficiency lies in its ability to handle high-dimensional feature spaces that are common in text data.
- **Face detection:** SVMs can classify facial patterns from non-face patterns effectively. By using Haar features and Principal Component Analysis (PCA) for dimensionality reduction, SVMs separate face and non-face images with a high level of accuracy.
- **Bioinformatics:** One of the areas where SVMs have gained popularity is in bioinformatics, especially in gene classification, protein structure prediction, and microarray data analysis. Due to the high dimensional nature of data in bioinformatics, SVMs' ability to cope with high dimensional and noisy data makes them suitable for these tasks.
- **Handwriting recognition:** Support Vector Machines perform well in recognizing characters in handwriting, especially when combined with the right feature extraction techniques. They are capable of handling the large databases commonly associated with handwritten text.

In summary, the implementation of machine learning algorithms like Decision Trees, Neural Networks, and Support Vector Machines offers promising prospects in various industries. Understanding the fundamentals of these algorithms will only lead to more innovative applications with even better results. As we continue to uncover new techniques and models, the impact of machine learning on real-world problems will keep advancing, opening new doors to endless possibilities.

6. Implementing Machine Learning Algorithms: Decision Trees, Neural Networks, and Support Vector Machines

Statistical methods, forecasting, and machine learning have become essential tools for many applications. Whether a business is optimizing logistics, a start-up is improving its recommendation system, or researchers are finding patterns in complex datasets, the power of these computational techniques cannot be denied. In this chapter, we will focus on three popular machine learning algorithms: Decision Trees, Neural Networks, and Support Vector Machines. We will discuss how they work, why they matter, and how to implement them in the real world.

6.1 Decision Trees

Decision trees are a family of machine learning algorithms that model decisions or decisions-making processes in the form of a tree structure. They can be used for both classification (categorical outcomes) and regression (continuous outcomes) problems, making them versatile tools for various real-world applications.

6.1.1 How Decision Trees Work

A decision tree is, as the name suggests, a tree-shaped structure composed of nodes and branches, which are organized in a hierarchical manner. The tree is built by splitting the dataset into subsets based on the values of the input features (predictor variables). At each node of the tree, a simple decision rule based on the input features is applied, which subsequently leads the data to the left or the right branch. Following along the branches, we reach the leaf nodes, where the outcome (class label or value) is predicted.

The algorithms for building a decision tree, such as ID3, C4.5, and CART, use a criterion (e.g., Information Gain, Gini Impurity) to determine the best possible feature and associated threshold for splitting the dataset at each node. The tree grows until a stopping criterion is met, such as reaching a minimum number of examples in the leaf nodes or reaching the maximum depth.

6.1.2 Decision Trees IRL

Decision trees can be found in various real-world applications, such as:

- **Medical diagnosis**: classification of patients into different medical conditions based on their symptoms and labs results.
- **Customer segmentation**: dividing customers into groups based on their sociodemographic and purchasing behavior.
- **Credit risk assessment**: predicting the likelihood of a borrower defaulting on their loan based on their financial profile.

To implement decision trees in your application, there are several libraries available in different programming languages. For instance, the `scikit-learn` library in Python provides an easy-to-use interface for working with decision trees and other machine learning algorithms.

6.2 Neural Networks

Neural networks are modeled after the biological neural networks that constitute animal brains. They are considered a part of deep learning, which is a subset of machine learning. Neural networks can be used to model complex patterns and relationships between input and output variables, making them suitable for tasks such as image recognition, natural language processing, and many others.

6.2.1 How Neural Networks Work

A neural network is composed of interconnected layers of artificial neurons or nodes. The first layer is called the input layer, the last layer is called the output layer, and layers between are called hidden layers. Each connection between nodes has an associated weight, which is adjusted during the training process to minimize the error between the actual and predicted outputs.

The nodes process the input data by applying a weighted sum of the inputs and then passing this value through an activation function, such as the ReLU or sigmoid function. The activation function essentially decides whether the node will fire its output or not, and defines the non-linearity of the model.

Training a neural network involves updating the weights and biases iteratively using algorithms such as backpropagation and gradient descent. The weights are adjusted so that the error between the actual and predicted output is minimized.

6.2.2 Neural Networks IRL

Neural networks have been successfully applied to a wide range of real-world problems, such as:

- **Image recognition**: identifying objects or scenes within images.
- **Natural language processing**: sentiment analysis, translation, and speech recognition.
- **Recommender systems**: suggesting items or content based on user preferences and behavior.

To implement neural networks in practice, there are several popular open-source libraries available, such as TensorFlow, Keras, and PyTorch, which offer user-friendly interfaces and extensive documentation.

6.3 Support Vector Machines

Support Vector Machines (SVM) are a family of supervised machine learning algorithms used mainly for classification and regression tasks. They are particularly useful for problems with high-dimensional datasets, small sample sizes, or nonlinear decision boundaries.

6.3.1 How Support Vector Machines Work

The main idea behind SVM is to find the best decision boundary (also called hyperplane) that separates the data points of different classes. In the case of a two-class problem, the optimal hyperplane maximizes the margin between the two classes, which can be thought of as the distance between the hyperplane and the nearest data points (called support vectors) from each class.

SVM can handle nonlinear decision boundaries by applying the kernel trick. This involves mapping the input data points into a higher-dimensional space using a kernel function, such as the radial basis function (RBF) or polynomial kernel, and then finding a linear decision boundary in that new space.

For regression tasks, SVM aims to find a hyperplane that approximates the target function within a specified margin of error, known as the ε-tube.

6.3.2 Support Vector Machines IRL

Support Vector Machines have been applied to a variety of real-world problems, including:

- **Text classification**: assigning documents to different categories based on their content.
- **Bioinformatics**: identifying genes, proteins, or other molecular structures associated with specific biological states or diseases.
- **Face detection**: locating the presence of human faces in images.

There are several libraries available for implementing SVM in practice, including the `scikit-learn` library in Python, which provides user-friendly tools for working with SVM and other machine learning algorithms.

Conclusion

Understanding and implementing Decision Trees, Neural Networks, and Support Vector Machines is crucial for many real-world applications when working with statistical methods, forecasting, and machine learning. By mastering these powerful algorithms, you will be well-equipped to tackle a wide range of complex problems and bring innovation to the projects and organizations you are involved in.

6. Implementing Machine Learning Algorithms: Decision Trees, Neural Networks, and Support Vector Machines

Machine learning has become an essential component of modern data analysis in various fields such as finance, healthcare, marketing, and more. This chapter focuses on three popular and powerful machine learning algorithms that can be applied to real-life problems: decision trees, neural networks, and support vector machines. Through the discussion of these techniques, we will provide an understanding of the underlying concepts behind each method, practical applications, and how to implement them using tools like Python and its libraries.

6.1 Decision Trees

A decision tree is a visual and analytical decision support tool that presents a branching structure divided into nodes. Following these branches (or paths) from the root node to the leaf nodes, a decision tree is capable of making predictions or decisions based on the input features specified.

6.1.1 How Decision Trees Work

The decision tree algorithm works by recursively splitting the dataset based on attribute values that result in the highest information gain. The information gain metric measures the reduction in entropy (i.e., randomness) due to the partitioning of data into sub-groups. The process continues until a stopping criterion is met, such as a threshold level for information gain or maximum tree depth.

6.1.2 Implementing Decision Trees in Python

Python provides several libraries for implementing decision trees, with the most common one being `scikit-learn`. Here is an example of using decision trees for classification:

```
# Import necessary libraries
from sklearn.datasets import load_iris
from sklearn.model_selection import train_test_split
from sklearn.tree import DecisionTreeClassifier
from sklearn.metrics import accuracy_score

# Load dataset
iris = load_iris()
X, y = iris.data, iris.target

# Split dataset into training and testing sets
X_train, X_test, y_train, y_test = train_test_split(X, y,
test_size=0.2, random_state=1)

# Create decision tree classifier and fit the model
clf = DecisionTreeClassifier()
clf.fit(X_train, y_train)

# Make predictions
y_pred = clf.predict(X_test)
```

```
# Calculate accuracy
accuracy = accuracy_score(y_test, y_pred)
print("Accuracy:", accuracy)
```

6.2 Neural Networks

Neural networks are advanced computational models inspired by the functioning of the human brain. They consist of an interconnected network of nodes (neurons) structured in different layers: input, hidden, and output layers. Neural networks excel at finding intricate patterns and generalizing information in large and complex datasets.

6.2.1 How Neural Networks Work

A neural network receives input data, which is passed through activation functions in the hidden layers, and the output layer provides predictions or classifications. The learning process is achieved through backpropagation and gradient descent, where the model adjusts its weights and biases to minimize the error between the actual and predicted outputs.

6.2.2 Implementing Neural Networks in Python

Python provides libraries like `TensorFlow` and `Keras` to easily implement neural networks. Here's an example of creating a simple neural network classifier for the MNIST dataset using `Keras`:

```
# Import necessary libraries
import numpy as np
```

```
from keras.datasets import mnist
from keras.models import Sequential
from keras.layers import Dense
from keras.utils import to_categorical

# Load MNIST dataset
(X_train, y_train), (X_test, y_test) = mnist.load_data()

# Preprocess data
X_train = X_train.reshape(60000, 784).astype("float32")
/ 255
X_test = X_test.reshape(10000, 784).astype("float32") /
255
y_train = to_categorical(y_train)
y_test = to_categorical(y_test)

# Create neural network model
model = Sequential()
model.add(Dense(512, activation="relu",
input_shape=(784,)))
model.add(Dense(10, activation="softmax"))

# Compile the model
model.compile(loss="categorical_crossentropy",
optimizer="adam", metrics=["accuracy"])

# Train the model
model.fit(X_train, y_train, epochs=10, batch_size=128)

# Evaluate the model
loss, accuracy = model.evaluate(X_test, y_test)
print("Accuracy:", accuracy)
```

6.3 Support Vector Machines

Support Vector Machines (SVM) is a powerful supervised learning algorithm for classification and regression tasks. Its key advantage is the ability to work well with high-dimensional datasets.

6.3.1 How Support Vector Machines Work

SVM algorithms work by finding the optimal hyperplane that separates the data points of two classes. SVM uses a kernel function to transform the data into a higher-dimensional space, making it possible to find complex decision boundaries. The objective is to maximize the margin between the closest points, known as support vectors.

6.3.2 Implementing Support Vector Machines in Python

Python provides the `scikit-learn` library for implementing SVM. Here's an example of using SVM for classification on the IRIS dataset:

```
# Import necessary libraries
from sklearn.datasets import load_iris
from sklearn.model_selection import train_test_split
from sklearn.svm import SVC
from sklearn.metrics import accuracy_score

# Load dataset
iris = load_iris()
X, y = iris.data, iris.target

# Split dataset into training and testing sets
X_train, X_test, y_train, y_test = train_test_split(X, y,
test_size=0.2, random_state=1)
```

```
# Create SVM classifier and fit the model
clf = SVC(kernel="linear", C=1)
clf.fit(X_train, y_train)

# Make predictions
y_pred = clf.predict(X_test)

# Calculate accuracy
accuracy = accuracy_score(y_test, y_pred)
print("Accuracy:", accuracy)
```

In summary, decision trees, neural networks, and support vector machines are three powerful and widely used machine learning algorithms. By learning how they work and how to implement them in Python, you can leverage their capabilities in various applications, such as image recognition, natural language processing, anomaly detection, and more.

Section: Real-World Applications of Statistics, Forecasting and Machine Learning

In this section, we dive into the real-world applications of statistics, forecasting and machine learning. We will explore different industries and areas where these techniques are particularly relevant, and look at specific use cases that demonstrate the power and utility of these methods in solving real-world problems. By the end of this section, you will have a deeper understanding of how you can apply these techniques to make more informed decisions and drive more successful outcomes in your own life and career.

1. Finance and Banking

Statistics and machine learning have long played a significant role in the finance and banking sectors. Risk management, portfolio optimization, and fraud detection are some of the primary areas where these methods are employed.

- **Risk Management**: Assessing and managing risks is a critical aspect of a financial institution's operations. Statistical models, time series analysis, and machine learning algorithms are used to measure market volatility, credit risk, operational risk, and liquidity risk. These techniques help financial analysts make more informed decisions on setting up risk-adjusted investment strategies and maintaining regulatory compliance.
- **Portfolio Optimization**: Modern Portfolio Theory (MPT) uses statistical methods to optimize the allocation of assets in an investment portfolio to achieve the highest possible return for a given level of risk. Time series forecasting and machine learning models can be used to predict the future performance of stocks, bonds, and other financial instruments, helping investors make more informed decisions about their investment strategies.
- **Fraud Detection**: The finance and banking industries face a significant threat from fraudulent activities such as credit card fraud, insider trading, and money laundering. Machine learning algorithms, such as neural networks and decision trees, can be used to analyze large amounts of transactional data to identify

suspicious patterns and flag potentially fraudulent activities in real-time.

2. Healthcare

Machine learning and statistical analysis are rapidly transforming the healthcare industry by improving diagnostics, treatment plans, and patient outcomes.

- **Disease Diagnosis and Prediction**: Machine learning algorithms, such as deep learning and support vector machines, are being used to analyze medical images, genetic data, and electronic health records to detect early signs of diseases like cancer, diabetes, and Alzheimer's. These predictive models can lead to earlier interventions, resulting in improved patient outcomes.
- **Drug Discovery**: The process of drug discovery and development is incredibly complex, expensive, and time-consuming. Machine learning algorithms sift through vast amounts of data to identify potential candidate molecules, predict their properties, and optimize their efficiency. By reducing the number of experiments and trials needed, machine learning can significantly accelerate the drug discovery process.
- **Personalized Medicine**: The field of personalized medicine aims to provide tailored treatments based on an individual's genetic makeup, lifestyle, and health history. Advanced statistical analysis and machine learning models are used to analyze genetic data, understand how different genetic variants impact specific conditions, and develop individualized treatment plans that lead to improved patient outcomes.

3. Marketing and Sales

Businesses across the globe are leveraging statistics, forecasting models, and machine learning techniques to drive customer engagement, increase revenue, and optimize marketing strategies.

- **Market Segmentation**: Statistical clustering techniques, such as k-means and hierarchical clustering, are used to segment customers based on demographics, purchasing behavior, and preferences. This segmentation helps businesses to target specific customer groups with tailored marketing campaigns, leading to higher conversion rates and increased customer satisfaction.
- **Sales Forecasting**: Time series analysis and machine learning models, such as ARIMA and LSTM neural networks, are employed to predict future sales based on historical data, allowing businesses to make better inventory management decisions, optimize supply chain operations, and set realistic sales targets.
- **Customer Churn Prediction**: Machine learning algorithms, such as logistic regression, random forests, and gradient boosting machines, can analyze customer behavior and transaction data to identify patterns that indicate an increased likelihood of churn. Early identification of customers at risk of churning enables businesses to implement targeted retention strategies, ultimately driving customer loyalty and revenue growth.

4. Transportation and Logistics

The transportation and logistics industry has experienced significant advancements by leveraging statistics, forecasting, and machine learning techniques.

- **Demand Forecasting**: Accurate demand forecasting is essential for optimizing transportation and logistics operations. Time series analysis and machine learning models, such as exponential smoothing state space models and recurrent neural networks, can provide accurate predictions of future demand, enabling companies to make better fleet management and route planning decisions.
- **Predictive Maintenance**: Statistical techniques, such as survival analysis and Weibull analysis, along with machine learning algorithms, like supervised learning and anomaly detection, are employed to predict when transportation equipment may fail or require maintenance. Implementing proactive maintenance strategies based on these predictions can reduce equipment downtime, minimize costly repairs, and enhance safety.
- **Route Optimization**: Machine learning models and optimization algorithms, such as genetic algorithms and simulated annealing, are used to determine the most efficient transportation routes, considering factors like traffic congestion, fuel consumption, and delivery deadlines. Enhanced route optimization leads to reduced costs, increased efficiency, and improved overall customer satisfaction.

These are just a few examples of how statistics, forecasting, and machine learning techniques are being applied across various industries to solve real-world problems. As technology continues to advance and improve, we can expect even more groundbreaking applications and innovations driven by these powerful methods.

Practical Applications of Statistics, Forecasting, and Machine Learning in Real Life

In today's fast-paced, data-driven world, the importance of leveraging statistics, forecasting techniques, and machine learning cannot be overstated. Analyzing data provides valuable insights for businesses and researchers, helping to improve upon existing processes, create new strategies, and make informed decisions. This subsection will explore the practical applications of statistics, forecasting, and machine learning in various real-world scenarios.

Business and Finance

Businesses often apply statistical analysis and forecasting to identify patterns and trends, thus allowing leaders to make informed decisions based on past data. Financial institutions employ a plethora of statistical models and machine learning algorithms to predict stock prices, assess credit risk, identify fraud, and more. Here are some applications within the industry:

- *Demand forecasting:* Companies use statistical models to predict customer demand for their products or services, which can help them optimize sales and inventory management strategies.
- *Marketing analytics:* By analyzing customer preferences and behavior, businesses can make more targeted marketing campaigns and secure better returns on investment.

- *Risk management:* Financial institutions and insurance companies assess risk through statistical analysis, making it easier to manage potential losses in various situations, such as lending, investment, or disaster management.

Health and Medicine

The healthcare industry depends heavily on statistical analysis to predict patterns of disease outbreaks, understand risk factors, personalize drug treatments, and assist in decision-making processes. Some examples include:

- *Clinical trials:* Statistical techniques are vital in designing and analyzing clinical trials, which determine the safety and efficacy of new drugs or medical procedures.
- *Epidemiology and public health:* By collecting and analyzing data on disease occurrence, public health officials can monitor outbreaks, evaluate interventions, and develop strategies for disease prevention.
- *Personalized medicine:* Machine learning algorithms can leverage genetic and clinical data to predict patients' responses to specific therapies, paving the way for more personalized and effective treatments.

Environmental Science and Sustainability

Statistics and machine learning play an essential role in understanding and managing the natural world effectively. From predicting weather patterns to optimizing sustainable practices, these techniques help address pressing global issues. Some applications in this area include:

- *Climate modeling and forecasting:* Scientists analyze vast datasets using statistical models and machine learning algorithms to predict future weather patterns, which is critical for understanding and mitigating climate change.
- *Ecology and biodiversity assessment:* By examining population dynamics, species interactions, and other ecological factors, researchers can develop conservation strategies, manage ecosystems, and predict the impacts of human activities on the environment.
- *Resource optimization:* Businesses, governments, and organizations use data-driven approaches to optimize the use of their resources, minimizing waste, and increasing overall efficiency.

Sports Analytics

The burgeoning field of sports analytics leverages statistical methods and machine learning to assess individual and team performance, evaluate strategies, and optimize decision-making. Some key areas of application include:

- *Player evaluation and scouting:* By analyzing performance data from games, coaches can make better decisions about team selection, player development, and game strategy.
- *Injury prevention:* Statistical analysis of player workload and injury data can help teams design more effective training programs to reduce injury risk.
- *Game strategy optimization:* Advanced analytics, including machine learning algorithms, can reveal insights about optimal strategies under different game conditions.

Entertainment

Machine learning and statistical analysis have also found their way into the entertainment industry, enhancing content creation, marketing, and user engagement:

- *Recommendation systems:* Machine learning algorithms analyze user preferences, history, and behavior to provide personalized recommendations for movies, songs, books, and other entertainment or e-commerce products.
- *Content analysis:* Machine learning can automatically identify themes, topics, and patterns within content, guiding creators in producing more engaging and appealing material for their audience.
- *Box office forecasting:* By analyzing historical data, social media buzz, and other factors, predictive models can provide valuable insights into how well movies or other forms of entertainment may perform financially.

In summary, the applications of statistics, forecasting, and machine learning in real-life scenarios are incredibly diverse and increasingly essential. These techniques continue to revolutionize various industries, paving the way for more efficient processes, informed decision-making, and innovation. As data continues to grow, so does the value and necessity of using these techniques to gain insights and make better decisions in our personal and professional lives.

Applying Machine Learning to Predictive Analytics

Introduction

Predictive analytics is a powerful tool that enables businesses, governments, and individuals to make data-informed decisions. By analyzing historical data, predictive models can forecast future trends, identify hidden patterns, and recommend actions to optimize outcomes. Machine learning (ML), a subset of artificial intelligence, has become a popular technique for building accurate and efficient predictive models.

In this section, we will explore various ways to apply machine learning in the real world to enhance predictive capacity across various domains, such as sales forecasting, churn prediction, fraud detection, and customer segmentation, among others. We'll also discuss critical techniques and considerations for successful ML deployment.

Sales Forecasting

A common application of machine learning in business is sales forecasting, which involves predicting future sales based on historical data. Accurate sales forecasts are vital for inventory management, resource allocation, and financial planning. Machine learning techniques, such as time series analysis, regression models, and deep learning, can handle diverse and complicated datasets to provide more precise predictions.

- **Time series analysis:** Time-series data is a sequence of data points collected over regular intervals of time. Sales data generally has a time component, making time series models like ARIMA,

Seasonal Decomposition, and Exponential Smoothing suitable for sales forecasting. However, these models may not accurately capture complex patterns and relationships present in the data.

- **Regression models:** Regression models identify relationships between dependent and independent variables. Multiple linear regression, decision trees, and support vector machines are examples of regression models that can predict sales based on factors such as seasonality, promotions, and economic indicators.
- **Deep learning techniques:** Neural networks, especially recurrent neural networks (RNN) and long short-term memory (LSTM) models, can handle large datasets and learn complex relationships among multiple variables. These deep learning models can improve sales forecasting accuracy in many scenarios.

Churn Prediction

Predicting customer churn, or the likelihood of a customer leaving a service or product, is crucial for customer retention. By identifying potential churners in advance, businesses can take proactive steps to retain customers and improve customer lifetime value. Machine learning techniques such as classification models can be used in churn prediction.

- **Logistic regression:** Logistic regression is a simple and widely used technique to predict the probability of an event occurring, based on input features. In the context of churn prediction, logistic regression can assess the likelihood of a customer churning based on factors such as duration of the relationship, frequency of interactions, and spending patterns.

- **Decision trees and random forests:** Decision tree models, such as Classification and Regression Trees (CART) and random forests, can effectively reveal complex relationships among different factors contributing to churn. Decision trees are easily interpretable, allowing businesses to understand what drives customers away and design targeted interventions.
- **Gradient boosting machines (GBM):** GBM is an ensemble technique that combines multiple weak models into a strong model by iteratively minimizing a loss function. It can handle missing data and imbalanced datasets, making it well-suited for churn prediction.

Fraud Detection

Detecting fraud in various sectors, including financial services, insurance, and eCommerce, is essential to minimize losses and protect customers. Traditional rule-based systems can be insufficient for detecting sophisticated and evolving fraud schemes. Machine learning models such as clustering, anomaly detection, and supervised classification can help identify suspicious activities and fraud patterns.

- **Clustering:** Clustering algorithms like K-means and DBSCAN group similar data points together. Unsupervised machine learning models such as clustering can identify unusual patterns or outlier groups that may represent fraudulent activity.
- **Anomaly detection:** Anomaly detection techniques, including autoencoders or isolation forests, recognize unusual behavior or data points that deviate significantly from the norm. Anomaly detection allows

for early identification of potential fraud, even if the data lacks labeled examples of fraud.

- **Supervised classification:** In cases where businesses have access to labeled fraud examples, supervised machine learning algorithms like logistic regression, support vector machines, and deep learning models can be trained to classify transactions as fraudulent or non-fraudulent.

Customer Segmentation

Understanding customer preferences and behaviors is the key to delivering relevant products, services, and marketing campaigns. Machine learning techniques such as clustering, principal component analysis (PCA), and collaborative filtering can help businesses segment their customers into meaningful groups and target them more effectively.

- **Clustering:** Similar to its use in fraud detection, clustering algorithms can group customers based on their shared attributes (demographics, spending patterns) and behaviors (product preferences, usage).
- **Principal Component Analysis (PCA):** PCA is a dimensionality reduction technique that helps visualize and interpret high-dimensional data. It can uncover latent variables that influence customer behaviors, facilitating more accurate customer segmentation.
- **Collaborative Filtering:** Collaborative filtering is a popular machine learning technique for recommendation systems. It segments customers based on their past interactions with products or services, enabling businesses to identify groups with common preferences and provide personalized recommendations.

Ensuring Successful ML Deployment

Regardless of the application, the success of machine learning models in real-life scenarios depends on several crucial factors:

- **Data quality and preprocessing:** Ensure that the data is cleaned, normalized, and transformed appropriately. Outliers, missing values, and inconsistent formats should be addressed during preprocessing.
- **Feature engineering and selection:** Focus on creating and selecting meaningful features that contribute to the model's predictive power. Redundant or irrelevant features may negatively impact the model's performance.
- **Model selection and validation:** Choose an appropriate machine learning model based on the problem's characteristics, such as data size, data type, and desired level of interpretation. Cross-validation and other model evaluation techniques should be used to assess a model's performance before deployment.
- **Continual monitoring and improvement:** Real-world data patterns evolve over time, and models should be regularly evaluated to ensure continued effectiveness. Periodically retrain models with updated data, monitor performance metrics, and adapt strategies as needed.

Conclusion

Machine learning techniques have the potential to revolutionize various applications of predictive analytics, from sales forecasting to fraud detection. By leveraging the power of algorithms like time series analysis, classification models, and deep learning, businesses and organizations can enhance their decision-making capabilities and stay ahead in an increasingly competitive and data-driven world.

Working with Real-World Data: Challenges, Strategies and Best Practices

When working with real-world data, it is important to understand that the data we deal with is often far from perfect. Data can be messy, incomplete, unstructured, and biased. In this subsection, we will discuss some common challenges faced when working with real-world data, as well as strategies and best practices for tackling these challenges and producing meaningful insights.

Addressing Messy and Incomplete Data

Real-world data can be fraught with issues such as missing values, duplicate entries, errors, and inconsistencies. In order to effectively perform statistical analysis, forecasting, and machine learning, we need to first address these issues.

Handling Missing Values

Missing values are a common occurrence in real-world datasets. There are several strategies to deal with them:

1. *Remove rows with missing values:* This is a simple method, but can lead to loss of valuable information if

a significant portion of your data contains missing values.

2. *Data imputation:* Replace missing values using a variety of techniques, such as mean, median or mode substitution, linear regression, or k-nearest neighbors.
3. *Utilize machine learning algorithms robust to missing data:* Certain algorithms, such as tree-based methods (Random Forests, XGBoost) can handle missing values natively without the need for explicit imputation.

Eliminating Duplicates and Errors

Duplicate entries and errors can skew results and mislead analyses. To tackle these issues:

1. *Use unique identifiers:* If possible, assign a unique identifier for each data entry to help identify and remove duplicate entries.
2. *Data validation:* Implement validation checks and constraints during data collection to minimize errors.
3. *Data cleansing:* Perform data profiling and exploratory analysis to identify and correct errors or inconsistencies in the data before analysis.

Taming Unstructured Data

Unstructured data, such as text, images, and videos, can be a rich source of information. In order to extract insights from unstructured data, it is necessary to convert it into a structured format:

1. *Text data:* Use natural language processing (NLP) techniques such as tokenization, stemming, lemmatization, and stopwords removal to preprocess text data. Employ advanced NLP techniques like topic

modeling, sentiment analysis, or named entity recognition to extract additional information.

2. *Image data:* Apply techniques such as image preprocessing and augmentation, feature extraction using convolutional neural networks (CNNs), or object detection algorithms to extract valuable information from images.
3. *Time-series data:* Aggregate and transform raw time-series data using relevant techniques such as moving averages, seasonality decomposition, or exponential smoothing to prepare it for further analysis and forecasting.

Mitigating Bias in Data

Real-world data often reflects inherent biases from various sources, such as sampling bias or measurement error. These biases can introduce systematic errors into your analyses and predictions. To mitigate bias:

1. *Data collection:* Ensure data is collected in a manner that is representative of the phenomenon of interest. Apply random sampling, stratified sampling, or other techniques to minimize sampling bias.
2. *Feature engineering:* Select features and data representations that are less likely to introduce or amplify biases.
3. *Model selection:* Choose models that are less susceptible to biased data, or use techniques such as regularization or ensemble learning to reduce the impact of biases on model predictions.

Splitting Data for Training, Validation, and Testing

When working with real-world data, it is crucial to ensure the statistical, forecasting or machine learning models are built using appropriate portions of the data to prevent overfitting and maintain a fair assessment of the models' performance. To do this:

1. *Randomly split data into training, validation, and testing sets:* A common approach is to use a 70-15-15 or 80-10-10 split, but the ratios may vary based on the size and nature of your data.
2. *Cross-validation:* Employ techniques such as k-fold or leave-one-out cross-validation to assess model performance and ensure that it generalizes well to unseen data.
3. *Evaluate multiple models and metrics:* Use a variety of models and performance metrics to build and evaluate statistical or machine learning models to minimize the impact of any one model's limitations.

Key Takeaways

Working with real-world data requires a thorough understanding of the potential issues and biases inherent in the data, as well as strategies and best practices to address them. By carefully handling missing values and errors, effectively working with unstructured data, mitigating bias, and properly splitting data for model training and evaluation, we can derive more accurate and meaningful insights from our data using statistical analysis, forecasting, and machine learning techniques.

Section 4: Applications of Statistics, Forecasting, and Machine Learning in the Real World

In this section, we will explore some real-world examples of how statistics, forecasting, and machine learning techniques are applied across various fields. By analyzing specific cases, we hope to illustrate the depth and importance of these principles in addressing real-world challenges.

4.1 Healthcare

Healthcare is one of the primary areas where statistics and machine learning techniques are being employed. Professionals in this field use data-driven approaches to improve patient outcomes, predict potential diseases, and optimize healthcare delivery. Some applications include:

- **Predictive analytics in healthcare**: Predictive analytics is the use of data, statistical algorithms, and machine learning techniques to identify the likelihood of future outcomes based on historical data. In healthcare, this helps professionals predict patient health status, reduce risks, and optimize treatments. Doctors can better diagnose diseases, devise treatment plans, and track patient progress.
- **Electronic Health Records (EHR) analysis**: EHR data contains valuable information about patient history, medications, and various health parameters. Analyzing EHR data can lead to better treatment

options, reduced risk of medical errors, and improved patient-centered care.

- **Medical imaging**: Machine learning models, especially deep learning algorithms, have proven to be highly effective in analyzing medical images. Applications include detecting tumors in radiographs, segmenting organs from MRI scans, and diagnosing retinal diseases from fundus images.

4.2 Finance

The finance sector is another area where statistics and machine learning play a significant role. Applications include predicting stock market trends, assessing credit risk, optimizing portfolios, and detecting fraud. Some specific examples are:

- **Algorithmic trading**: Traders and finance professionals use sophisticated statistical techniques to forecast and analyze market trends, price movements, and trader behavior. Machine learning models learn from historical data and make predictions that help traders make informed decisions.
- **Credit scoring**: Financial institutions use statistical methods and machine learning algorithms to assess the creditworthiness of borrowers. These models analyze an individual's credit history, financial behavior, and demographic information to determine the risk associated with loaning money to the individual.
- **Fraud detection**: Using machine learning models to identify unusual patterns in financial transactions can alert institutions to potential fraud. By detecting anomalies in real-time, financial institutions can mitigate losses and protect consumers.

4.3 Marketing

Marketers leverage data and machine learning to better understand customer behavior, segment customers, personalize advertisements, and optimize pricing strategies. Applications in marketing include:

- **Customer segmentation**: Using clustering algorithms and other machine learning techniques, marketers can segment customers based on their behavior, preferences, and demographic information. This enables targeted marketing campaigns, increasing customer satisfaction, and driving sales.
- **Sentiment analysis**: Machine learning models, particularly natural language processing techniques, are applied to analyze customer feedback and reviews. Marketers can use this information to identify customer sentiment towards products and services, enabling them to make improvements and build positive relationships with customers.
- **Demand forecasting**: Marketers use forecasting techniques to predict product demand and optimize inventory levels. By analyzing historical data, external factors, and market trends, companies can better meet customer needs and manage their resources efficiently.

4.4 Transportation

In the transportation sector, data-driven approaches are being used to optimize traffic flow, reduce emissions, and improve mobility. Applications include:

- **Traffic prediction and routing**: Machine learning models are used to predict traffic conditions and suggest optimal routes to drivers. This improves traffic flow and reduces congestion, saving time and fuel for drivers.

- **Autonomous vehicles**: Self-driving cars rely heavily on artificial intelligence and machine learning algorithms for decision-making, object detection, and navigation. Advanced statistical models and sensor data enable vehicles to navigate complex road environments with high levels of accuracy and safety.
- **Public transportation optimization**: Data-driven methods help optimize public transportation schedules, routes, and capacity to ensure timely and efficient movement of people. This results in improved service quality and better utilization of resources.

These examples illustrate just a few applications of statistics, forecasting, and machine learning in various industries. As technology continues to advance, the potential for even more groundbreaking applications grows, offering the opportunity to revolutionize the way we live, work, and interact in countless ways.

7. Feature Selection and Dimensionality Reduction Techniques

7.1 Feature Selection and Dimensionality Reduction Techniques

In this subsection, we will delve deeper into two essential techniques in the field of data science, namely, Feature Selection and Dimensionality Reduction. These practices enable better and efficient data management, streamlined processes and improved training models, thus enhancing the overall performance of Machine Learning algorithms.

7.1.1 Feature Selection: Methods and Approaches

The process of selecting the most relevant features or variables from the dataset is called Feature Selection. Irrelevant or less important features, known as noise, might affect the accuracy of the machine learning algorithms. Eliminating such features improves the efficiency, reduces complexity and yields better performance.

There are three main approaches used for feature selection:

1. **Filter Methods**: In this technique, the features are ranked based on the relevance index or statistical measures, and the top-ranked features are selected. Popular filter methods are correlations, mutual information, and chi-square. These methods are independent of the algorithms employed, resulting in reduced overfitting odds.
2. **Wrapper Methods**: A wrapper method employs a machine learning model to test different feature combinations to assess their performance. The performance measure can involve accuracy, F1-score, or a specific metric relevant to your project. Some examples of wrapper methods are forward selection, backward elimination, and recursive feature elimination.

3. **Embedded Methods**: These methods examine feature selection and model construction simultaneously. They involve techniques like LASSO, Elastic Net, and decision tree-based algorithms such as Random Forest and XGBoost. Embedded methods have the advantage of accounting for the training model's interactions, resulting in optimal feature selection.

7.1.2 Dimensionality Reduction: Methods and Techniques

Dimensionality Reduction is a technique that involves the transformation of the high-dimensional dataset into lower dimensions without significant loss of information. It's a useful technique for dealing with the curse of dimensionality and visualization issues.

Mainly, there are two types of Dimensionality Reduction techniques:

1. **Linear Methods**: Linear methods transform the dataset through linear transformations. Some popular linear methods are:

- **Principal Component Analysis (PCA)**: PCA forms the basis for many dimensional reduction techniques. By identifying the axes with maximum variance, it projects the data into a new coordinate system, thus eliminating underlying correlation and reducing dimensions.
- **Linear Discriminant Analysis (LDA)**: LDA, mostly used in the classification tasks, aims to maximize the separation between different classes by finding the linear combination of features, allowing clear visualization of separate class entities.

- **Factor Analysis**: This method identifies the root factors underlying the original dimensions. For example, it may identify groups of correlated features that form a common factor.

2. **Non-linear methods**: In real-world scenarios, the data is not always linear, and linear transformation techniques may not provide accurate results. Non-linear methods, such as t-Distributed Stochastic Neighbor Embedding (t-SNE) and Uniform Manifold Approximation and Projection (UMAP), are suitable for such situations. These methods focus on preserving the local structure in the lower-dimensional space, making them useful for visualization purposes.

7.1.3 Choosing the Right Method for Your Application

Deciding the ideal feature selection or reduction technique depends on multiple factors such as dataset size, underlying structure, and the machine learning task. Smaller datasets may benefit more from filter and wrapper methods, while large-scale datasets could rely on embedded and dimensionality reduction techniques. Visualizing the dataset after applying dimensionality reduction methods can indicate the optimal number of features. Ultimately, a cross-validation procedure and performance assessment of various models can help determine the best-suited technique for your project.

In conclusion, feature selection and dimensionality reduction techniques are critical to enhancing the efficiency of machine learning algorithms. Implementing these methods enables more manageable data, reduces resource utilization, improves interpretability, and results in better overall performance. As all real-life applications and data-driven projects are diverse, assessing multiple feature selection and dimensionality reduction methods is recommended to select the optimal approach.

7.1 Feature Selection and Dimensionality Reduction Techniques

Before diving into the world of forecasting and machine learning, it is important to understand and appreciate the power of Feature Selection and Dimensionality Reduction Techniques. In this subsection, we will discuss the importance of both, the difference between them, specific techniques, and their applications in real-life scenarios.

7.1.1 Importance of Feature Selection and Dimensionality Reduction

Feature Selection and Dimensionality Reduction techniques serve an essential purpose in the stages of data preprocessing and model building. Here's why they are of paramount importance:

1. **Curse of Dimensionality**: High-dimensional datasets can pose a challenge to traditional machine learning algorithms, as they often struggle to find meaningful patterns, and are more prone to overfitting. These techniques enable the reduction of the number of features, mitigating the effects of this issue and decreasing the risk of overfitting the model.

2. **Computational Efficiency**: As fewer features are involved, both feature selection and dimensionality reduction can reduce the computational requirements of machine learning algorithms, making them run faster and become more efficient.
3. **Improved Model Performance**: By removing irrelevant features, noise, and redundant data, feature selection enhances the prediction ability of the model by optimizing the selected set of features, leading to better performance of the algorithms.
4. **Data Interpretation**: A lower-dimensional dataset is easier to visualize and interpret, helping in the identification of meaningful patterns or the understanding of the relationships between the variables.

7.1.2 Feature Selection vs. Dimensionality Reduction

Although they share similarities, Feature Selection and Dimensionality Reduction are not interchangeable terminologies.

Feature Selection is the process of selecting a subset of the most important features that contribute to the predictive power of the model while ignoring the irrelevant ones. In other words, feature selection aims to select a subset of "original" features that can effectively replace the entire feature set without compromising model performance.

Dimensionality Reduction, on the other hand, refers to the process of reducing the number of features (variables) in a dataset by creating a new set of features using a combination of the original variables. The primary goal here is to represent the data in a lower-dimensional space, projecting the selected features into a new feature space.

7.1.3 Techniques of Feature Selection and Dimensionality Reduction

There are numerous methods available for both feature selection and dimensionality reduction. It is essential to select the most appropriate technique depending upon your data and problem domain. Some popular methods include:

1. **Filter Methods**: These methods evaluate the relevance of the features independently of any machine learning algorithm. The feature selection process is based on statistical measures such as correlation (e.g., Pearson, Spearman), mutual information, Chi-Square, etc.
2. **Wrapper Methods**: These methods assess the value of features based on the performance of a specific machine learning algorithm. Techniques like forward feature selection, backward feature elimination, and recursive feature elimination are popular wrapper methods.
3. **Embedded Methods**: These methods integrate feature selection as a part of the training process of a machine learning algorithm. Examples include LASSO and Ridge regression, and Decision Trees/Random Forests using feature importance measures.
4. **Principal Component Analysis (PCA)**: A popular linear dimensionality reduction technique, PCA aims to project the data onto a lower-dimensional subspace while preserving its variance.
5. **t-Distributed Stochastic Neighbor Embedding (t-SNE)**: This is a nonlinear dimensionality reduction

technique that works well for visualizing high-dimensional data in two or three dimensions.

7.1.4 Real-life Applications

Feature Selection and Dimensionality Reduction Techniques have proven their significance and practicality in various real-life applications. Here are a few:

1. **Image Recognition**: Reducing the number of features while preserving essential information can help improve the efficiency of image recognition tasks.
2. **Medical Diagnostics**: In medical science, detecting and understanding the most important biomarkers allows researchers and medical practitioners to diagnose and treat diseases more effectively.
3. **Customer Segmentation**: Marketing and sales departments can use dimensional reduction of customer data for effective market segmentation, targeting or positioning, and understanding customer behavior.
4. **Anomaly Detection**: The process of finding outliers or anomalies becomes more manageable and computationally plausible using dimensionality reduction techniques in high-dimensional data.
5. **Pharmaceutical Research**: In order to identify the most significant features that impact the effectiveness or outcome of drugs, researchers can use feature selection and dimensionality reduction techniques on complex and high-dimensional datasets.

In conclusion, mastering Feature Selection and Dimensionality Reduction Techniques should be considered an essential part of your data science toolbox. Implementing the right techniques can lead to improved model performance, better insights, and a more practical approach to solve complex machine learning and forecasting problems in real life.

7. Feature Selection and Dimensionality Reduction Techniques

In real-life applications of statistics, forecasting, and machine learning, there's often a huge amount of data involved. This data can have many features, which can make working with the data more complex, difficult to understand, and computationally expensive. Therefore, selecting the most important features and reducing the dimensionality of the data is an essential step in the modeling process. This section will go over different methods and techniques for feature selection and dimensionality reduction and their practical implications.

7.1 Importance of Feature Selection and Dimensionality Reduction

Feature selection and dimensionality reduction are crucial for various reasons:

1. **Improving model performance**: Some features may provide no useful information or be irrelevant to the model, leading to noisy or redundant input data. Removing these features can help to improve the model's performance.

2. **Simplifying models**: Reducing the number of features simplifies the model, making it easier to interpret and explain.
3. **Reducing computational complexity**: Fewer features means less computational time and resources required for training models.
4. **Avoiding overfitting**: Including too many features in a model can lead to overfitting, where the model is too complex and adapts too well to the training data. This may result in poor performance on new, unseen data.

7.2 Types of Feature Selection Methods

There are various methods of feature selection, each with its advantages and drawbacks. Below are common feature selection techniques:

1. **Filter methods**: These methods use statistical measures, such as correlation or mutual information, to evaluate the relationship between each feature and the target variable. The features with the strongest relationship to the target are selected. Examples of filter methods include:
    - Pearson's correlation coefficient
    - Chi-square test
    - Information gain (mutual information)
2. **Wrapper methods**: These methods rely on the performance of a given machine learning model to evaluate the importance of features. The idea is to "wrap" the feature selection process around the model and use it as a feedback mechanism to determine the most relevant subset of features. Examples of wrapper methods include:
    - Recursive feature elimination (RFE)
    - Forward feature selection

○ Backward feature elimination

3. **Embedded methods**: These methods are built into specific machine learning algorithms that automatically perform feature selection as part of the model training process. Examples of embedded methods include:

○ Lasso regularization (L1 regularization)

○ Ridge regularization (L2 regularization)

○ Decision tree-based models (such as Random Forest and XGBoost)

7.3 Dimensionality Reduction Techniques

Dimensionality reduction methods differ from feature selection techniques because they work by combining or transforming the original features, rather than selecting a subset of them. This can be particularly useful when dealing with a large number of features that are strongly correlated, as removing redundancy can lead to better model performance. Common dimensionality reduction techniques include:

1. **Principal Component Analysis (PCA)**: This unsupervised linear technique is used to reduce the dimensionality of the data by finding the directions (i.e., principal components) along which the variance of the data is maximized. The transformed data is represented using a lower-dimensional set of uncorrelated features (i.e., principal components).
2. **Linear Discriminant Analysis (LDA)**: LDA is a linear, supervised method used for dimensionality reduction primarily for classification tasks. LDA finds the linear combinations of features that maximize separation between classes, while minimizing the within-class variance.

3. **t-Distributed Stochastic Neighbor Embedding (t-SNE)**: t-SNE is a non-linear technique used for reducing high-dimensional data to a lower-dimensional space while preserving the relationships between data points. This technique is useful for visualizing high-dimensional data, particularly in cases where linear methods such as PCA are insufficient.
4. **Autoencoders**: Autoencoders are artificial neural networks used for unsupervised dimensionality reduction or feature learning. These networks are trained to reconstruct their input data by encoding it into a lower-dimensional representation and then decoding it back to the original dimensions.

7.4 Practical Guidelines for Feature Selection and Dimensionality Reduction

When applying feature selection and dimensionality reduction methods to real-world datasets, analysts should consider the following guidelines:

1. **Evaluate methods based on the specific problem**: The effectiveness of a feature selection or dimensionality reduction method will depend on the nature of the data and the problem being addressed. It's essential to evaluate the performance of different methods within the context of a specific problem or dataset.
2. **Combine methods**: Often, the best results are achieved using a combination of methods. For example, filter methods can help remove irrelevant features, while wrapper or embedded methods can further fine-tune the feature selection process based on the specific objectives of a given model.
3. **Consider the trade-offs**: When reducing the dimensionality of data or selecting a subset of

features, there are often trade-offs between model complexity, computational resources, and model performance. It's important to carefully consider these factors when deciding on an appropriate approach.

4. **Validate results**: Use proper evaluation techniques, such as cross-validation or separate validation datasets, to ensure the selected features or reduced dimensions yield stable and accurate results across different datasets.

In conclusion, understanding and applying feature selection and dimensionality reduction techniques is essential for successful real-world applications of statistics, forecasting, and machine learning models. By appropriately selecting the most relevant features and reducing the dimensionality of input data, practitioners can improve model performance and interpretability, lower computational costs, and avoid overfitting.

7. Feature Selection and Dimensionality Reduction Techniques

An essential step while developing machine learning models is selecting the most prominent features from a large pool of existing ones. This step not only helps in enhancing the model's performance but also simplifies it, making it easier to comprehend and execute. In this section, we'll discuss various techniques for feature selection and dimensionality reduction, providing a comprehensive insight into these crucial processes in real-life applications.

7.1 Importance of Feature Selection and Dimensionality Reduction

Before diving into the specific techniques, let's first understand why feature selection and dimensionality reduction are essential in real-world applications:

1. **Avoid Overfitting**: Ensuring that a model is not overly complex reduces the chances of overfitting. By selecting only the most relevant features, we ensure that the model focuses on critical information while avoiding noise.
2. **Speed up model training and execution**: Reducing the number of features leads to a drop in required computational resources, thereby speeding up the training and execution of models.
3. **Enhance model understanding and reduce maintenance cost**: A model with fewer features is generally easier to comprehend, enabling better knowledge transfer amongst different stakeholders. Additionally, maintaining such models is less resource-intensive.

7.2 Feature Selection Techniques

Several techniques can help identify the essential features for our models. Some of these techniques are as follows:

1. **Filter Methods**: These techniques employ statistical measures to rank features based on their relationship with the target variable. Filter methods include:
   - Correlation coefficient

- Chi-squared test
- Mutual information
- Variance threshold

2. **Wrapper Methods**: These methods use iterative procedures to evaluate different subsets of features to identify the best fit for our model. Some of the commonly used wrapper methods include:
   - Forward selection
   - Backward elimination
   - Recursive feature elimination
3. **Embedded Methods**: These methods use machine learning algorithms to identify the best features as a part of the model training process itself. Some popular embedded methods include:
   - LASSO (Least Absolute Shrinkage and Selection Operator) regression
   - Ridge regression
   - Decision trees and their ensembles

7.3 Dimensionality Reduction Techniques

Dimensionality reduction techniques transform the original dataset into a lower-dimensional space, compactly representing the essential information. Here are few widely used dimensionality reduction techniques:

1. **Principal Component Analysis (PCA)**: PCA is a linear transformation method that identifies the orthogonal axes (or principal components) explaining the maximum variance in the data. By retaining the top few components, we can reduce the dimensions while preserving most of the information.

2. **Linear Discriminant Analysis (LDA)**: LDA, similar to PCA, is a linear transformation technique, but with a significant focus on maximizing separability between different classes. LDA is specifically suitable for supervised learning tasks.
3. **Non-linear dimensionality reduction techniques**: These techniques attempt to capture the complex, non-linear relationships in the data by building manifold representations. Some popular methods are:
   - t-Distributed Stochastic Neighbor Embedding (t-SNE)
   - Isometric Feature Mapping (Isomap)
   - Locally Linear Embedding (LLE)

7.4 Feature Selection and Dimensionality Reduction in Practice

By understanding the various techniques mentioned above, practitioners can decide which method is most suitable for their specific use case. Here are some general guidelines for approaching feature selection and dimensionality reduction IRL:

1. **Understand the data**: Spend time analyzing the data to identify any inherent relationships, correlations, or redundancies that might aid in feature selection or dimensionality reduction.
2. **Establish clear objectives**: Knowing the model's goals, constraints, and optimum performance criteria serve as a useful guide when selecting features or reducing dimensions.
3. **Apply multiple techniques**: There is no one-size-fits-all technique; It's recommended to try different feature selection or dimensionality reduction methods

to determine the most appropriate one for your specific use case.

4. **Perform cross-validation**: Regularly cross-validate your results to ensure the model's stability, consistency, and resistance to overfitting.
5. **Communicate and collaborate**: Engage with domain experts or colleagues to evaluate the model's features and discuss the implications of different techniques on the model's interpretability and performance.

In conclusion, feature selection and dimensionality reduction play a vital role in developing efficient and effective machine learning models for real-world applications. Investing time in understanding these techniques and carefully selecting the most appropriate one for your use case can significantly impact the model's success.

7. Feature Selection and Dimensionality Reduction Techniques

Feature selection and dimensionality reduction are essential techniques for preparing your data, improving the performance of machine learning models, and understanding the underlying patterns within your data. Both play a pivotal role in real-world applications of statistics, forecasting, and machine learning. In this section, we will discuss various feature selection and dimensionality reduction techniques, their importance, and the practical scenarios in which they can be used.

7.1 Why are Feature Selection and Dimensionality Reduction Important?

Before diving into specific techniques, let's understand why feature selection and dimensionality reduction are crucial components of data analysis and machine learning:

1. **Improve Model Performance**: Including irrelevant features can negatively affect the performance of machine learning models. By selecting the most relevant features and reducing the dimensionality, you can improve the accuracy and efficiency of your models.
2. **Reduce Computational Complexity**: Reducing the number of features can significantly reduce the computational complexity of most machine learning algorithms, resulting in faster training and prediction times.
3. **Prevent Overfitting**: The use of many features can lead to overfitting, a common issue in machine learning where a model learns from noise instead of the underlying pattern. Feature selection and dimensionality reduction can help to prevent this by reducing the data's complexity.
4. **Enhance Interpretability**: Reducing the number of features can make your model easier to understand and interpret, which is particularly important in industries where explainability is essential.

7.2 Feature Selection Techniques

Feature selection is the process of choosing the most relevant features from the original dataset. There are various feature selection techniques, such as filter methods, wrapper methods, and embedded methods. Let's look at some of these techniques in more detail:

1. **Filter Methods**: Filter methods evaluate the relevance of the features independently of any machine learning algorithm. Common filter methods include correlation coefficients, chi-square test, mutual information, and information gain. Filter methods are computationally efficient and easy to implement but can be prone to selecting redundant features.
2. **Wrapper Methods**: Wrapper methods use a machine learning algorithm to evaluate the usefulness of subsets of features. Common methods include forward selection, backward elimination, and recursive feature elimination. Wrapper methods can find the best subset of features for a specific algorithm but can be computationally expensive.
3. **Embedded Methods**: Embedded methods incorporate feature selection as part of the machine learning algorithm. Examples of embedded methods include LASSO regression, Elastic Net, and decision tree algorithms. Embedded methods can be more efficient than wrapper methods and account for both feature relevance and selected model.

7.3 Dimensionality Reduction Techniques

Dimensionality reduction is the process of reducing the data's dimensionality while retaining its essential properties. Popular dimensionality reduction techniques include Principal Component Analysis (PCA), Singular Value Decomposition (SVD), and t-Distributed Stochastic Neighbor Embedding (t-SNE). Let's explore some of these techniques further:

1. **Principal Component Analysis (PCA)**: PCA is a popular linear dimensionality reduction technique that identifies linear combinations of features called principal components. These components capture the maximum variance in the data while maintaining orthogonality (perpendicularity) to each other. PCA can be used for data visualization, noise reduction, and speeding up machine learning algorithms.
2. **Singular Value Decomposition (SVD)**: SVD is another linear dimensionality reduction technique that decomposes a matrix into three components: a matrix of left singular vectors, a diagonal matrix of singular values, and a matrix of right singular vectors. Like PCA, SVD can be used for data visualization, noise reduction, and improving machine learning algorithm efficiency.
3. **t-Distributed Stochastic Neighbor Embedding (t-SNE)**: Unlike PCA and SVD, t-SNE is a non-linear dimensionality reduction technique primarily used for data visualization. It transforms high-dimensional data into low-dimensional data while preserving the distance between nearby points and the separation between dissimilar points. t-SNE is particularly useful for visualizing complex datasets with multiple clusters or groups.

7.4 Practical Applications of Feature Selection and Dimensionality Reduction

Feature selection and dimensionality reduction techniques have numerous real-world applications across various industries. Some practical examples include:

1. **Finance**: Reducing dimensionality can help identify the key risk factors in investment portfolios,

improving the accuracy of risk forecasts and facilitating better investment decisions.

2. **Healthcare**: Selecting relevant features can improve the performance of predictive models for disease diagnosis and patient monitoring, leading to more accurate diagnoses and treatment plans.
3. **Marketing**: Utilizing dimensionality reduction techniques like PCA can help identify the most important factors that influence consumer behavior, allowing marketers to target the right customer segments and improve customer satisfaction levels.
4. **Natural Language Processing (NLP)**: Feature extraction methods, like Latent Semantic Analysis (LSA), which uses SVD, can help identify important concepts in text data and enable more accurate semantic understanding and topic modeling.
5. **Image Processing**: Dimensionality reduction techniques can be useful in image processing tasks such as compression, object detection and recognition, and pattern recognition. For example, PCA can be used for lossy image compression, reducing the data size while maintaining image quality.

In conclusion, feature selection and dimensionality reduction techniques are vital tools in the arsenal of data scientists and machine learning practitioners, allowing them to deal with complex, high-dimensional data, improve the performance of their models, and gain better insights into the underlying patterns and relationships within the data. By mastering these techniques, you can unlock the full potential of your data and create more effective, efficient, and interpretable machine learning models.

Modeling Customer Churn: Combining Statistics, Forecasting, and Machine Learning Techniques

As businesses become more reliant on data-driven decision-making, they are continually searching for ways to understand their customer base and improve their products and services. One crucial aspect of this endeavor is predicting and preventing customer churn – or the loss of customers over time. In this section, we will discuss how you can model customer churn using a combination of statistical, forecasting, and machine learning techniques, and how this model can potentially save your organization millions of dollars in lost revenue.

Step 1: Define the Problem and Collect Data

Before diving into the analysis, it is essential to clearly define the problem you are trying to solve. For this exercise, our goal is to predict which customers are most likely to churn in the next month. This will allow us to target specific customers with marketing efforts or other retention strategies.

Once the problem is defined, the next step is to collect the data necessary for analysis. You will need historical customer data, including demographics, transaction history, and any other customer-specific features that you believe may be valuable in predicting churn.

Step 2: Perform Exploratory Data Analysis (EDA)

The primary goal of EDA is to understand the underlying structure and relationships within your data. Begin by visualizing different aspects of the data, such as customer age distribution, average transaction values, and the correlation between features. This will give you an idea of which factors may be most important in determining churn rates.

Step 3: Pre-process Data

Before applying any machine learning algorithms, it's essential to pre-process your data. This includes handling missing values, scaling features, and encoding categorical variables. Depending on the size of your dataset, you may also need to consider techniques such as dimensionality reduction or feature selection to improve the computational efficiency of your models.

Step 4: Identify Potential Churn Indicators

Using the insights gained from EDA and pre-processing, begin identifying potential churn indicators. These are features that have a strong relationship with customer churn rates. Examples may include customer tenure, frequency of purchases, or average transaction value. You may also need to create new features that better capture the relationships in your data. For example, the ratio of a customer's income to their average transaction value may be a more effective churn predictor than either variable alone.

Step 5: Train and Evaluate Models

Now that you have cultivated a list of potential churn indicators, it's time to begin training and evaluating different predictive models. Examples of machine learning algorithms that can be used for this task include logistic regression, decision trees, and support vector machines. Regardless of the algorithm you choose, remember to rigorously evaluate the performance of each model using techniques such as cross-validation and ROC curves. This will help you identify the best model for your specific business scenario.

Step 6: Ensemble Forecasting

To improve the robustness and generalizability of your model, consider using ensemble forecasting techniques. This involves training multiple models and then combining their predictions to generate a final forecast. Examples of ensemble forecasting methods include bagging, boosting, and stacking. Each of these techniques has its own advantages and disadvantages, so it's important to experiment with different approaches to determine which works best for your specific problem.

Step 7: Implement the Churn Prediction Model

After selecting the best model, implement it within your organization's customer relationship management (CRM) system or other relevant infrastructure. This will allow your marketing and customer service teams to identify high-risk customers and tailor their interactions accordingly. Continually monitor the model's performance metrics and update the model with new data to ensure its continued effectiveness.

Step 8: Measure the Impact

Finally, measure the impact of your churn prediction model on customer retention rates and calculate the associated financial benefits. This may involve comparing the retention rates before and after implementing the model or running experiments to directly measure the impact of retention-focused interventions.

By combining the power of statistical analysis, forecasting, and machine learning techniques, your organization can create a robust and accurate customer churn prediction model. This predictive insight will enable you to proactively address customer retention concerns, providing an opportunity to potentially save millions of dollars in lost revenue.

Integrating Statistics, Forecasting, and Machine Learning for Real-Life Problem-Solving

In this section, we will explore the interconnections between statistics, forecasting, and machine learning when applied to real-life problems. We will discuss how to identify the most suitable technique for each situation, ensuring that both accuracy and efficiency are optimized. Let's take a closer look at the key components of each approach and demonstrate how they may be combined to solve complex challenges.

Bridging the Gap: Statistics, Forecasting, and Machine Learning

Undoubtedly, each of these domains - statistics, forecasting, and machine learning - has its benefits when it comes to analyzing data and making predictions. They complement each other in numerous ways:

- **Statistics** helps to identify patterns and relationships within a dataset, enabling us to make informed decisions about past and present events. Through descriptive summaries and inferential analyses, we gain a clearer understanding of the structure and variance of the data, which ultimately helps us craft our problem-solving strategy.
- **Forecasting** builds on statistical analysis to make future predictions based on the observed data. Forecast models can be simple or complex, depending on the nature of the data and the desired outcome. In many cases, forecasting techniques are employed to predict trends, customer behavior, or market demand.
- **Machine Learning** takes data analysis and prediction to the next level by using algorithms and models that learn from data, automating the process and continually improving its accuracy. Machine learning techniques can be supervised, unsupervised, or reinforcement-based, depending on the nature of the problem and the data.

By harnessing the power of each approach, we can create a well-rounded data analysis toolkit that allows us to effectively tackle a wide array of real-life problems.

Identifying the Right Technique for Each Problem

To determine the most suitable approach for a given problem, we must consider several factors, such as the quantity and quality of the data, the specific goals and constraints, and the desired level of accuracy. Here are some guidelines for choosing the appropriate method based on these factors:

1. **Data Quality and Quantity**: Before diving into complex models or algorithms, it's essential to evaluate the data's quality and volume. High-quality, well-structured data is a prerequisite for accurate and effective analysis. The more data you have to work with, the more you can fine-tune the techniques you choose to utilize.
2. **Scope and Goals**: Clearly define the problem you aim to solve and the goals you want to achieve. Are you trying to gain insights into past events, or do you want to make predictions about the future? Knowing the scope and goals enables you to focus on relevant techniques and avoid wasting time on unnecessary or ineffective methods.
3. **Accuracy and Complexity**: Keep in mind that more complex techniques are not always better. Simpler methods may yield accurate results while being easier to understand, implement, and communicate. However, sometimes advanced models or algorithms are needed to improve accuracy, even if they increase the solution's complexity.
4. **Time and Resource Constraints**: Consider how much time and effort you are willing to invest in data analysis and model development. Machine learning, especially deep learning techniques, can be

computationally expensive and require significant resources to fine-tune and deploy. Balancing these constraints with your goals should help you identify the most cost-effective and efficient approach.

Case Study: Predicting House Prices

To demonstrate the integration of statistics, forecasting, and machine learning, let's consider a case study where we aim to predict house prices.

1. **Data Quality and Quantity**: To begin, we must gather a dataset containing various factors that affect the housing prices, such as the location, number of bedrooms, age of the property, and local amenities. The larger and more comprehensive the dataset, the higher the potential accuracy of our predictions.
2. **Scope and Goals**: Our goal in this case is to predict future house prices based on the observed data. Thus, we will primarily focus on forecasting and machine learning techniques, using statistics as an essential preliminary analysis tool.
3. **Accuracy and Complexity**: We might start with a simple linear regression model, a statistical method that predicts the relationship between the house price and multiple variables. However, if this model doesn't yield the desired level of accuracy, we can explore more complex techniques such as decision trees or neural networks.
4. **Time and Resource Constraints**: As we progress from simple to complex models, we should also consider the additional computational resources and time required to implement, fine-tune, and deploy each technique. Balancing these factors will ensure that we select the most efficient and effective approach to predict house prices.

By integrating statistics, forecasting, and machine learning, we can develop a robust, data-driven framework for predicting house prices that can be applied to similar real-life problems requiring accurate future predictions.

Chapter 4: Demystifying the Differences: Statistics, Forecasting and Machine Learning in Practice

4.1 Understanding the Roots: Statistics, Forecasting and Machine Learning

Before diving into the practical applications of the different fields, it is crucial to understand what each entails, their distinctions, and how they complement one another. In this section, we will explore the fundamentals and differences between statistics, forecasting, and machine learning, preparing the foundation for later discussions on real-world applications.

- **Statistics** is the branch of mathematics that deals with the collection, analysis, interpretation, presentation, and organization of data. It includes the planning of experiments, the study of probability, and the derivation of estimators for various types of random distributions. The ultimate goal of statistics is to uncover patterns and relationships in data, utilizing techniques such as hypothesis testing, correlations, and regressions to make informed inferences.
- **Forecasting** is a subfield of statistics that revolves around predicting the future value of a specific variable

using historical data. It relies on various methods of analysis, including time-series modeling (e.g., autoregressive integrated moving average or ARIMA models), seasonal decomposition, and exponential smoothing. Forecasting allows businesses, governments, and institutions to understand potential future scenarios, plan accordingly, and respond proactively to rapidly changing environments.

- **Machine Learning** is a subset of artificial intelligence where computer algorithms improve upon themselves automatically by analyzing data and learning from it. These algorithms often draw from statistical models and pattern recognition techniques to "learn" from the data, adapting their output as they receive additional inputs. Machine learning can be primarily divided into two categories: supervised learning (where the algorithm learns from labeled data) and unsupervised learning (where the algorithm finds patterns in unlabeled data). Machine learning covers a wide variety of techniques, such as neural networks, decision trees, clustering, and natural language processing.

4.2 Applications in the Real World: How They Overlap and Differ

While each field has its own unique strengths and benefits, it is essential to understand where their applications overlap, differ, and even complement each other. The following examples showcase the wide-ranging applications of statistics, forecasting, and machine learning:

- **Healthcare:** Understanding disease patterns is fundamental to improving public health outcomes. Epidemiologists often use statistical analysis to identify various risk factors and preventative measures, whereas forecasters can analyze trends in disease incidence to predict and mitigate future outbreaks. Meanwhile, machine learning algorithms can classify medical images, detect diseases earlier, and even prioritize treatment options for individual patients.

- **Finance:** Financial institutions rely on accurate predictions for stock prices, exchange rates, and overall market movements. Time-series forecasting techniques are commonly used for short-term predictions, while machine learning models, such as random forests and deep learning, can be employed for complex long-term predictions involving multiple factors.
- **Marketing:** Companies use an array of techniques to analyze customer behavior, predict demand, and recommend targeted products or services. Statistical methods, such as regression analysis, can quantify the relationship between marketing activities and sales performance. In contrast, machine learning algorithms are instrumental in developing complex recommendation systems that analyze vast amounts of customer data to suggest the most relevant items in real-time.
- **Weather forecasting:** The predictability of the atmosphere is crucial for various applications, ranging from agriculture to transportation. Traditional statistical forecasting methods like regression analysis can be beneficial in identifying relevant correlations between weather variables. However, machine learning algorithms, such as neural networks, can discern more intricate patterns in meteorological data, leading to more accurate forecasts, particularly in the context of climate change.
- **Manufacturing:** Statistical process control principles are frequently employed to monitor and

maintain product quality. Time-series forecasting techniques can help production planners anticipate future factory demand and optimize scheduling. Simultaneously, machine learning algorithms can predict equipment maintenance needs and enhance the overall efficiency of production processes.

4.3 Choosing the Right Approach: Key Factors to Consider

The selection of the most suitable method for a particular application largely depends on the problem to be solved, the nature of the data, and the available resources. The following questions can guide the process of determining the appropriate approach:

- *What is the primary goal?* If the primary goal is to make inferences or identify relationships between variables, relying on statistical analysis is the most appropriate approach. Conversely, if the goal is to predict future values or make recommendations, forecasting or machine learning techniques may better serve the purpose.
- *What type of data is involved?* Discrete data, like categorical responses, might call for statistical tests such as the chi-square test or logistic regression. Continuous data, like time series, often require forecasting techniques, while complex, high-dimensional data could benefit from machine learning approaches.
- *Which techniques would be computationally feasible?* Highly complex machine learning models can be resource-intensive and might not be suitable for certain applications with limited computational power or real-time responsiveness requirements. Conversely, basic statistical models may not capture intricate

patterns in the data and might provide suboptimal results. Balancing accuracy and computational feasibility is essential.

In summary, understanding the differences and similarities between the fields of statistics, forecasting, and machine learning is vital to effectively apply them in real-world situations. By carefully considering the problem at hand, type of data, and computational resources, practitioners can tailor their analyses and models to serve their unique needs and unlock valuable insights from data in any domain.

Real World Applications of Statistics, Forecasting, and Machine Learning

One of the greatest strengths of statistics, forecasting, and machine learning (ML) is their wide applicability in various industries and fields. In the real world, these techniques are used to solve complex problems, optimize processes, and make informed decisions. Let's explore some of these applications in different sectors.

1. Healthcare

In healthcare, the use of predictive analytics and machine learning has been revolutionary. These methods have several applications, including:

- *Disease Prediction*: Predicting the likelihood of illness for a patient based on factors like age, medical history, and genetics. This information can help doctors take preventative measures to minimize the risk of certain diseases.

- *Drug Development*: Using ML algorithms to analyze vast amounts of data in the drug development process, researchers can identify new drug candidates and streamline the process, ultimately bringing cheaper drugs to market faster.
- *Medical Imaging*: Machine learning algorithms can identify and classify medical images at a remarkable speed, allowing for faster diagnosis and treatment of various conditions.

2. Finance

The finance sector has been an early adopter of statistical and machine learning techniques for several purposes:

- *Fraud Detection*: Banks, credit card companies, and financial institutions use machine learning to identify anomalous transactions and detect patterns indicative of fraudulent activities.
- *Credit Scoring*: Lenders leverage data analytics to evaluate and predict the creditworthiness of borrowers by examining factors like repayment history, income, and debt levels.
- *Algorithmic Trading*: Many trading firms employ advanced algorithms to perform high-frequency trading, where investment decisions are made at lightning-fast speeds based on real-time market data.

3. Transportation

Statistical and machine learning techniques have transformed transportation systems with applications such as:

- *Route Optimization*: Delivery companies use ML algorithms to optimize routes and minimize delivery times, saving fuel and improving overall efficiency.
- *Traffic Prediction*: Authorities and navigation apps leverage data from various sources to predict traffic patterns, enabling better traffic management and reducing congestion.
- *Autonomous Vehicles*: Machine learning and AI are at the heart of self-driving car technology, as these vehicles rely on algorithms to understand their surroundings and make intelligent decisions on the road.

4. Manufacturing

In manufacturing, the adoption of Industry 4.0 relies heavily on statistical and machine learning applications, including:

- *Predictive Maintenance*: Analyzing sensor data from equipment can identify patterns that indicate when a failure is likely to occur, enabling proactive maintenance and reducing downtime.
- *Quality Control*: Machine learning models can detect defects in products with high accuracy, improving the overall quality of products and reducing waste.
- *Supply Chain Optimization*: Data-driven models can improve procurement, inventory management, and demand forecasting, leading to a more efficient and cost-effective supply chain.

5. Marketing and Advertising

Today's marketing landscape involves leveraging customer data and advanced analytics to create effective marketing campaigns:

- *Customer Segmentation*: Clustering techniques can identify groups of customers with similar preferences, allowing marketers to target their messaging more effectively.
- *Recommendation Systems*: ML-powered recommendation engines suggest products and services that are likely to appeal to individual consumers, leading to increased customer satisfaction and higher conversion rates.
- *Ad Performance*: Data analytics can assess the success of advertising campaigns, providing insights on which ads perform best and guide strategic decisions regarding ad spending.

6. Energy and Environment

Sustainable development is greatly enhanced by the application of statistics and machine learning:

- *Climate Change Prediction*: ML models can analyze historical weather data and other environmental factors to forecast climate trends and assess the potential impacts of climate change.
- *Energy Demand Forecasting*: Accurate prediction of energy consumption levels helps utility companies and policymakers plan energy generation and distribution resources more effectively.
- *Optimizing Renewable Energy*: Machine learning techniques can optimize the output of solar panels and wind turbines by adjusting their positioning and other parameters to maximize energy generation.

These examples only scratch the surface of the many ways statistics, forecasting, and machine learning techniques are applied in real-world situations. As technology continues to advance, the potential for these methods to positively impact various industries and fields is truly limitless.

Combining Statistics, Forecasting, and Machine Learning to Solve Real-World Problems

In the age of big data and digital transformation, the demand for tools that can help individuals, organizations, and even entire societies make sense of the massive amounts of information has skyrocketed. It's within this context that the fields of statistics, forecasting, and machine learning have risen to prominence.

In this subsection, we'll explore how these three disciplines can be combined to solve complex, real-world problems. We'll walk you through several practical examples that demonstrate the value of incorporating statistical analyses, predictive models, and machine learning algorithms into a single, cohesive framework.

Understanding the Components

Statistics: This field is concerned with the collection, analysis, interpretation, presentation, and organization of data. Statistics offers a variety of techniques to analyze and derive meaningful insights from data, which can then be used to inform decision-making processes.

Forecasting: Forecasting is the process of making predictions about the future based on historical data and analysis. This field is heavily reliant on statistical methods and typically involves analyzing historical data patterns to anticipate future trends or outcomes.

Machine Learning: Machine Learning is a subset of Artificial Intelligence that enables computers to learn from and make decisions based on data without explicit programming. In other words, machine learning algorithms can recognize patterns in data and make inferences or predictions based on these patterns.

Real-World Applications

Now that we have a basic understanding of the components, let's examine how these various disciplines can be combined to create powerful, real-world solutions:

Health Care

In health care, a significant challenge is making accurate diagnoses, predicting patient outcomes, and determining optimal treatments based on patient-specific data. By combining statistical techniques with forecasting and machine learning, medical professionals can analyze massive amounts of patient records to identify patterns related to specific conditions, forecast the patient's disease progression, and recommend tailored treatment plans.

For example, machine learning algorithms can be used to predict whether a tumor is benign or malignant based on features extracted from medical images.

Similarly, historical data on patients with similar diagnoses can be statistically analyzed to estimate the likelihood of a successful treatment plan or assess the risk of relapse or complications.

Finance

The financial industry is yet another domain where combining statistical analyses, forecasting, and machine learning can be of immense value. For instance, a common challenge is predicting the future value of stocks, bonds, and other financial instruments.

By statistically analyzing historical price data for various assets, a forecasting model can be created to predict future values. Further, machine learning algorithms can improve upon these forecasts by identifying complex interactions between different financial variables and dynamically adapting to new data points.

These predictions can be used to support investment decisions, assess risk, or assist in the creation of automated trading systems.

Supply Chain Management

Supply chain management involves the coordination and organization of resources required to produce and deliver goods and services efficiently. Combining statistical methods, forecasting techniques, and machine learning algorithms can lead to significant improvements in supply chain operations.

For example, analyzing historical sales data can help predict future demand for specific products, enabling businesses to optimize inventory levels and minimize stockouts. Machine learning algorithms can further refine these forecasts by considering additional variables, such as regional trends and seasonal fluctuations.

In warehouses and distribution centers, machine learning can be used to optimize picking and packing processes, recognizing patterns in order fulfillment data, and recommending adjustments to improve efficiency and accuracy.

These examples are only a small snapshot of the vast array of real-world applications where a combination of statistical analyses, forecasting, and machine learning can lead to genuine improvement and innovation. By recognizing the complementary strengths of these fields and strategically integrating them into a unified framework, individuals and organizations can harness the full potential of the data at hand, making better-informed decisions and ultimately driving success in their respective goals.

8. Real-life Applications: Finance, Marketing, Healthcare, and Manufacturing

8. Real-life Applications: Finance, Marketing, Healthcare, and Manufacturing

8.1 Finance

Statistics, forecasting, and machine learning techniques have found numerous important applications in the finance sector, making it one of the most data-driven industries. Here, we look at a few significant use cases of these methods in finance.

8.1.1 Risk Management

Banks and financial institutions face various risks, such as credit risk, market risk, and operational risk. Statistical methods play an essential role in identifying, quantifying, and mitigating these risks. For example, Value at Risk (VaR) is a widely-used statistical method to assess potential losses in the financial markets due to market risk. VaR estimates the maximum loss a portfolio can experience within a given timeframe for a specified confidence level. Machine learning models, like neural networks and decision trees, can also be used to predict potential credit risks based on customers' historical data.

8.1.2 Algorithmic Trading

Machine learning algorithms have revolutionized trading in the stock market. High-frequency trading, sentiment analysis, and predictive modeling are some of the popular applications of ML algorithms in algorithmic trading. ML models can analyze large volumes of historical stock market data, identify patterns, and make predictions with high accuracy. Traders can benefit from these real-time insights and make informed trading decisions.

8.1.3 Fraud Detection

Transactions in the financial sector must be secure and tamper-proof. Machine learning techniques use anomaly detection to identify suspicious activities and potential frauds. By analyzing historical transaction data, machine learning algorithms can detect irregularities and alert the concerned parties. This proactive approach to fraud detection helps in reducing financial losses and developing a more secure transaction environment.

8.2 Marketing

In a world driven by data, marketing has also embraced the power of statistics, forecasting, and machine learning techniques to access profound insights and drive better decision-making.

8.2.1 Customer Segmentation

Using clustering algorithms and demographic data, businesses can segment their customers into different groups based on their purchasing behavior, preferences, and geolocation. This enables companies to tailor their marketing strategies, targeting specific segments with the most appropriate products, offers, and promotions. Statistics and machine learning techniques can also help identify customer churn risk and enable businesses to customize marketing efforts for customer retention.

8.2.2 Marketing Mix Modeling

Marketing mix modeling uses statistical methods to analyze how different marketing channels influence sales, customer behavior, and overall business performance. Companies can utilize these insights to optimize their marketing budget, allocate resources effectively, and improve return on investment (ROI). Machine learning methods, such as time-series analysis, multivariate regression, and decision trees, can be employed in predicting the impact of marketing campaigns on future sales.

8.3 Healthcare

Statistics, forecasting, and machine learning techniques have been instrumental in improving healthcare outcomes, reducing costs and errors, and making healthcare more accessible.

8.3.1 Medical Diagnosis and Prognosis

Machine learning algorithms have shown promising results in diagnosing and prognosticating various diseases, including breast cancer, heart diseases, and diabetes. By analyzing medical images, electronic health records, and patient demographic data, ML models can detect the presence of disease or predict the risk of developing a certain condition with high accuracy. This enables healthcare providers to deliver personalized care, prescribe appropriate treatments, and monitor patients effectively.

8.3.2 Drug Discovery and Development

The process of drug discovery and development is time-consuming and expensive. Machine learning algorithms can help identify potential drug candidates, optimize clinical trials, and predict the success or failure of a drug in the market. By sifting through vast volumes of chemical, biological, and patient data, ML models can guide drug developers in making data-driven decisions, thereby accelerating the drug discovery process and reducing costs.

8.4 Manufacturing

Manufacturing industry can significantly benefit from the application of statistical techniques, forecasting, and machine learning methods.

8.4.1 Quality Control and Process Optimization

Statistical process control (SPC) techniques are widely used in manufacturing to monitor the quality of products and improve production processes. Machine learning models, like neural networks and decision trees, can create a predictive maintenance system that identifies faulty equipment before it fails, minimizing downtime and unexpected breakdowns. Advanced analytics can also help improve production processes by identifying inefficiencies, predicting demand, and optimizing supply chain operations.

8.4.2 Predictive Maintenance

Machine learning algorithms can be applied to monitor the condition of equipment, detect anomalies, and predict the probability of failure. These predictive maintenance models use data from sensors, maintenance records, and work orders to determine when a machine is likely to fail or require maintenance, allowing manufacturers to schedule maintenance proactively, reduce downtime, and increase operational efficiency.

In conclusion, statistics, forecasting, and machine learning techniques have become integral tools across various industries, from finance and marketing to healthcare and manufacturing. As data-driven decision-making continues to gain prominence, we can expect these methods to play an even more significant role in shaping the future of these sectors.

8. Real-life Applications: Finance, Marketing, Healthcare, and Manufacturing

Statistics, forecasting, and machine learning are essential tools that are widely used across different industries, such as finance, marketing, healthcare, and manufacturing. In this chapter, we will discuss some important real-life applications of these techniques and how they help organizations make informed decisions, predictions, and streamline processes.

8.1 Finance

The financial domain is an area where statistics, forecasting, and machine learning find extensive utility. Some of the key applications in finance are:

1. **Portfolio Optimization**: An investor is often interested in maximizing the return of a portfolio while minimizing risk. Techniques like the Modern Portfolio Theory, which uses statistical properties like mean and

variance to find the optimal portfolio allocation, are often used in portfolio management.

2. **Credit Risk Modeling**: Credit risk modeling involves the estimation of the probability of default by borrowers or issuers of debt instruments. Machine learning techniques, such as logistic regression, decision trees, and neural networks, are employed for estimating credit risk.
3. **Algorithmic Trading**: The use of algorithms for executing trades in financial markets has become increasingly popular. Statistical techniques and machine learning models, such as Support Vector Machines (SVM) and Deep Learning (DL), are used for predicting asset prices, which in turn, form the basis for algorithmic trading strategies.
4. **Fraud Detection**: Identifying and eliminating fraud is a critical challenge in the financial services sector, and machine learning algorithms play a crucial role in detecting suspicious patterns, flagging abnormal transactions, and preventing financial crimes.

8.2 Marketing

Marketing is another area where statistics, forecasting, and machine learning are vital. Some of the major applications in marketing are:

1. **Customer Segmentation**: Dividing the customer base into segments based on shared characteristics, such as purchasing behavior or demographics, is an essential task for marketers. Clustering techniques, such as k-means or hierarchical clustering, are popular methods for achieving customer segmentation.
2. **Targeted Marketing**: By analyzing historical data, marketers can use machine learning algorithms to predict customers' likelihood to purchase a particular

product or respond to a specific offer. This information allows marketers to direct campaigns towards customers who are most likely to generate positive outcomes.

3. **Market Basket Analysis**: Market Basket Analysis aims to identify patterns and relationships between products purchased together. Techniques such as the Apriori algorithm enable marketers to discover product associations and utilize those insights to create cross-selling or bundling strategies.
4. **Churn Prediction**: The ability to predict and mitigate customer churn is essential for any business. Machine learning techniques, such as Random Forests and Gradient Boosting, are widely used to forecast which customers are more likely to end their relationship with the company, allowing for targeted retention strategies.

8.3 Healthcare

The healthcare sector benefits significantly from the advancements in statistics, forecasting, and machine learning. Some of the prominent applications include:

1. **Disease Diagnosis**: Machine learning algorithms, such as Convolutional Neural Networks (CNN), are used for image classification and pattern recognition tasks in diagnosing conditions like cancer or heart diseases based on medical images (X-Rays, MRIs, etc.).
2. **Genomics**: Analyzing genomic data to understand the function of different genes and their role in various diseases is a key use-case in healthcare. Machine learning techniques, such as Deep Learning and SVM, are employed to predict the gene-disease associations or categorize patients based on their genetic profiles.

3. **Drug Discovery**: The drug discovery process involves finding potential drug molecules that can act as effective therapies for specific diseases. Techniques like molecular docking, quantitative structure-activity relationships (QSAR), and machine learning models are used for identifying promising drug candidates.
4. **Predictive Analytics**: Healthcare providers can use machine learning models to predict patient outcomes, identify at-risk individuals, and optimize treatment strategies. Techniques like Logistic Regression and Random Forests are used to forecast outcomes such as hospital readmissions or susceptibility to a particular condition.

8.4 Manufacturing

The manufacturing industry relies heavily on statistics, forecasting, and machine learning for process optimization, quality control, and demand planning. Some of the significant applications in manufacturing are:

1. **Quality Assurance**: Statistical techniques like Statistical Process Control (SPC) help monitor and control manufacturing processes, ensuring that the quality standards are met. Machine learning models can detect abnormal patterns in the production data, flagging potential quality issues for further investigation.
2. **Predictive Maintenance**: Machine learning models can predict when a piece of equipment is likely to fail or require maintenance, allowing organizations to optimize their maintenance schedules and reduce downtime. Techniques such as the Long Short-Term Memory (LSTM) and Recurrent Neural Networks

(RNN) are commonly used in predicting equipment failure.

3. **Supply Chain Optimization**: Forecasting models, such as ARIMA or Prophet, are widely used for demand planning in manufacturing. Accurate demand forecasts enable manufacturers to optimize their inventory levels, minimize stockouts, and efficiently allocate resources along the supply chain.

4. **Process Optimization**: Manufacturing processes produce a vast amount of data, which can be utilized to optimize operations. Machine learning algorithms, such as SVM or Deep Learning, can identify patterns and relationships in the data, enabling engineers to make data-driven decisions and enhance process efficiency.

In conclusion, the applications of statistics, forecasting, and machine learning are far-reaching in various industries. The continuous development and advancements in these areas have a vital impact on improving decision-making processes, predictive capabilities, and overall efficiency, driving innovation and growth in finance, marketing, healthcare, and manufacturing sectors.

8. Real-life Applications: Finance, Marketing, Healthcare, and Manufacturing

8.1. Finance

The financial industry has been at the forefront of leveraging the power of statistical, forecasting, and machine learning algorithms. Several areas within the financial realm stand to benefit from these techniques, including:

1. **Credit Scoring**: Lending institutions (such as banks and credit card companies) use machine learning models to assess the creditworthiness of potential borrowers. These models employ statistical techniques to identify patterns and relationships from historical borrower data, which can then be used to calculate a credit risk score. A higher risk score typically indicates a higher likelihood for default and vice versa.
2. **Trading Algorithms**: Algorithmic trading, also known as automated trading, involves using computer programs to execute trades at high speeds and volumes, based on predefined trading strategies. These strategies are often built using machine learning algorithms and statistical models to identify profitable trading opportunities in the markets. For instance, neural networks can be used to predict stock prices, which can then guide buy and sell decisions.
3. **Fraud Detection**: Financial institutions use machine learning algorithms to identify anomalous transactions or behaviors that might indicate fraud. These algorithms analyze vast amounts of transactional data in real-time to spot patterns, trends, and abnormalities, which can then trigger investigation processes or automated incident responses.
4. **Portfolio Optimization**: Financial portfolios typically comprise various assets with different risk and return potential. Machine learning algorithms can assist in optimizing the allocation of assets in a portfolio, with the aim of achieving an optimal balance between risks and returns. These models can assess historic and real-time data to recommend the appropriate investment mix for each investor.

5. **Risk Management**: Financial institutions deal with different types of risks, with credit risk and market risk being two of the key areas. Machine learning and statistical models can help assess and quantify these risks, enabling organizations to take necessary precautions and hedge their exposures. In this regard, models like VaR (Value-at-Risk) and stress testing are widely used in the industry.

8.2. Marketing

Marketing strategies can be significantly enhanced by the use of statistic, forecasting, and machine learning techniques, such as:

1. **Customer Segmentation**: Businesses can use machine learning algorithms and statistical techniques to analyze customer data and classify them into distinct groups based on their similarities. This can help organizations tailor their marketing efforts more effectively by targeting each group's needs and preferences.
2. **Predictive Analytics**: Marketers can use forecasting models to predict customer behavior, product demand, or market trends. These predictions can provide valuable insights that can inform marketing decisions, allowing organizations to anticipate and capitalize on future opportunities.
3. **Churn Prediction**: One of the key challenges for businesses is retaining customers. Machine learning models can help predict the likelihood of customers churning and take necessary actions to prevent it. For example, organizations can preemptively reach out to at-risk customers, offering incentives, or addressing potential causes of dissatisfaction.

4. **Recommendation Engines**: E-commerce, online streaming, and various other platforms use machine learning algorithms to generate personalized product or content recommendations to users based on their browsing history, preferences, and past transactions. This helps improve customer satisfaction and engagement, leading to increased retention and revenue.

8.3. Healthcare

The healthcare industry benefits from the use of statistical, forecasting, and machine learning algorithms in the following ways:

1. **Disease Diagnosis**: Machine learning models can analyze medical images, such as X-rays, MRIs, and CT scans, to identify patterns and features indicative of diseases or abnormalities. This can assist in timely diagnosis and treatment and reduce human error.
2. **Drug Discovery**: The drug development process is complex and cost-intensive. Machine learning algorithms can expedite the process by analyzing vast amounts of biological, chemical, and clinical data to identify potential drug candidates and predict their efficacy more accurately.
3. **Personalized Medicine**: Machine learning models can be used to analyze a patient's genetic data and predict their response to treatments or medications. This can guide doctors in prescribing treatments tailored to individual patients, leading to better health outcomes and reduced adverse drug effects.
4. **Healthcare Resource Allocation**: Forecasting models can predict the demand for healthcare resources, such as hospital beds, medical staff, and equipment, in various geographic locations or during

specific timeframes (e.g., flu season or during outbreaks). This can help healthcare providers allocate resources effectively to meet the anticipated demand.

8.4. Manufacturing

In manufacturing, statistical, forecasting, and machine learning algorithms can contribute considerably to process optimization, quality enhancement, and production planning:

1. **Predictive Maintenance**: Machine learning models can predict equipment failure by analyzing sensor data and identifying early signs of wear and tear. This can help prevent unexpected breakdowns, minimize downtime, and optimize maintenance schedules.
2. **Quality Control**: Machine learning algorithms can analyze images or other data collected during the manufacturing process to detect defects, anomalies, or deviations from desired specifications. This can help ensure product quality while reducing waste and rework.
3. **Demand Forecasting**: Accurate demand forecasts can aid in production planning and inventory management. Machine learning models can analyze historical sales data, market trends, and external factors to generate more accurate and granular demand forecasts.
4. **Supply Chain Optimization**: Machine learning algorithms can help optimize the supply chain by analyzing factors such as raw material availability, production capacity, transportation times, and other constraints. Manufacturers can use these insights to make data-driven decisions and increase efficiency.

By incorporating statistical, forecasting, and machine learning techniques in various domains, we can make better decisions, optimize processes, and ultimately drive innovation and success in these industries.

8. Real-life Applications: Finance, Marketing, Healthcare, and Manufacturing

8.1 Finance

In finance, applying statistics, forecasting, and machine learning algorithms play a pivotal role in various aspects, including risk assessment, portfolio management, trading, and fraud detection. Financial institutions and experts harness the power of data analytics to make informed decisions and predictions about market trends and individual stocks.

- **Risk Assessment**: Credit scores, loan defaults, and investment risks are some of the many aspects that heavily rely on risk assessment. Statistical models and machine learning algorithms are used to predict the risks associated with lending to individual borrowers, investing in particular stocks or bonds, or creating a specific investment portfolio.
- **Portfolio Management**: Financial advisors and portfolio managers use different strategies to optimize investment portfolios, minimize risks, and maximize returns. Machine learning algorithms help forecast the performance of individual assets and balance the overall risk in the portfolio. Additionally, algorithms like modern portfolio theory (MPT) can be used to

determine the best asset allocation for an investor's needs.

- **Trading**: High-frequency trading (HFT) and algorithmic trading use sophisticated computer programs to place orders in the markets rapidly. These programs make decisions based on statistical analysis and machine learning algorithms that analyze vast amounts of data, news, and market trends in order to identify profitable trading opportunities.
- **Fraud Detection**: Banks and financial institutions are adept at detecting fraudulent activities, such as credit card fraud or insider trading, by analyzing large volumes of transaction data with the help of machine learning algorithms. These algorithms are designed to recognize anomalous behavior or patterns among transactions and flag them for further investigation.

8.2 Marketing

Marketing professionals use statistics, forecasting, and machine learning techniques to understand customer behavior, segment markets, target specific customer groups, and optimize campaign strategies.

- **Customer Segmentation**: Clustering algorithms and statistical models can analyze vast amounts of data on customer demographics, preferences, and purchasing habits. This information allows marketing teams to create targeted campaigns and customized offers for various customer segments.
- **Predictive Analytics**: Predictive models help marketing professionals forecast customer churn, product demand, and the impact of marketing campaigns. By understanding these trends, marketers can strategize and budget more effectively, allocate

resources efficiently, and ultimately boost their return on investment (ROI).

- **A/B Testing**: Marketing campaigns often involve multiple variables, such as ad designs, email subject lines, or promotional offers, that need to be optimized for maximum effectiveness. A/B testing uses statistical hypothesis techniques to compare and analyze the performance of different campaign variables and identify the most successful combinations.
- **Sentiment Analysis**: Machine learning models, such as natural language processing (NLP), can be employed to analyze text data from customer feedback, product reviews, and social media to gauge consumer sentiment. This data provides valuable insights into customer preferences and can inform decisions about product development, marketing campaigns, and customer engagement.

8.3 Healthcare

Statistics, forecasting, and machine learning methodologies have a profound impact on healthcare, driving advancements in personalized medicine, disease prediction, medical imaging analysis, and drug development.

- **Personalized Medicine**: Machine learning algorithms can analyze genomic data on a patient-by-patient basis, helping researchers to understand how individual genes interact with medications and identify the best treatment options for specific patients.
- **Disease Prediction**: Machine learning models can be used to predict disease outbreaks or the individual likelihood of disease development by analyzing various factors such as genetic information, medical records, and environmental data.

- **Medical Imaging Analysis**: Deep learning and computer vision techniques are revolutionizing medical imaging analysis by automating the identification of diseases and abnormalities in x-ray, CAT, and MRI images.
- **Drug Development**: Computational models and machine learning algorithms can significantly reduce the time and cost of drug development by predicting drug toxicity, optimizing the chemical structure of drug candidates, and assisting in the identification of potential new drug targets.

8.4 Manufacturing

In the manufacturing sector, data-driven techniques are critical for optimizing production processes, managing supply chains, and ensuring quality control.

- **Predictive Maintenance**: Machine learning models use sensor data and historical maintenance records to predict when equipment is likely to fail or require maintenance. By scheduling maintenance proactively, manufacturers can minimize downtime and reduce costs.
- **Supply Chain Optimization**: Forecasting algorithms and machine learning models enable manufacturers to predict raw material shortages or delays, allowing them to adapt their production schedules and reorganize their supply chains dynamically.
- **Quality Control**: Computer vision, image processing, and machine learning models can be employed to automate the inspection process and detect defects in manufactured products. By reducing human error and ensuring a consistently high standard of quality throughout the production process,

manufacturers can increase customer satisfaction and minimize losses due to defects.

- **Process Optimization**: Statistical process control (SPC) and machine learning algorithms can be used to analyze manufacturing processes and identify variables that impact efficiency or product quality. By optimizing these variables, manufacturers can streamline their operations and maximize productivity.

In conclusion, the application of statistics, forecasting, and machine learning techniques has far-reaching implications across various industries, including finance, marketing, healthcare, and manufacturing. As data continues to grow in both volume and complexity, the potential for these methodologies to drive innovation and efficiency increases exponentially.

8. Real-life Applications: Finance, Marketing, Healthcare, and Manufacturing

In this section, we will explore some real-life applications of statistics, forecasting, and machine learning in various industries such as finance, marketing, healthcare, and manufacturing. These use cases highlight the importance of these techniques in making data-driven decisions and creating efficient solutions for various business problems.

8.1 Finance

The finance industry has heavily relied on statistical analysis and machine learning techniques to make better investment decisions for decades. Some key applications in this domain are as follows:

8.1.1 Risk Management

Banks and financial institutions use statistical models to assess the default probabilities and credit risks associated with potential borrowers. Techniques such as time-series analysis, Monte Carlo simulations, and survival analysis help institutions quantify and manage credit risk effectively.

8.1.2 Algorithmic Trading

Stock trading has witnessed significant automation due to the application of machine learning algorithms. High-frequency trading (HFT) employs algorithms to make trading decisions and submit orders within milliseconds. These algorithms can analyze large volumes of data in real-time to identify trading opportunities.

8.1.3 Portfolio Optimization

Investment managers leverage statistical models and optimization techniques to construct optimal portfolios that maximize returns while minimizing portfolio risk. Modern portfolio theory, founded by Harry Markowitz Utilizes mean-variance optimization to allocate weights to different assets in a portfolio.

8.1.4 Fraud Detection

Machine learning techniques, particularly classification algorithms, help identify fraudulent transactions by monitoring customer behavior and detecting unusual patterns. Models such as logistic regression, decision trees, and neural networks have been successfully applied in catching frauds and reducing financial crimes.

8.2 Marketing

Organizations have started to utilize the power of data-driven marketing strategies to engage customers and increase revenues. Applications of statistics and machine learning in marketing include:

8.2.1 Customer Segmentation

Clustering algorithms are widely used to segment customers based on their demographics, behavior, and preferences. This enables marketers to create targeted marketing campaigns and reach out to different customer segments more effectively.

8.2.2 Market Basket Analysis

Association rule mining helps discover patterns among products purchased by customers. Retailers use this information to design promotional strategies, generate personalized recommendations, and optimize store layouts.

8.2.3 Sentiment Analysis

Natural language processing (NLP) techniques such as text mining and sentiment analysis help capture consumer opinions and feedback on various platforms.

This helps businesses identify areas of improvement and adjust their marketing strategies to improve brand perception.

8.2.4 Churn Prediction

Predictive analytics and machine learning models are employed to forecast customer churn. By identifying customers at the risk of leaving or canceling their subscriptions, organizations can direct targeted retention efforts and minimize customer attrition.

8.3 Healthcare

The healthcare industry has witnessed rapid adoption of data analytics and machine learning tools to improve the diagnosis, treatment, and prevention of diseases. Some key applications include:

8.3.1 Disease Diagnosis

Machine learning algorithms, particularly deep learning techniques like convolutional neural networks (CNN), have shown great promise in diagnosing diseases based on medical images, such as lung cancer from chest X-rays or skin cancer from images of skin lesions.

8.3.2 Drug Discovery

Machine learning vastly optimizes the drug discovery process by analyzing massive amounts of patient data and identifying key biological characteristics associated with a disease. This helps in selecting potential drug candidates and predicting the outcomes of clinical trials.

8.3.3 Personalized Medicine

Machine learning techniques enable the development of precision medicine by integrating patient-level data (genomics, clinical, and lifestyle) to create tailored treatments for each individual. Personalized medicine allows medical practitioners to select the most effective treatment options for individual patients.

8.3.4 Epidemic Forecasting

Statistical models and machine learning techniques are employed to track and predict the spread of infectious diseases. These forecasts help governments and health organizations to plan and allocate resources more efficiently, thus improving public health outcomes.

8.4 Manufacturing

Manufacturing processes have greatly benefited from the introduction of advanced data analytics and machine learning techniques to optimize production and improve product quality. Some notable applications include:

8.4.1 Quality Control

Machine learning algorithms like image recognition and pattern recognition help identify defects and deviations in the manufacturing process, thus ensuring optimal quality control at every stage of production.

8.4.2 Predictive Maintenance

IoT sensors and advanced analytics enable manufacturers to monitor equipment performance and predict potential failures before they occur. Timely maintenance helps to reduce operational costs and prevent equipment downtime.

8.4.3 Supply Chain Optimization

Data-driven forecasting models are used to predict demand and inventory levels, allowing manufacturers to optimize their supply chains and reduce costs. Additionally, machine learning models can identify inefficiencies in the supply chain and suggest improvements to enhance overall performance.

8.4.4 Process Optimization

Machine learning models can be used to identify and optimize the key parameters and variables affecting the manufacturing process, leading to increased output and reduced waste. Techniques such as design of experiments (DOE) and response surface methodology (RSM) are widely adopted for process optimization.

In conclusion, statistics, forecasting, and machine learning techniques are essential tools in today's data-driven world. Industries such as finance, marketing, healthcare, and manufacturing are leveraging these techniques to improve decision-making, streamline operations, and gain a competitive advantage. As more organizations embrace these tools, we can expect even greater innovations and advancements that will shape the future of these industries.

References

1. Hinton, G., Deng, L., Yu, D., Dahl, G.E., Mohamed, A., Jaitly, N., Senior, A., Vanhoucke, V., Nguyen, P., Sainath, T.N., and Kingsbury, B., 2012. Deep neural networks for acoustic modeling in speech recognition: The shared views of four research groups. IEEE Signal Processing Magazine, 29(6), pp.82-97.
2. Johnson, K.W., Torres Soto, J., Glicksberg, B.S., Shameer, K., Miotto, R., Ali, M., Ashley, E., and Dudley, J.T., 2018. Artificial intelligence in cardiology. Journal of the American College of Cardiology, 71(23), pp.2668-2679.
3. Smithant, I., Dunnmon, J., and Suh, S., 2016. Cross-domain use of pneumonia to predict pathologic response to neoadjuvant therapy. In Radiological Society of North America Annual Meeting (Vol. 27, p. 835). Radiological Society of North America (RSNA).
4. Vaughn-Cooke, M., 2016. Manufacturing process monitoring: A comprehensive quantitative model of process monitoring. Journal of manufacturing association, 301, pp.303-310.
5. World Health Organization, 2013. The global burden of disease: 2004 update. World Health Organization.

Combining Time-Series Forecasting and Machine Learning to Enhance Real-World Applications

Understanding time-series data has become vital in many areas of our lives, from predicting the stock market's behavior to anticipating a machine's maintenance requirements. With recent advancements in statistics, forecasting methods, and machine learning, we can improve our comprehension of time-series data and optimize various real-world applications. In this subsection, we discuss the principles of time-series forecasting, machine learning algorithms, and how they can be integrated to enhance their performance in handling real-life problems.

Time-Series Forecasting

Time-series forecasting deals with generating predictions based on historical data points, over time. The objective is to forecast future data points given past observations. This analysis involves a significant role in business planning and decision-making processes.

A few common techniques used in time-series forecasting are:

1. **Moving Average (MA)**: Calculates the average of data points within a specific window in time, sliding through the data.
2. **Exponential Smoothing (ES)**: Similar to moving average, but this method assigns exponentially decreasing weights to past observations, giving higher importance to more recent observations.
3. **Autoregressive Integrated Moving Average (ARIMA)**: A powerful forecasting model that considers three components—autoregression, integration, and moving average— enabling the model to adapt to non-stationary time-series data.

4. **Seasonal Decomposition of Time Series (STL)**: Decomposes a time series into its trend, seasonal, and residual components, which can be forecast separately before recombining them into a final prediction.

Machine Learning for Time-Series Data

The emergence of machine learning has provided new ways to analyze time-series data. Some popular machine learning models applied to time-series problems are:

1. **Recurrent Neural Networks (RNNs)**: Neural networks that can process variable-length sequences by maintaining a hidden state representing the historical information.
2. **Long Short-Term Memory (LSTM)**: A type of RNN that can learn long-term dependencies in the data and is less prone to issues like vanishing and exploding gradients.
3. **Gated Recurrent Units (GRU)**: Similar to LSTMs but with a simplified architecture that combines the hidden and memory cells, making training faster.
4. **Prophet**: A forecasting model developed by Facebook that offers robust performance with simple out-of-the-box configurations and handles missing values and outliers effectively.

Integrating Time-Series Forecasting and Machine Learning

While traditional statistical methods offer a strong foundational approach to time-series forecasting, incorporating machine learning techniques can often enhance performance. Some ways to combine these approaches are:

Feature Engineering and Selection

Applying domain knowledge to create new features can significantly help machine learning models capture complex patterns in the data. Furthermore, feature selection techniques can aid in selecting the most informative features and reducing overfitting.

Model Stacking and Ensemble Methods

Multiple models can be combined or 'stacked' to create an ensemble that outperforms individual models. Time-series forecasting models and machine learning techniques can be used to create a diverse set of predictions. The final forecast can be obtained through an average or weighted average of these predictions.

Hyperparameter Tuning and Model Selection

Both forecasting methods and machine learning models have hyperparameters that need optimization to achieve the best performance. Hyperparameter tuning using methods like grid search, random search, or Bayesian optimization can be employed to find the best hyperparameters for both approaches.

Evaluation and Model Comparison

Comparing the performance of different models and their combinations may provide valuable insights into the best methodology for a specific problem. Common evaluation metrics for time-series forecasting are Mean Absolute Error (MAE), Mean Squared Error (MSE), and Root Mean Squared Error (RMSE).

In conclusion, combining time-series forecasting and machine learning techniques can lead to better and more reliable predictions for real-world applications. Practitioners should consider the problem at hand, the available data, and computational resources when integrating these approaches to optimize performance. As technology advances, we expect to see even more sophisticated and powerful integration of forecasting methods and machine learning techniques, leading to improved decision-making and higher efficiencies across various industries.

Real-World Applications of Statistics, Forecasting, and Machine Learning

In recent years, statistics, forecasting, and machine learning have become essential tools across various industries to solve complex problems and make data-driven decisions. Applications of these techniques can be found in fields as diverse as healthcare, finance, marketing, sports, and agriculture. This subsection will explore several real-world applications of these quantitative methods and discuss their impact on everyday life.

Healthcare

Healthcare is a critical industry, characterized by increasing amounts of data due to advancements in medical technology, wearable devices, and electronic health records. These vast amounts of data can be used to identify trends, optimize treatment options, and create predictive models to improve patient outcomes. Key applications include:

- **Disease prediction and prevention**: Utilizing patient data to generate disease risk models, which can be used to identify at-risk individuals, prioritize preventative measures, and guide clinical decision-making.
- **Drug development and personalized medicine**: Advanced statistical techniques and machine learning algorithms can be employed to analyze the data from clinical trials and genomic research, enabling the development of personalized therapies tailored to each individual's unique genetic makeup.
- **Hospital resource optimization**: Implementing forecasting models to predict patient volume, enabling hospitals and other healthcare facilities to optimize resource allocation, reduce wait times, and improve overall patient experience.

Finance

The finance industry can harness the power of statistics, forecasting, and machine learning to guide investment decisions, manage risk, and optimize trading strategies. Key applications include:

- **Portfolio optimization**: Analyzing historical market data to construct optimal portfolios that minimize risk and maximize returns, using sophisticated risk models and machine learning algorithms.
- **Fraud detection**: Employing advanced analytics techniques to identify suspicious activities and transactions that signal potential fraudulent behavior.
- **Algorithmic trading**: Leveraging forecasting models and machine learning techniques to build automated trading strategies based on historical price data, market trends, and other relevant variables.

Marketing

Marketing professionals increasingly rely on quantitative methods to target customers effectively, drive sales, and maximize revenue. Key applications include:

- **Customer segmentation**: Applying clustering algorithms and other statistical techniques to analyze customer data, enabling marketers to identify distinct target groups based on factors such as demographics, interests, and purchasing behavior.
- **Sales forecasting**: Utilizing historical sales data and other relevant variables to generate accurate sales forecasts, allowing businesses to manage inventory, allocate resources efficiently, and plan marketing campaigns.
- **Predictive analytics**: Leveraging machine learning algorithms to predict customer behavior, such as likelihood to respond to promotions, churn, or make repeat purchases, enabling more efficient targeting and improved customer retention.

Sports

From enhancing team performance to informing decision-making, statistics and machine learning are increasingly important components of sports management and analysis. Key applications include:

- **Player performance analysis**: Utilizing statistical models and machine learning techniques to assess player performance metrics, enabling coaches to develop targeted training plans and make informed roster decisions.
- **Injury risk prediction**: Employing predictive algorithms to assess individual athletes' injury risk profiles, guiding injury prevention programs and athlete management strategies.
- **Game outcome forecasting**: Analyzing historical game data to make predictions about future match outcomes and inform betting markets, fantasy sports, and other applications.

Agriculture

Advanced analytics can support agriculture stakeholders by increasing crop yield, minimizing resource waste, and optimizing farming practices. Key applications include:

- **Crop yield prediction**: Leveraging historical production data, climatic variables, and other relevant factors to generate crop yield forecasts, helping farmers optimize planting and harvesting decisions.
- **Precision agriculture**: Utilizing machine learning algorithms and sensor data to assess field and crop conditions, enabling targeted application of fertilizers,

pesticides, and irrigation, reducing waste and environmental impacts.

- **Supply chain optimization**: Employing forecasting models to predict demand for agricultural products and optimize logistics, ensuring timely delivery and minimizing spoilage.

In conclusion, statistics, forecasting, and machine learning play a crucial role in many aspects of modern life. By harnessing the power of these quantitative methods, we can optimize decision-making, gain insights from complex datasets, and drive innovation across various industries. As technology advances and our ability to collect and process data grows, the importance of these tools will only continue to increase.

Evaluating Models in the Real World: Performance Measures, Over- and Underfitting, and Cross Validation

In this subsection, we will explore how to evaluate the effectiveness of statistical and machine learning models in real-life applications. We will discuss important concepts such as performance measures, overfitting, underfitting, and cross validation. These are essential to understand how well a model generalizes to new, unseen data, and ultimately, determine its success in solving the problem at hand.

Performance Measures

An important aspect of building and selecting a suitable model is determining how well it performs.

Performance measures are criteria used to assess the quality of a model by comparing its predictions to the actual outcomes. There are several performance measures available, and the choice depends on the problem type and the specific requirements of the application. Some common performance measures for regression and classification problems are:

- **Mean Absolute Error (MAE)**: This represents the average of the absolute differences between the predicted and actual values in a regression problem. It is a simple and intuitive measure of model performance.
$$ \text{MAE} = \frac{1}{n}\sum_{i=1}^{n}\left|y_i - \hat{y}_i\right| $$
- **Mean Squared Error (MSE)**: Similar to MAE, this metric represents the average of the squared differences between the predicted and actual values in a regression problem. MSE is more sensitive to outliers, as it gives more weight to larger errors.
$$ \text{MSE} = \frac{1}{n}\sum_{i=1}^{n}(y_i - \hat{y}_i)^2 $$
- **Root Mean Squared Error (RMSE)**: This performance measure is the square root of MSE. RMSE represents the same units as the target variable, making it easier to interpret in a regression problem.
$$ \text{RMSE} = \sqrt{\frac{1}{n}\sum_{i=1}^{n}(y_i - \hat{y}_i)^2} $$
- **Accuracy**: In classification problems, accuracy represents the proportion of correctly classified instances out of the total instances.
$$ \text{Accuracy} = \frac{\text{number of correct predictions}}{\text{total number of predictions}} $$
- **Precision**: Precision measures the proportion of true positive predictions (e.g., the number of

successfully identified relevant items) out of all positive predictions made by the model.

$$ \text{Precision} = \frac{\text{True Positives}}{\text{True Positives + False Positives}} $$

- **Recall**: Also known as sensitivity or true positive rate, recall measures the proportion of relevant items that are successfully identified by the model.

$$ \text{Recall} = \frac{\text{True Positives}}{\text{True Positives + False Negatives}} $$

Overfitting and Underfitting

As we build and refine models, we must be aware of two common issues: overfitting and underfitting.

- **Overfitting**: This occurs when a model performs well on the training data but poorly on new, unseen data. An overfitted model has learned the training data too well, likely capturing noise and random fluctuations, resulting in a lack of generalization to new inputs.
- **Underfitting**: Conversely, underfitting occurs when a model does not capture the underlying patterns in the training data, leading to poor performance on both the training and test data. An underfitted model is too simplistic and requires more complexity to accurately represent the relationships in the data.

The goal is to strike a balance between underfitting and overfitting, achieving a model that generalizes well to new data. This can be accomplished by applying techniques such as regularization, as well as selecting appropriate model complexity based on the available data.

Cross Validation

To effectively evaluate model performance and avoid overfitting, we often use a technique called cross validation. Cross validation is a process that divides the data into multiple smaller subsets called folds, and iteratively trains and evaluates the model on these folds. The most common form of cross validation is k-fold cross validation, where the data is divided into k equal-sized folds.

During each iteration, one fold is held out as the validation set, while the remaining k-1 folds are used to train the model. This process is repeated k times, each time with a different fold as the validation set. Finally, the model's performance is averaged across all k iterations.

Cross validation is a powerful technique that not only helps in model evaluation but also aids in model selection and hyperparameter tuning. By providing a more reliable estimate of model performance, cross validation can help prevent overfitting and ensure that the chosen model generalizes well to new, unseen data.

In conclusion, understanding and implementing these concepts – performance measures, overfitting, underfitting, and cross validation – are crucial steps in effectively applying statistics, forecasting, and machine learning models in real-life situations. By carefully considering these factors, we can develop robust models that provide valuable insights and solutions to complex problems.

Applying Statistics, Forecasting and Machine Learning to Real-Life Problems

As we continue to collect more data from various aspects of our lives, the importance of using statistics, forecasting, and machine learning to better understand, predict, and make informed decisions grows. In this subsection, we will explore some of the practical applications of these concepts in real-life problems.

Predicting the Stock Market

Financial markets are complex systems with large amounts of data, with thousands of stocks, bonds, and indices to analyze. Investors and analysts have long used statistical models and machine learning techniques to predict the movement of these securities and make sound investment choices. These models can be applied to several aspects of the stock market, such as predicting stock prices, identifying suitable investment opportunities, and estimating the risk associated with potential investments.

Some common machine learning models used in this field are linear regression, neural networks, decision trees, and time series forecasting techniques like ARIMA (Autoregressive Integrated Moving Average) and LSTM (Long Short-Term Memory) neural networks. While these models have their respective advantages and limitations, they collectively offer valuable insights into the ever-changing dynamics of financial markets.

Recommendations Systems

Almost all e-commerce platforms and streaming services use recommendation systems to personalize the user experience and increase user engagement. By gathering and analyzing user data, such as viewing or purchasing history, search queries, and demographic information, these systems can predict the user's preferences and make suitable recommendations. For instance, Amazon can suggest products based on your browsing patterns, and Netflix can show you movies or TV shows that you might enjoy.

Machine learning algorithms like collaborative filtering, content-based filtering, and hybrid models (e.g., matrix factorization) are widely utilized in these recommendation systems. These algorithms aid service providers in better understanding the user's preferences and delivering relevant content, increasing the chances of gaining customer satisfaction and loyalty.

Healthcare

In healthcare, statistics, forecasting, and machine learning can help identify and diagnose diseases more accurately, predict patient outcomes, and optimize the allocation of healthcare resources. Some of these applications include:

- Medical imaging: Machine learning models, such as convolutional neural networks (CNNs), have been successfully used in identifying diseases from medical images, like X-rays, MRI scans, and mammograms.
- Drug discovery: Discovering new drugs is a time-consuming and expensive process. Machine learning algorithms can help identify novel drug candidates faster and with greater accuracy by analyzing the vast amount of data generated in the drug discovery process.
- Hospital readmissions: Forecasting models can predict the likelihood of patient readmissions, allowing healthcare providers to create personalized care plans and reduce unnecessary costs.
- Disease outbreak prediction: By analyzing historical data and considering factors such as weather, population density, and travel patterns, machine learning models can accurately predict disease outbreaks like influenza, enabling public health officials to take preventive measures in a timely manner.

Weather Forecasting

Accurate weather forecasts are essential for various sectors, including agriculture, transportation, and disaster management. Modern weather forecasting relies heavily on statistical models and machine learning techniques to process enormous amounts of data collected from satellite imagery, weather stations, and other sources.

Some popular forecasting models include numerical weather prediction (NWP) models, which use mathematical equations to simulate the atmosphere's behavior, and machine learning models like random forests and artificial neural networks. These models allow meteorologists to make more reliable short-term and long-term weather forecasts, significantly impacting planning and decision-making processes in various industries.

Fraud Detection

Fraud detection is an essential aspect of several industries, including banking, insurance, and telecommunications. Machine learning algorithms, such as decision trees, logistic regression, and neural networks, can provide valuable insights into customers' transaction patterns and flag any suspicious behavior, potentially indicating fraud.

By implementing these techniques, organizations can significantly improve their fraud detection capabilities, reducing financial losses and promoting customer trust.

Conclusion

As technology evolves, the use of statistics, forecasting, and machine learning in real-life applications will undoubtedly continue to expand. The examples provided in this subsection are only a small representation of the endless possibilities that exist in the field. By understanding these concepts and applying them to specific problems, we can create innovative solutions and improve decision-making processes in various aspects of our everyday lives.

Managing Uncertainty and Volatility with Machine Learning

In the real world, data is often messy, incomplete, and subject to various sources of uncertainty. This means that the assumptions we hold about patterns and relationships in the data are frequently undermined by unanticipated factors. As a result, it is imperative to consider uncertainty and volatility when applying statistics, forecasting and machine learning models.

In this section, we will discuss how to manage uncertainty and volatility in order to optimize the performance of your models in real-life scenarios. This will include techniques for measuring and accounting for uncertainty, as well as practical tips for improving the robustness of your analyses and predictions.

Understanding Uncertainty and Volatility

Before diving into the practical techniques, it is important to understand the concept of uncertainty and volatility in the context of data analysis and machine learning. Uncertainty refers to the lack of complete knowledge or information about a given situation, which may be due to the complexity of the underlying system, the absence of certain data points, or the presence of nonsystematic factors (or noise). Volatility, on the other hand, is the degree of variability or dispersion in a given process, which makes it more challenging to predict future outcomes accurately.

In both cases, the uncertainties and volatility present in our data impose limits on the reliability of our inferences, forecasts and predictions. The goal, therefore, is to develop methods for identifying and quantifying these uncertainties and volatility in order to improve the robustness and reliability of our models.

Quantifying Uncertainty

One way to quantify uncertainty in a dataset is by calculating the variance, which measures the spread or dispersion of individual data points around the mean. This can help identify the degree of variability and inconsistency in our data and point to potential issues that may impact the accuracy of our predictions.

Another approach is to estimate confidence intervals or prediction intervals for our estimates and forecasts, which provide a range within which we expect the true value to lie with a certain degree of confidence. This is particularly useful in cases where we have a small sample size or where there is a large degree of variability in our data.

For machine learning models, one can calculate the uncertainty of predictions by estimating the variance of the predictions across multiple models or bootstrapped samples of the data. This can be achieved using ensemble methods, such as bagging and bootstrapped aggregating (also known as "bagging"), which involve training multiple models on different subsets of the data and combining their predictions to produce a more robust and accurate estimate.

Dealing with Volatility

When dealing with volatile data, it is crucial to use appropriate smoothing techniques to reduce the impact of short-term fluctuations and noise on our predictions. Some popular methods for addressing volatility in time series data include:

- Moving averages: Calculate the average value of the data over a specified window or time period, which can help reduce the impact of short-term fluctuations and highlight longer-term trends.
- Exponential smoothing: Apply a weighting factor to the data such that more recent observations are given greater importance, which allows the model to adapt more quickly to changes in the underlying process.
- Kalman filters: Use a state-space model to track the underlying trends in the data while accounting for the influence of noise and other sources of uncertainty.

When working with machine learning models, incorporating regularization techniques, such as LASSO or Ridge regression, can help reduce the impact of noise and prevent overfitting by encouraging simpler models that are less sensitive to small fluctuations in the data.

Evaluating the Performance of Your Models

It is essential to evaluate the performance of your models using appropriate metrics and validation techniques, such as cross-validation, to assess how well they generalize to previously unseen data. This can help you identify potential issues related to overfitting, as well as assess the uncertainty and volatility in your predictions.

Moreover, by comparing the performance of different models, you can determine which are better suited to handling the particular sources of uncertainty and volatility in your data, and select the best model accordingly.

Conclusion

In real-life scenarios, uncertainty and volatility are ever-present challenges. In order to create reliable and robust statistical and machine learning models, it is vital to understand, quantify, and manage these challenges effectively. Use these techniques to improve the reliability of your inferences, forecasts and predictions in the face of uncertain and volatile data, and ensure the performance and relevance of your models in real-world applications.

9. Ethical Considerations and Bias Prevention in Statistical Analysis and Machine Learning

9.1 Recognizing and Addressing Bias in Statistical Analysis and Machine Learning

In real-world applications of statistics, forecasting, and machine learning, it is crucial to recognize and address the potential biases that may arise at each stage of the data analysis process - from data collection to model development and evaluation. Bias can lead to erroneous conclusions or predictions, perpetuate pre-existing inequities, and ultimately erode trust in data-driven decision-making. In this subsection, we discuss several types of bias, their sources, and recommended practices for mitigating their impact.

9.1.1 Types of Bias and their Sources

1. **Sampling Bias**: This occurs when the sample used for analysis is not representative of the population from which it has been drawn. For instance, using an online survey to study a highly diverse population with varying levels of internet access can lead to selection bias. The results from such an analysis might only reflect the perspectives of a particular group, such as young people or those living in urban areas, rather than the entire population.
2. **Measurement Bias**: This arises when the tools or methods employed to collect data are inherently flawed or biased. For example, researchers measuring customer satisfaction may inadvertently introduce bias by providing vague survey questions or using leading language in interviews.
3. **Confirmation Bias**: Confirmation bias occurs when analysts interpret or prioritize data in ways that confirm their preconceptions, rather than objectively evaluating all relevant evidence. This can manifest in the form of data snooping, overfitting, or selective reporting of findings.
4. **Algorithmic Bias**: This occurs when biases are inadvertently introduced at the model development stage or amplified through machine learning algorithms. If training data contains biases or if the choice of features and their respective weights in the model cause systematic errors, the resulting model may generate biased predictions.

9.1.2 Best Practices for Mitigating Bias in Statistical Analysis and Machine Learning

1. **Ensure Data Representativeness**: Before undertaking any analysis, carefully assess the sample characteristics and ensure that it is representative of the target population. If necessary, consider employing stratified sampling, weighted adjustments, or oversampling techniques to adjust for under-represented groups.
2. **Leverage Multiple Data Sources**: Comparing and contrasting data from different sources can help identify potential biases and improve overall data quality. This may involve combining primary data (collected by the researcher) with secondary data (obtained from other sources) or making use of data triangulation techniques, such as cross-sectional, longitudinal, and sequential analysis.
3. **Perform Rigorous Data Preprocessing**: Cleaning and preprocessing the data before conducting any analysis forms an integral part of reducing bias in the results. This includes handling missing data, dealing with outliers, and transforming variables, such as normalizing or standardizing the data.
4. **Test for Bias**: Use statistical tests, such as the chi-square test, t-test, or F-test, to examine whether observed differences in sample data are due to random chance or inherent bias.
5. **Opt for Robust Estimators**: When estimating model parameters, prefer using estimators that are less sensitive to outliers or deviations in the underlying data distribution. These robust estimators may include the trimmed mean, Winsorized mean, or median absolute deviation.

6. **Develop Fair and Explainable Models**: In machine learning applications, prioritize the use of models and algorithms that are interpretable, transparent, and fair - this means treating different groups fairly and providing explanations for model decisions. Techniques such as feature importance analysis or employing explainable AI frameworks like LIME or SHAP can help.
7. **Perform Fairness and Bias Audits**: Routinely audit and evaluate models for fairness, both before deploying them and throughout their operational use. Consider using performance measures and analytical techniques specifically designed to assess fairness, such as disparate impact analysis or the equalized odds ratio.
8. **Involve Stakeholders and Foster Diversity**: Engaging stakeholders in the development, implementation, and evaluation of statistical or machine learning models can help identify and address biases more effectively. Moreover, fostering diversity in research teams can bring diverse perspectives, identify potential sources of bias, and counteract unconscious biases.

In summary, ethical considerations and bias prevention are crucial aspects of using statistical analysis and machine learning in real-world applications. By recognizing different types of bias, understanding their sources, and employing best practices to mitigate them, we can ensure more accurate and fair models and improve data-driven decision-making.

9.1 Understanding and Addressing Bias in Statistical Analysis and Machine Learning

9.1.1 Defining Bias

Bias, in the context of statistical analysis and machine learning, refers to the presence of systematic errors when making predictions, which could lead to unfair outcomes, skewed perceptions, or reinforcing stereotypes. The reason behind the bias could be the selection of the training dataset, improper handling of data, or algorithmic constraints that may lead to discriminatory practices.

9.1.2 Sources of Bias

There could be multiple sources of bias present in a statistical or machine learning system. Some of the most common sources of bias are:

1. **Data Collection**: Biased sampling of a population could lead to an over-representation or under-representation of certain groups, giving distorted results when the model is generalized to a broader population.
2. **Measurement Errors**: Incorrect or incomplete data collection mechanisms can result in biased datasets, and the predictions made from them could be erroneous.
3. **Labeling Bias**: When utilizing supervised learning techniques, biased labeling occurs when data

annotators unknowingly incorporate their stereotypes, prejudices, or misconceptions into the data labels.

4. **Algorithms**: Choice of algorithm, and its assumptions and constraints, can lead to biased predictions. For instance, some algorithms may assign more significant importance to specific features, leading to unfair outcomes.

9.1.3 Recognizing Bias

It is crucial to acknowledge that bias is inherent in the real world, and therefore, completely eliminating it from data or models might be impossible. However, to ensure that statistical analysis or machine learning models remain ethical and trustworthy, it is vital to recognize the existence of bias and address it effectively. Some methods for recognizing bias include:

1. **Descriptive Analysis**: By doing a thorough analysis of the data using basic descriptive statistics, visualizations, and cross-tabulations, it is often possible to identify inconsistencies or imbalances, which may indicate the presence of bias.
2. **Domain Expertise**: Leveraging domain knowledge to understand better the context of the data can also help identify biases. Engaging with domain experts can provide a perspective beyond the available data, and help detect potential sources of bias in the prediction process.
3. **Bias Detection Metrics**: Utilizing quantitative metrics to measure the level of bias present in the dataset/models can help in identifying the existence of bias. Examples of popular bias detection metrics include Disparate Impact (DI) and Equal Opportunity Difference (EOD).

9.1.4 Addressing Bias

Once the presence of bias is identified, it is essential to address it to improve the fairness and robustness of the models. Some actions that can be taken to mitigate bias are:

1. **Data Preprocessing Techniques**: Re-sampling or re-weighting can counterbalance sampling biases by oversampling under-represented groups or undersampling over-represented groups. Another data preprocessing technique is the application of transformation functions to the features of the dataset that may have a biased distribution. These methods aim to balance out the dataset and reduce the impact of bias on model outcomes.
2. **Algorithmic Approaches**: Designing fair algorithms or modifying existing ones to include fairness constraints can help in addressing bias. Some popular approaches are Fair Adversarial Learning, Constrained Optimization, and Reweighting Techniques.
3. **Post-hoc analysis and adjustments**: After the model has been trained, biases can still be reduced or even eliminated through various techniques like recalibration, cost-sensitive learning, or threshold adjusting.
4. **Performance Monitoring**: Regularly monitoring the model's performance in terms of fairness indicators and making necessary adjustments to account for any changes in the data distribution or user-feedback can help mitigate bias in the long run.

9.1.5 Ethical Considerations

While it is essential to address bias in statistical analysis and machine learning, it is equally critical to ensure that measures taken to mitigate bias are ethical and legally compliant. Transparency about the approach and processes employed to address bias, accountability for any issues that arise despite the best efforts, and stakeholders' engagement to ensure the responsible and ethical use of these technologies would go a long way in fostering trust and delivering fair predictions.

In conclusion, understanding, acknowledging, and addressing bias effectively goes a long way in ensuring that statistical analysis and machine learning models remain ethical and prevent the perpetuation of discrimination or unfair outcomes. It is the responsibility of data scientists, statisticians, and decision-makers to remain vigilant about bias, critically examine the models and their impact across diverse groups, and take corrective actions when needed.

9.1 Understanding and Mitigating Bias in Statistical Analysis and Machine Learning

In the realm of statistical analysis and machine learning, we often work with large data sets and complex models in order to make predictions, understand patterns, and draw conclusions about the underlying processes. However, the results we produce are only as accurate and fair as the data and techniques we use. This is why ethical considerations and bias prevention play such a crucial role in ensuring the integrity and reliability of our work. As practitioners of these fields, we must be aware of potential sources of bias, understand how to recognize them, and develop strategies to mitigate their impact on our analyses and predictions.

9.1.1 Defining Bias

Bias, in the context of statistical analysis and machine learning, refers to the presence of systematic errors in the data, models or analysis procedures, leading to results that deviate from the truth or unfairly favor certain groups or outcomes. Bias can originate from various sources, such as data collection and sampling procedures, model development, and subjective human decision-making. When unchecked, biases may propagate through multiple stages of the analysis and severely compromise the accuracy, fairness, and ethical nature of the conclusions and predictions we draw.

9.1.2 Sources of Bias

Bias can be introduced in different stages of the analysis process, and often results from a combination of factors. Some common sources of bias include:

9.1.2.1 Data Collection and Sampling

When collecting and sampling data, we may inadvertently introduce biases by selecting cases or observations that are not representative of the processes we intend to study. These biases can arise in various ways, such as:

- **Selection bias**: If we collect data only from certain sources, groups or individuals, we inadvertently exclude others, potentially leading to an unbalanced or incomplete view of the underlying processes.

- **Measurement bias**: Systematic errors in data collection instruments or procedures, such as survey questionnaires or data entry, can introduce measurement bias, affecting the accuracy and reliability of the collected data.
- **Survivorship bias**: By only considering cases that have "survived" certain processes or conditions, we may overlook others that did not make it to our dataset due to various factors, leading to an overrepresentation of "successful" cases or outcomes.

9.1.2.2 Model Development

Bias can also be introduced during the model development process, when we create, train and validate our statistical and machine learning models. Some potential sources of bias include:

- **Overfitting**: When a model learns the noise in the training data rather than the true underlying patterns or relationships, it may overfit, resulting in poor generalization and biased predictions.
- **Underfitting**: Conversely, when a model does not capture the complexity of the underlying data, it may underfit, leading to biased and unreliable predictions.
- **Algorithmic bias**: The algorithms we use for model development may themselves be biased, as they may have been designed or tuned based on certain assumptions that do not hold true in our specific data and analytical context.

9.1.2.3 Human Decision-Making

Finally, bias can also result from human intervention in various stages of the analysis, be it during data collection, preprocessing, model development or interpretation of results. Some examples of human-driven biases include:

- **Confirmation bias**: When humans seek, interpret or prioritize evidence that confirms their pre-existing beliefs or hypotheses, they may inadvertently introduce confirmation bias into the analysis process.
- **Anchoring bias**: If we rely too heavily on the initial pieces of information we encounter when making decisions, we may anchor our subsequent judgments to these early data points, leading to a biased decision-making process.
- **Cognitive biases**: Other cognitive biases, such as recency bias, groupthink, and hindsight bias, among others, can influence our decision-making and analytical processes, contributing to overall bias in our work.

9.1.3 Strategies for Bias Prevention and Mitigation

Recognizing the potential sources of bias and understanding their implications are the first steps toward mitigating their impact on our statistical analyses and machine learning models. Several strategies can be employed to reduce or eliminate bias, which include:

9.1.3.1 Ensuring Representative Data Collection and Sampling

- Plan and design data collection procedures carefully to ensure that they capture a representative view of the processes, populations or groups of interest.

- Use stratified or random sampling techniques to minimize selection bias.
- Regularly assess and ensure the quality and accuracy of data collection instruments and procedures to minimize measurement errors.

9.1.3.2 Improving Model Development and Selection

- Use techniques such as cross-validation to assess the generalization performance of models and guard against overfitting or underfitting.
- Evaluate the suitability of the algorithms and techniques used for model development, considering their assumptions, biases, and limitations.
- Consider using ensemble methods, which combine the predictions of several base models, to increase the robustness and reduce the bias of the final predictions.

9.1.3.3 Mitigating Human Biases

- Encourage critical thinking and questioning of pre-existing assumptions, beliefs, and hypotheses to avoid confirmation bias.
- Train and encourage team members to be aware of cognitive biases and seek objective evidence and external inputs to counteract them.
- Create opportunities for diverse perspectives and inputs in the decision-making process, which can help identify and counteract potential biases.

9.1.4 Concluding Remarks

Biases play an inevitable role in statistical analysis and machine learning, and it is our responsibility as practitioners to recognize and mitigate their impact on our work. By understanding the sources of bias, employing appropriate strategies to minimize their presence, and continuously monitoring and validating the accuracy and fairness of our results, we can ensure that our work contributes positively to science, industry, and society, and addresses the ethical concerns underlying these fields.

9.1 Understanding and Identifying Bias

Bias, in the context of statistical analysis and machine learning, refers to the presence of systematic errors in predictions or estimation due to inappropriate or incomplete representations of the data. In real-life applications, biases can lead to misleading results and negatively impact decision-making processes. Therefore, ethical considerations must be taken into account to prevent potential negative consequences of bias and ensure fairness, accountability, and transparency.

9.1.1 Sources of Bias

Bias can originate from various sources, including the following:

1. **Data collection and sampling bias**: This occurs when the data collected for analysis or model training is not a representative sample of the population. Skewed sample distributions can lead to biased predictions or inferences.
2. **Measurement bias**: Inaccuracies in data measurement or recording can introduce bias. For

example, systematic errors in measuring instruments or self-reporting survey responses can distort the true relationships between variables.

3. **Labeling bias**: In supervised machine learning algorithms, the quality of the training data labels directly impacts the learning process. Biased labels, either due to human errors or subjective judgments, can result in biased model predictions.
4. **Algorithmic bias**: Even with unbiased data, the choice of the algorithm, model architecture, or specific parameters can lead to biased results. In some cases, a particular algorithm may inherently favor a specific data pattern or feature over others.
5. **Confirmation bias**: When conducting analysis or model evaluation, analysts may selectively focus on information that confirms their pre-existing beliefs, leading to biased interpretation of results.

9.1.2 Strategies to Mitigate Bias

To ensure ethical analysis and model development, it is crucial to adopt methodologies addressing potential bias sources. The following approaches can be helpful to prevent, identify, and mitigate bias:

1. **Data collection and preprocessing**: Collect data from diverse sources, and ensure the sample represents the target population. Conduct a thorough exploratory data analysis (EDA) to understand the data distribution, detect potential issues, and apply necessary transformations.
2. **Feature selection and engineering**: Adopt techniques for identifying important features and removing irrelevant or redundant ones. Prevent overfitting by selecting an appropriate balance between model complexity and generalization.

3. **Model selection**: Be aware of the inherent biases in specific algorithms and choose a model that best aligns with the problem and data characteristics. Consider using ensemble techniques, combining predictions from multiple models, to reduce individual model biases.
4. **Evaluation**: Use robust evaluation metrics and cross-validation techniques to assess model performance on different data subsets. Perform additional bias analysis, such as disparate impact analysis or counterfactual analysis, to further identify and address potential biases.
5. **Continual learning and improvement**: Regularly update models with new data, keeping up with changes in the population or circumstances. Encourage feedback from stakeholders and end-users to identify potential issues and improve models accordingly.

9.1.3 Ensuring Transparency and Accountability

In addition to identifying and mitigating biases, it is crucial to ensure transparency and accountability in statistical analysis, forecasting, and machine learning application development. This can be achieved by the following measures:

1. **Documentation**: Clearly document data sources, collection methods, preprocessing steps, model selection rationale, model evaluation results, and any assumptions made during the process. This allows for external validation, peer review, and replicability.
2. **Interpretability**: Choose interpretable models or incorporate explainability techniques to help stakeholders and end-users understand how the

model makes predictions or inferences, and build trust in the system.

3. **Openness**: Share analysis, code, and results with the community for peer review, to ensure the findings are scrutinized and validated by a diverse audience.
4. **Collaboration**: Work with ethics committees, domain experts, and other stakeholders in model development and deployment stages to ensure that ethical considerations and potential biases are properly addressed.

By incorporating these ethical considerations into the development and deployment of statistical analyses, forecasting, and machine learning models, practitioners can contribute to building fair, transparent, and accountable systems for real-life applications. Additionally, these actions can help in addressing the challenges related to bias prevention, ensuring better decision-making processes, and enhancing the overall impact of these technologies on society.

9. Ethical Considerations and Bias Prevention in Statistical Analysis and Machine Learning

9.1 Identifying and Addressing Bias in Data Collection

Bias in data collection is often the root cause of unethical outcomes in statistical analysis and machine learning implementations. Ensuring that the data being processed is representative and free from any discriminatory factors is crucial to the development of dependable models. This section outlines key considerations for identifying and addressing bias in data collection.

- **Sampling bias**: Sampling bias occurs when the data being used does not accurately represent the overall population. It can lead to misleading conclusions or results that don't translate well to real-world scenarios. To combat sampling bias, ensure that data being collected represents the entire population of interest. This can be achieved through stratified sampling techniques to select a balanced sample or through oversampling to balance underrepresented classes.
- **Measurement bias**: Measurement bias can be introduced during the process of data collection or when capturing the values of certain variables. This can result in systematic errors that impact the accuracy of statistical models. While not all measurement bias can be eliminated completely, awareness of potential error sources can help to minimize the likelihood of their occurrence.
  - Verify that measurement instruments are well-calibrated, and consider potential inaccuracies due to observer bias or measurement equipment limitations.
- **Selection bias**: Selection bias can occur when certain observations are more likely to be represented in the data set than others. This can be caused by factors ranging from inability to access certain participants to varying response rates among different demographic groups. To minimize the effect of selection bias, investigators can employ random sampling methods as well as consider employing techniques like propensity score matching and inverse

probability weighting to control for potential confounding factors.

- **Omitted variable bias**: Omitted variable bias arises when a key variable or factor influencing the target outcome is excluded, either unintentionally or due to data limitations. This results in an unclear relationship between the explanatory variables and the outcome. To address this, it is crucial to have a clear understanding of the domain area and experimental design to try and include all relevant variables.
- **Data quality**: Data collected from various sources may contain inconsistent entries, duplicate records, or missing values. All of these issues can introduce bias and affect the statistical validity of the obtained results. To enhance data quality:
  - Implement data cleaning procedures, including outlier detection, data normalization, and missing data imputation.
  - Encourage and maintain transparency in data collection methods.
- **Handling bias in algorithms and models**: Sometimes, statistical algorithms or machine learning models can introduce or exacerbate existing biases in the data. Researchers and practitioners need to continually examine and challenge the assumptions made by their chosen models and be vigilant about potential sources of bias. Some popular techniques to mitigate algorithmic bias can include:
  - Ensuring diversity in the training data.
  - Creating model evaluation metrics that take fairness and equity into account.
  - Utilizing machine learning techniques specifically designed for fairness, like adversarial debiasing or fair Adaboost.

If bias is suspected during or after the analysis, it is essential to transparently communicate limitations and potential biases that may have been introduced in the process. This fosters a culture of honesty and is valuable for ensuring that the results of the analysis are ethically acceptable and scientifically accurate.

By addressing biases and ethical considerations early on in the data collection and analysis process, researchers and practitioners ensure a more reliable foundation for their overall statistical analysis or machine learning project, while building trust between users and system stakeholders. With the continual development of AI and data-driven technologies, adopting a proactive and thoughtful approach to addressing bias has become more important than ever.

Integrating Statistics, Forecasting, and Machine Learning in Real Life

In this subsection, we will dive into how to effectively integrate statistics, forecasting, and machine learning techniques into real-life applications. By understanding the power and limitations of these approaches, we can make better decisions and gain valuable insights in various fields such as business, finance, healthcare, and social sciences.

1. Understanding the Data

The first step in applying these techniques is obtaining a good understanding of the data at hand. This includes:

- *Data collection*: Gathering reliable and relevant data is crucial for any analysis. Ensuring the data is representative of the population or phenomenon being studied is essential for accurate analysis and decision making.
- *Data preprocessing*: Real-world data is often messy, incomplete, and noisy. Preprocessing techniques such as outlier detection, missing value imputation, and feature scaling are necessary to address these issues and ensure the validity of the results.
- *Exploratory data analysis (EDA)*: Visualizing and summarizing the data helps in identifying patterns, trends, and relationships among variables. This step can guide the selection of appropriate statistical and machine learning methods for a specific problem.

2. Building and Validating Models

Once we have a clear understanding of the data, we can proceed with building and validating models that address specific questions or problems. This process involves:

- *Model selection*: Choosing the appropriate statistical or machine learning algorithm is crucial for obtaining meaningful results. This decision should be based on the nature of the data, the problem being addressed, and the desired level of interpretability and prediction accuracy.
- *Model training*: Fitting the chosen model to the data allows us to learn its parameters and quantify the relationships among variables. This can involve techniques such as least squares regression, maximum likelihood estimation, or gradient descent optimization.

- *Model validation*: Assessing the validity and accuracy of the model is essential for ensuring that the results are reliable and useful. Validation techniques include cross-validation, bootstrapping, and comparing the performance of different models on a holdout set.

3. Interpreting Results and Making Decisions

With a well-fitting model in hand, we can proceed with interpreting the results and making decisions based on them. This process may involve:

- *Statistical inference*: Estimating the values of unknown population parameters, testing hypotheses, deriving confidence intervals, and quantifying uncertainty in the results.
- *Forecasting*: Predicting future outcomes or trends based on the relationships identified in the historical data. This can involve time series analysis, scenario analysis, or simulation-based techniques such as Monte Carlo simulation.
- *Machine learning*: Utilizing trained models to make predictions, classify new data points, identify patterns, and uncover hidden relationships in the data. Examples include image recognition, natural language processing, and recommender systems.
- *Decision making*: Using the results from the analysis to make informed decisions, whether in business, finance, healthcare, or social sciences. This could involve scenario analysis, cost-benefit analysis, or optimization techniques.

4. Iterating and Updating Models

As new data becomes available or conditions change, it is essential to update the models and reevaluate their accuracy and relevance. This could involve a continuous improvement process such as:

- *Model refinement*: Updating the model to incorporate new data, variables, or methodologies to improve its performance.
- *Monitoring performance*: Regularly evaluating the model's performance using performance metrics such as accuracy, precision, recall, or F1 score, to ensure that it remains valid and accurate over time.
- *Retraining and fine-tuning*: Reassessing and adjusting the model's parameters based on new data or changed conditions to maintain its performance.

By integrating statistical, forecasting, and machine learning techniques in real-life applications, we can leverage the power of data-driven decision making to address complex problems and make informed choices. By understanding the limitations and strengths of these techniques and continuously validating and updating our models, we can ensure that our decisions are based on accurate, reliable, and relevant insights.

Real-World Applications of Statistics, Forecasting, and Machine Learning

In recent times, statistics, forecasting, and machine learning (ML) have become integral to various aspects of modern life. This increased relevance is due to the growth of big data and the advancements in computing power, which have enabled the application of these techniques in multiple fields. In this subsection, we will explore some of the key real-world scenarios where statistics, forecasting, and ML are being employed to solve complex problems and drive advancements.

1. Healthcare and Biomedical Research

With the increasing volume of health-related data being generated daily, the domain of healthcare and biomedical research has become a significant beneficiary of statistics, forecasting, and ML techniques. Some of these applications include:

- **Disease Diagnosis and Prognosis**: ML algorithms, especially deep learning and neural networks, are being utilized to analyze medical images such as X-rays and MRIs to identify patterns and diagnose diseases more accurately than traditional methods. Moreover, these techniques can also be employed to predict disease progression and suggest effective treatment plans.
- **Drug Discovery and Personalized Medicine**: ML algorithms can expedite the drug discovery process by predicting the efficacy and safety of candidate molecules. Furthermore, these techniques can also help in developing personalized treatment plans that consider the genetic makeup and health history of individual patients.
- **Genomics and Epigenomics**: Statistics and ML algorithms are being harnessed to analyze vast datasets generated through human genomics and epigenomics research. This analysis aids in understanding the role of genetic variations in disease susceptibility and the development of targeted therapies.

2. Finance and Economics

The finance and economics sectors are embracing the power of statistics, forecasting, and ML for various purposes:

- **Stock Market Prediction**: Advanced statistical models and ML techniques, such as time series analysis and deep learning, can help in predicting stock market trends and making more informed investment decisions.
- **Credit Risk Analysis**: ML algorithms such as decision trees, logistic regression, and neural networks are being utilized to analyze the creditworthiness of borrowers and thereby mitigate the risk associated with loans and other financial products.
- **Fraud Detection**: ML algorithms can analyze massive datasets on financial transactions to identify patterns and anomalies indicative of fraudulent activities.
- **Economic Forecasting**: Various statistical and econometric models are employed to forecast macroeconomic indicators, such as GDP growth, inflation, and unemployment rates. These forecasts help inform monetary and fiscal policy decisions.

3. Marketing and Customer Analytics

Organizations across industries are leveraging statistics, forecasting techniques, and ML to enhance their marketing efforts and better understand their customers:

- **Customer Segmentation**: ML algorithms, such as clustering and classification techniques, help businesses group customers based on their demographic information, purchasing patterns, and other relevant factors.

- **Sentiment Analysis**: Natural Language Processing (NLP), a branch of ML, can analyze customer reviews and social media posts to determine customer sentiments towards a specific product or brand, enabling companies to make data-driven decisions on product improvement and marketing strategies.
- **Demand Forecasting**: Time series analysis and regression models can help businesses predict product demand, allowing them to optimize their supply chain and inventory management processes.
- **Churn Prediction**: ML models can identify patterns that indicate customer churn, enabling businesses to take preventive measures and retain valuable customers.

4. Transportation and Urban Planning

Statistical and ML techniques play a vital role in tackling transportation and urban planning challenges:

- **Traffic Prediction**: Using historical traffic data and patterns, ML algorithms can forecast congestion levels, allowing traffic management authorities to optimize traffic flow and implement data-driven policies.
- **Autonomous Vehicles**: Advanced ML algorithms, such as deep learning and reinforcement learning, are driving the development of autonomous vehicles that can navigate complex traffic situations with minimal human intervention.
- **Smart City Infrastructure**: Statistical and ML techniques can aid in analyzing urban data to optimize energy consumption, waste management, and other critical aspects of city planning.

In conclusion, the applications of statistics, forecasting, and machine learning are virtually limitless, impacting virtually every industry and domain. The rapid evolution of these techniques, combined with the increasing availability of data and computational power, has set the stage for further advancements and innovations that will continue to reshape our world. Aspiring professionals seeking to make an impact in their respective fields must strive to develop expertise in these quantitative and analytical tools and techniques.

Real-Life Applications of Statistical Techniques and Machine Learning

In today's increasingly data-driven world, knowledge of statistical techniques and machine learning algorithms is an invaluable skill set. These powerful tools have widespread applications across various fields and industries, and their efficacy in solving complex problems and generating valuable insights has led to their usage in a plethora of scenarios. In this section, we will explore some prevalent real-life applications of statistical techniques and machine learning, which showcase their transformative potential.

1. Healthcare and Medicine

The healthcare industry generates a massive volume of data from medical records, clinical trials, patient history, genetics, and devices. Incorporating statistical analysis and machine learning can lead to improved medical diagnostics and treatment plans. Key applications include:

- Disease prediction: Identifying high-risk individuals, detecting diseases in their early stages, and personalizing treatment options.
- Drug discovery: Predicting drug safety and efficacy, optimizing drug dosage, and speeding up the time to market for new medications.
- Genomics: Analyzing genetic data to determine the relationship between genes and diseases, providing a foundation for personalized medicine.
- Medical imaging: Automatic analysis of medical images such as MRI, CT scans, and X-rays, aiding in accurate and faster diagnosis.
- Telemedicine: Leveraging machine learning techniques for remote health monitoring, preventive care, and disease management.

2. Finance and Banking

Statistical techniques and machine learning algorithms play a crucial role in the finance and banking sector, enabling better decision-making, fraud detection, and risk prediction. Examples include:

- Credit scoring: Determining the creditworthiness of an individual through statistical analysis and machine learning models, leading to informed lending decisions.
- Algorithmic trading: Analyzing large volumes of historical data to identify patterns and trends, facilitating automated trade executions.
- Fraud detection: Identifying unusual patterns in financial transactions and flagging them for possible fraud, resulting in loss prevention and stronger security.

- Risk management: Analyzing historical financial data to predict and mitigate potential risks, leading to optimized investment strategies.

3. Retail and E-commerce

Companies in retail and e-commerce rely heavily on data-driven decision-making. Statistical and machine learning techniques enable enhanced customer experience, improved business performance, and optimized logistics. Notable applications include:

- Recommender systems: Leveraging user behavioral data and preferences to provide personalized product suggestions, leading to higher conversion rates and customer satisfaction.
- Demand forecasting: Predicting sales and inventory needs to optimize stock levels and reduce waste.
- Pricing optimization: Analyzing market trends and competitor pricing to determine the optimal pricing strategy, maximizing revenue and profit.
- Segmentation and targeting: Identifying distinct customer groups with similar preferences and behaviors, enabling more effective marketing and promotional campaigns.

4. Transportation and Logistics

Efficient transportation and logistics management are instrumental for businesses and urban planning. Statistical methodologies and machine learning algorithms play a significant role in optimizing these processes. Some applications include:

- Route optimization: Analyzing historical traffic data and patterns to identify optimal routes, saving time and fuel costs.
- Traffic prediction: Forecasting traffic flow and congestion, enabling better traffic management and city planning.
- Fleet management: Predicting vehicle maintenance needs, optimizing fuel consumption, and enhancing driver safety.
- Autonomous vehicles: Leveraging machine learning algorithms for sensor-based data analysis, facilitating real-time decision-making and control for self-driving cars.

5. Energy and Environment

The ongoing global effort to find sustainable energy solutions and combat climate change is driving the need for sophisticated data analysis. Statistical techniques and machine learning aid the development and management of renewable energy sources, environmental monitoring, and conservation strategies. Key applications include:

- Renewable energy forecasting: Predicting solar and wind power generation based on weather data, leading to optimized energy generation and distribution plans.
- Energy consumption prediction: Analyzing historical data to determine future energy consumption patterns, enabling better demand-side management.
- Climate modeling: Simulating complex climate systems and predicting future climate change scenarios to guide policy-making and adaptation strategies.

6. Sports and Entertainment

In recent years, sports teams and organizations have started leveraging data analytics and machine learning. Key applications are:

- Performance analysis: Analyzing player performance data and developing optimal training strategies to improve athlete output.
- Injury prediction: Identifying factors contributing to injury risk and implementing preventive measures.
- Game strategy: Using player and team statistics to inform coaching decisions and game plans.
- Fan engagement: Analyzing fan data to enhance the overall experience, optimize marketing campaigns, and drive revenue.

In conclusion, statistical techniques and machine learning methods hold great promise and transformative potential across various domains. Continued investment in the development and application of these tools will unlock new opportunities and shape the landscape of our future.

Combining Statistical Approaches, Forecasting Techniques, and Machine Learning to Enhance Real-World Applications

When approaching the real world, having an understanding of statistics, forecasting, and machine learning provides valuable insights that can help a great deal in decision-making, optimization, and prediction. This section aims to showcase how combining these approaches can enhance various real-life applications, such as business processes, scientific research, and technological advancements.

1. Business Analytics and Decision Making

A key aspect of running a successful business is making data-driven decisions that will impact growth, efficiency, and customer satisfaction. To achieve this, businesses can leverage statistical analysis, forecasting, and machine learning to analyze data and gather actionable insights.

A. Demand Forecasting and Supply Chain

For businesses involved in manufacturing, retail, or logistics, understanding the demand for their products and ensuring that inventory levels are maintained is crucial. Statistical analysis techniques can be used to identify trends in historical sales data, while forecasting models (such as time series analysis or exponential smoothing) can predict future demand. This information can then be fed into machine learning algorithms that can help optimize supply chain and inventory management decisions, such as deciding when to order from suppliers or when to schedule production runs.

B. Customer Segmentation and Targeting

Understanding customers' needs and preferences is paramount for any business. Statistical techniques (such as cluster analysis or principal component analysis) can be used to identify customer demographics, preferences, or engagement patterns. Forecasting models can predict how specific customer groups will react to certain marketing campaigns or promotional offers, while machine learning algorithms (such as recommendation engines) can help businesses tailor their ad content, website experience, or product recommendations to individual customers, thus maximizing conversions and customer satisfaction.

2. Healthcare and Medicine

In healthcare and medicine, accurate predictions and up-to-date information can directly translate into better patient diagnosis, treatment, and outcomes. Statistical analysis and machine learning can enhance various aspects of medical research, diagnostics, and care.

A. Medical Diagnosis and Imaging

Statistical techniques can be applied to analyze large medical datasets, identify patterns and correlations, and discover potential biomarkers for diseases. Machine learning algorithms, such as deep learning neural networks or support vector machines, can be used to analyze medical images (such as MRIs, CT scans, or X-rays) and provide accurate diagnoses, aiding physicians in making informed decisions in treatment.

B. Drug Discovery and Personalized Medicine

The drug discovery process traditionally involves extensive experimentation and testing. Statistical approaches, such as experimental design and hypothesis testing, can be applied to optimize the experimentation process, while machine learning algorithms can analyze large datasets to identify potential drug candidates and predict their efficacy in treatment. Moreover, forecasting techniques combined with genomic data analysis can help healthcare professionals provide personalized medicine, tailoring treatments based on individual patient profiles and needs.

3. Climate Change and Environmental Conservation

Combating the negative effects of climate change and preserving our environment are both increasingly urgent tasks. Statistical analysis, forecasting, and machine learning can contribute greatly to these fields, enhancing our understanding of natural phenomena and improving our action plans for the future.

A. Climatic Trends and Weather Forecasting

Statistical techniques, such as regression analysis or time series analysis, can be used to study historical climate and weather data, detecting trends and patterns in global temperatures, greenhouse gas emissions, or sea-level rises. Forecasting models, such as the General Circulation Model (GCM) or the Weather Research and Forecasting (WRF) model, can provide short- to long-term predictions of climate and weather patterns. Coupling these forecasts with machine learning algorithms, such as artificial neural networks, can improve predictions and inform mitigation strategies, adaptation plans, or policy-making.

B. Biodiversity Conservation and Ecosystem Management

Protecting biodiversity and preserving ecosystems are essential to maintaining our planet's health. Statistical techniques can be used to estimate population sizes, analyze species distributions, or model species interactions within ecosystems. Forecasting models can predict the impact of climate change or human actions on these ecosystems, while machine learning (for example, reinforcement learning) can optimize conservation strategies or ecosystem restoration plans, ensuring the best possible outcomes for our environment.

Conclusion

In conclusion, the combination of statistical approaches, forecasting techniques, and machine learning can greatly enhance our understanding and decision-making processes in various real-world applications. Armed with the power of data-driven insights, individuals, businesses, and governments can make better decisions, optimize their operations, and foresee potential challenges, ultimately resulting in better outcomes and a more prosperous future for all.

Combining Human Expertise with Automated Algorithms in Real-Life Applications

More often than not, we find ourselves delving into the world of data analytics to make informed decisions across various fields. While automated algorithms offer an excellent way to process and analyze massive amounts of data, human expertise remains indispensable in contextualizing, evaluating, and implementing the insights derived from these algorithms. In this subsection, we discuss some practical ways that human expertise can help interpret statistical analyses, forecasts, and machine learning models to derive optimum real-life solutions.

Enhancing Validation and Interpretation of Algorithm Outputs

While automated algorithms are capable of processing vast datasets and providing numerous insights, human expertise is essential in validating and interpreting these outputs. Contextualizing quantitative results, identifying nuances, and mitigating biases require human judgment to ensure accurate analysis and appropriate recommendations.

For instance, a machine learning model might identify a pattern that links a certain demographic to higher or lower performance. However, it requires human judgment to ensure that the pattern is not an artifact from bias present in the data, and that its interpretation is fair and does not propagate discrimination. Additionally, subject matter experts can provide valuable feedback on the relevance and feasibility of algorithm outputs, further fine-tuning the analysis process.

Bridging the Gap between Theory and Practical Implementation

Applying statistical methods and machine learning models in real-life situations requires a deep understanding and appreciation of the practical implications involved. Human expertise can bridge the gap between theoretical models and practical constraints, ensuring that statistical and machine learning predictions are realistic, feasible, and actionable.

For example, a machine learning model used in traffic management might suggest specific traffic restrictions with the aim of reducing congestion. However, local authorities must consider practical implications, such as the availability of alternative routes, the potential effect on local businesses, and public opinion. In this case, domain experts and local stakeholders must work together to evaluate the proposed solutions and weigh the trade-offs before implementing the recommendations.

Facilitating Effective Cross-disciplinary Collaboration

The fusion of statistical and machine learning approaches often necessitates collaboration between experts from various domains to ensure that the resulting outputs are precise and reliable. Subject matter experts bring domain knowledge to the table, helping data scientists understand the context and intricacies of the problem at hand. Conversely, data scientists teach domain experts how to harness the potential of algorithms to gain valuable insights from their data.

This collaborative environment fosters a fruitful exchange of ideas and allows the development of customized solutions tailored to address specific challenges faced in different fields. For instance, collaboration between healthcare professionals and data scientists can lead to predictive models that identify at-risk patients, while combining marketing insights with machine learning algorithms can optimize advertisement placements and maximize return on investment.

Balancing Ethical Considerations

Applying statistical and machine learning models in real-life situations must be guided by ethical considerations. Human expertise plays a crucial role in recognizing potential ethical issues and ensuring that the outcomes and recommendations do not compromise individual privacy, perpetuate unfair biases, or inflict unintended harm.

For instance, a machine learning model may identify a certain group of customers as being more likely to default on their loans. In such a scenario, human judgment is required to ensure that the resulting credit policies do not discriminate unfairly against this group. Furthermore, transparency and accountability should be maintained throughout the analysis and decision-making processes to allow stakeholders and regulators to evaluate the fairness and validity of the outcome.

In conclusion, combining human expertise with automated algorithms offers the best of both worlds –

the capacity to process massive amounts of data with the nuanced human understanding required to generate valuable, ethical, and practical real-life solutions. By enhancing validation and interpretation, bridging the gap between theory and practice, facilitating cross-disciplinary collaboration, and balancing ethical considerations, human expertise plays an essential role in unlocking the full potential of statistics, forecasting, and machine learning in real-life applications.

10. Future Developments in Statistics, Forecasting and Machine Learning: Trends and Challenges

10.1 Technology Convergence and Collaboration

Advancements in multiple technology domains such as Artificial Intelligence (AI), data mining, statistics, forecasting, and machine learning are all aimed at making sense of massive amounts of data to help solve real-world problems. With data becoming more and more central to decision making and problem-solving, the need for these technologies to work together and deliver coherent solutions becomes essential. In this subsection, we will explore the ongoing developments and potential challenges as these technologies converge and collaborate to drive humanity into the future.

10.1.1 Increased Interdisciplinary Research and Applications

The interdisciplinary nature of this technology convergence implies that there will be a necessary increase in collaboration between experts from different domains. Statisticians, data miners, AI specialists, and other professionals will need to work closely to develop effective solutions. The integration of these fields will enable organizations to build data-driven decision-making processes driven by the best aspects of all these technologies.

One obvious example of this trend is the rise in the use of machine learning in statistical forecasting models. Conventional forecasting methods like ARIMA and Exponential Smoothing are being supplemented by or integrated with more advanced machine learning algorithms like Recurrent Neural Networks (RNN) and Long Short-Term Memory (LSTM) networks. This allows forecasters to leverage the strengths of both methods by creating hybrid models that can handle an increasingly complex and vast data landscape.

The key challenge in interdisciplinary research and applications is developing and maintaining a shared understanding and vocabulary between diverse groups of experts. As these fields converge, continued efforts towards standardization, communication, and knowledge dissemination will be critical to fostering a truly collaborative environment that can drive innovation.

10.1.2 Automation and Algorithmic Improvements

As the potential applications and scenarios to be tackled by statistics, forecasting, and machine learning grow in complexity, so too will the need to develop and deploy increasingly sophisticated algorithms. One expected development is the increased focus on automating the process of model selection, parameter tuning, and data processing. Automation reduces the amount of manual intervention required, which in turn minimizes the chance for human bias or error to infiltrate the analysis.

Furthermore, as the volume of data continues to grow, there is increasing pressure on the development of algorithms that can efficiently process large-scale datasets. The field of machine learning in particular has seen significant advancements in recent years, with the development of new algorithms and improvements to existing ones that can reduce the time, computational resources, and in some cases, the amount of labeled data required to produce accurate predictions.

These advancements also bring about new challenges related to the explainability and interpretability of the models being developed. As models grow more complex and automated, the need for human intuition and understanding does not disappear. In fact, it becomes even more crucial for ensuring that these systems remain accountable, transparent, and ethically responsible.

10.1.3 Data Privacy and Security

As more and more organizations and institutions in various sectors leverage data-driven decision-making strategies, there is an increasing need to address concerns related to data privacy and security. Combining methods from statistics, forecasting, and machine learning has led to extremely effective analytical methods for extracting insights from data, but they have also increased concerns around user information confidentiality.

There are ongoing efforts in the fields of cryptography and privacy-preserving machine learning to develop techniques and solutions that allow for data analysis, while ensuring sensitive information remains secure. These techniques include homomorphic encryption, secure multi-party computation, and differential privacy. The challenge here is to strike a balance between maintaining data privacy and allowing organizations to gain valuable insights and make informed decisions.

10.1.4 Educational Initiatives and Workforce Transformation

As we move into the future, the workforce that deals with statistics, forecasting, and machine learning will need to be well equipped to handle these evolving technologies. Educational and training programs must adapt to these changes by incorporating interdisciplinary perspectives and providing ongoing education on new techniques and methodologies. Formulating curricula, courses, and programs that teach students the essential skills for working in this evolving landscape will be essential.

The demand for professionals skilled in these areas will continue to grow, which may strain the workforce if an adequate number of capable individuals are not available. Organizations and institutions must invest in reskilling and upskilling their employees as well as implementing interdisciplinary educational initiatives to equip them with the necessary skills to face future challenges.

In conclusion, statistics, forecasting, and machine learning are three fields that are undergoing significant advancements and will continue to closely collaborate in the future. Key future developments will likely include increasing interdisciplinary research, automation, algorithmic improvements, improved data privacy and security, and a focus on adapting educational frameworks. The future of these fields is promising, but successfully realizing this potential will be dependent on overcoming several significant and complex challenges.

10. Future Developments in Statistics, Forecasting and Machine Learning: Trends and Challenges

10.1. Real-World Applications and the Importance of Interdisciplinary Collaboration

As the world becomes increasingly data-driven, the significance of statistical methods, forecasting models, and machine learning (ML) algorithms continues to grow. Their importance transcends disciplines and industry sectors, with applications ranging from finance, healthcare, transportation, and energy, among others. In this section, we touch on some future trends and challenges of these approaches, while emphasizing the importance of interdisciplinary collaboration for their successful implementation.

10.1.1. Increased Complexity and Heterogeneity of Data

One of the primary trends that the field of statistics, forecasting, and machine learning will have to contend with is the increasing complexity and heterogeneity of data. Organizations and individuals are continuously generating diverse datasets that include text, images, audio, and video files, as well as interrelated and temporal data. This means that more sophisticated techniques will be necessary to extract valuable insights from these complex datasets, and this is where machine learning, deep learning, and advanced statistical methods come into play.

10.1.2. Integration of AI and ML in Decision-Making Processes

As more organizations begin to integrate AI and ML into their decision-making processes, there will be an even greater reliance on accurate forecasts and actionable insights. This compels researchers to develop more robust and reliable statistical models and machine learning algorithms.

One trend that we can expect to see in this regard is the increased use of explainable AI (XAI). As decision-makers implement AI and ML solutions, they will want to understand how the models make their predictions. This promotes accountability, transparency and trust in the algorithms, ensuring that ethical considerations are maintained and errors are reduced.

10.1.3. Edge Computing and the Emergence of IoT

The rapid growth of the Internet of Things (IoT) is poised to have a profound impact on the applied fields of statistics, forecasting, and machine learning. The vast amounts of data produced by IoT devices offer significant opportunities for real-time analytics, but also present challenges in terms of latency, bandwidth limitations, and privacy concerns.

Edge computing, which involves processing data closer to the source, will likely become increasingly relevant for tackling some of these challenges. Researchers will need to develop resource-efficient algorithms that can be deployed on edge devices, allowing for real-time prediction and forecasting without overwhelming network infrastructure.

10.1.4. Interpretable Machine Learning, Causal Inference, and Ethical Challenges

As machine learning achieves broader adoption and is increasingly integrated into critical decision-making processes, the importance of interpretability and understanding causal relationships becomes even more significant. This is relevant not only for model diagnostics and optimization but also for addressing ethical and fairness concerns in AI.

The need to understand the underlying causal mechanisms and to develop fair, transparent and accountable algorithms presents both opportunities and challenges for statisticians and machine learning researchers. The growing interest in interpretable machine learning techniques and causal inference may help bridge the gap between model accuracy and its explainability, ensuring that ML models align with the ethical standards expected in critical applications.

10.1.5. The Importance of Interdisciplinary Collaboration

The rapid advancement of technologies and techniques in the fields of statistics, forecasting, and machine learning requires collaboration between domain experts, statisticians, and computer scientists. Cross-disciplinary teams are crucial for tackling complex real-world problems and ensuring that the models and algorithms developed are applicable, interpretable, and ethically sound.

Collaboration promotes the sharing of ideas, methods, and perspectives, ultimately leading to more meaningful insights that can drive innovation and influence decision-making. By encouraging interdisciplinary learning and communication, statisticians and machine learning practitioners can better understand the challenges and requirements of various fields, facilitating the development of more relevant and impactful solutions.

10.2. Conclusion

The future of statistics, forecasting, and machine learning is filled with exciting opportunities, as well as significant challenges. By staying up-to-date with emerging trends, collaborating with experts from other disciplines, and addressing ethical and fairness considerations, practitioners and researchers in these fields will be well-equipped to navigate the complex landscape of real-world applications and contribute meaningfully to the advancement of knowledge and technology.

10.5 Future Developments in Statistics, Forecasting and Machine Learning: Trends and Challenges

The future of statistics, forecasting, and machine learning is vast, as these areas are essential in creating data-driven solutions that address various challenges in the world today. Innovations in technology, computational resources, and algorithms keep propelling the field of data analysis to new heights. This section will delve into the exciting trends and challenges poised to shape the future of these domains and how they will be intertwined with different sectors to drive transformation and innovation.

10.5.1 Growing Data and Complexity

With the rise of the Internet of Things (IoT), mobile devices, sensors, and social media, data creation is exploding. Every minute, vast amounts of data are generated, representing rich sources of knowledge waiting to be mined. Data professionals will increasingly need the knowledge and skills to handle massive datasets efficiently. Big data analytics and distributed computing frameworks, such as Apache Hadoop and Spark, will play a crucial role in facilitating data processing, thereby refining statistical modeling and machine learning techniques.

10.5.2 Neural Networks and Deep Learning

Neural networks, a type of machine learning that simulates the human brain's functioning, have been instrumental in significant advancements in various applications such as image recognition, natural language processing (NLP), and game playing. Deep learning, a subfield of neural networks, has become increasingly popular, as researchers explore new architectures and training methodologies. We can expect the complexity of neural networks to escalate, enhancing performance and widening the scope of their application.

10.5.3 Reinforcement Learning and Transfer Learning

Reinforcement Learning (RL) and Transfer Learning are active areas of research that promise to revolutionize the way systems learn and gain intelligence. In RL, an agent learns from its interaction with an environment based on a reward feedback mechanism, enabling it to develop strategies to optimize outcomes. Transfer Learning, on the other hand, involves applying knowledge learned in one context to solve related problems, facilitating faster convergence and improved performance. These approaches have far-reaching potential, including the development of "artificial general intelligence" (AGI) systems capable of efficiently learning multiple tasks and outperforming humans in various domains.

10.5.4 Cross-disciplinary Integration

As the application of statistics, forecasting, and machine learning continues to expand, we will witness increased integration with other fields of study such as physics, biology, and social sciences. This interdisciplinary fusion will bolster the exchange of knowledge and methods, and enhance the breadth and depth of data-driven discoveries. For example, applications of machine learning in drug discovery and genomics are becoming more prevalent, propelling advancements in personalized medicine.

10.5.5 Ethics and Fairness

As data-driven systems impact human lives to a greater extent, ensuring ethical and fair behavior within these systems will become increasingly important. Algorithmic bias, transparency, and accountability will be the focus of considerable debate and research among academics, practitioners, and policymakers. Developing ethical frameworks and assessment tools to safeguard against discrimination, privacy infringement, and other potential harms will be paramount.

10.5.6 Infrastructure and Scalability

The massive scale and realtime nature of data generation require robust hardware and software infrastructure to ensure proper maintenance, storage, and processing capabilities. Cloud computing and high-performance computing (HPC) will likely continue playing a vital role in addressing these requirements. Additionally, efficient and cost-effective data storage technologies, such as object storage and data lake architecture, will become prominent as data management challenges evolve.

10.5.7 Human-Machine Interaction

As AI and machine learning systems become more intelligent and autonomous, fostering human-machine collaboration to leverage the strengths and mitigate the weaknesses of both parties will be essential. Innovations in human-computer interaction, such as augmented reality, natural language processing, and computer vision, will continue transforming how humans and machines work together, creating synergy and accelerating problem-solving.

In conclusion, the future of statistics, forecasting, and machine learning presents a fascinating landscape full of opportunities and challenges. As technology advances at an unprecedented pace, data-driven solutions are becoming indispensable in addressing complex issues affecting humanity. Staying informed, adaptable, and receptive to innovation in these domains is key to unlocking their potential and transforming the world for the better.

10.2 The Role of Interdisciplinary Approaches in Advancing Statistical and Machine Learning Techniques

As we progress further into the 21st century, computational methodologies and techniques arising from Statistics, Forecasting, and Machine Learning (ML) will continue to permeate nearly every aspect of human life. In a constantly-evolving world, predicting future trends and challenges is often a difficult task. However, one thing remains certain: interdisciplinary approaches will play a critical role in the ongoing process of developing new and improved methods in fields like Statistics and Machine Learning. By bridging the gap between diverse areas of expertise, researchers and practitioners will gain access to innovative ideas and novel applications that can significantly advance the state-of-the-art for these powerful tools.

10.2.1 Interactions Between Industry and Academia

In the future, more and more professionals will be expected to possess a solid foundation in statistical and ML techniques. Ensuring that people acquire these skills requires close collaboration between industry and academia. Educational institutions play a crucial role in preparing future employees and researchers by offering cutting-edge coursework and training opportunities. Meanwhile, industrial organizations can provide valuable feedback and support by sponsoring research projects, sharing valuable data, and offering internships and co-op placements.

Such partnerships between the two spheres should continue to be strengthened in the coming years. This will not only ensure a steady flow of well-prepared professionals entering the workforce, but also foster ongoing innovation in the development and implementation of Statistical and Machine Learning techniques.

10.2.2 Robustness and Privacy Enhancements

As Statistical and Machine Learning techniques become more ubiquitous across different sectors, the need for developing robust and privacy-preserving methods will increase. Generating predictions and insights from data can sometimes entail potential risks, including breaches of confidentiality or biased outcomes that carry adverse consequences. For this reason, greater attention must be placed on designing algorithms that are not only effective but also respect individuals' privacy and minimize the likelihood of producing harmful results.

Emerging strategies, such as Differential Privacy and Federated Learning, are gaining traction as potential solutions to these issues. By continually iterating and refining the implementation of these methods, developers can provide more secure ways of handling sensitive information while still allowing for robust analysis and prediction capabilities.

10.2.3 The Rise of AutoML and Neural Architecture Search

One noticeable trend in recent years has been the increasing focus on developing algorithms that can design and optimize Machine Learning models autonomously. This involves methods like Hyperparameter Search and Neural Architecture Search, with the goal of automating much of the process that goes into designing accurate and efficient models.

These efforts are expected to continue into the future, driven by the idea that human experts can only keep track of a limited number of factors at once. By harnessing computational power and sophisticated algorithms, a broader search space for potential model designs can be explored, uncovering new and better-performing solutions. These methods can also prove especially valuable in identifying models that perform well on new, unseen tasks or datasets.

10.2.4 Human-AI Collaboration and Expanding the Domain of Applications

To maximize the potential of Statistics, Forecasting, and Machine Learning, the focus on human-AI collaboration will continue to grow in the future. Researchers are increasingly devoted to helping people better understand and utilize the information and predictions generated by statistical or ML models. This implies the need for more interpretable techniques or dedicated user interfaces that can present insights in an intuitive and actionable manner.

Besides improving human-AI interactions, another important challenge is to extend the range of real-world domains where these techniques can be applied. This includes tackling unconventional or historically difficult problems, such as natural disaster forecasting or tracking global pandemics. By targeting such high-impact areas, the power of statistical and ML methods can be harnessed to make meaningful and positive change in people's lives.

In conclusion, anticipating the future of Statistics, Forecasting, and Machine Learning is a complex task. Nevertheless, the role of interdisciplinary approaches and ongoing collaboration between academia and industry, combined with growing attention to robustness, privacy, AutoML, and human-AI collaboration, will undoubtedly play a pivotal role in shaping advancements in these areas. As we continue to innovate and expand the horizons of these fields, the potential to enhance our understanding of the world and improve decision-making across various domains will be virtually limitless.

10.1 Emerging Technologies and Paradigms in the Field of Statistics, Forecasting and Machine Learning

As the field of statistics, forecasting, and machine learning continues to evolve, several key trends are shaping its future. These developments pose exciting opportunities for improving and expanding the application of these disciplines, as well as challenges in understanding and navigating the rapidly changing landscape. This section will discuss some of the most promising developments, focusing on how they may impact the field and what challenges they might present for those working in this area.

10.1.1 The Rise of Big Data and Real-Time Analytics

The explosion of data in recent years has changed the face of statistics, forecasting, and machine learning. With access to massive datasets, these fields have the potential to develop more accurate models, make more informed decisions, and provide unprecedented insights into various industries and aspects of life. However, the sheer volume of data also presents challenges: how can we efficiently process, store, and analyze such vast quantities of data?

One solution to this challenge is the rise of real-time analytics, which focuses on processing data as it is generated, rather than relying on historical data. This approach enables practitioners to make proactive decisions, quickly identify patterns and trends, and respond to events as they unfold. Real-time analytics also plays a significant role in the growing field of streaming analytics, where data is continuously analyzed to generate insights and make decisions.

10.1.2 Deep Learning and Artificial Neural Networks

Deep learning, a subset of machine learning, utilizes artificial neural networks to train computers to recognize patterns, make decisions, and perform other complex tasks. These networks, inspired by the structure and function of biological neural networks, have demonstrated remarkable success in areas such as image recognition, natural language processing, and game playing.

Deep learning has the potential to revolutionize forecasting and statistics by enabling more accurate predictions and providing novel insights into complex relationships within data. However, challenges remain in training and deploying deep learning models, particularly in terms of computational power and understanding their inner workings. As deep learning continues to advance, it will be crucial for practitioners in statistics, forecasting, and machine learning to stay current on this rapidly evolving area.

10.1.3 The Internet of Things and Sensor Data

The internet of things (IoT) – the network of interconnected devices and objects – is a rapidly growing and evolving field, providing an extensive array of data to inform statistical models and forecasts. IoT devices and sensors collect vast amounts of real-time data in various industries, including agriculture, healthcare, transportation, and energy management.

The rise of IoT and sensor data presents unique opportunities for the application of statistics, forecasting, and machine learning, allowing for more granular and accurate modeling and prediction. However, the sheer volume of data generated, combined with the need for real-time analysis, presents significant challenges in terms of data storage, processing, and transmission.

10.1.4 The Ethical, Privacy, and Security Implications of Data Science

As data becomes increasingly available and integrated into decision-making processes, concerns about the ethical, privacy, and security implications of data collection and use are critical. From digital surveillance and facial recognition to algorithmic biases and autonomous vehicles, the growing power and influence of data-driven decisions raise questions about the responsible use of data and the implications for individual privacy and societal well-being.

For practitioners in statistics, forecasting, and machine learning, understanding the ethical, privacy, and security dimensions of their work is essential. This may involve considering potential biases in data sources, ensuring responsible data use and storage, and engaging with ethical frameworks and guidelines in their fields.

10.1.5 The Integration of Domain Expertise with Technical Skills

As the field of statistics, forecasting, and machine learning expands and diversifies, the need for interdisciplinary collaboration will continue to grow. Experts in various domains – from ecology and public health to finance and policy – will need to work closely with data scientists and statisticians to develop impactful models and predictions. This collaboration helps ensure that technical expertise is appropriately applied to real-world problems, making the most significant impact on industry and society at large.

Additionally, domain-specific knowledge is invaluable for ensuring the interpretability of machine learning models, a key challenge in the field. Experience in the target domain can help to validate models, identify potential pitfalls and biases, and guide the development of more accurate and meaningful models.

In conclusion, the future developments in statistics, forecasting, and machine learning present both exciting opportunities and formidable challenges. By staying informed about these trends and engaging with the interdisciplinary and ethical dimensions of their work, practitioners will be better equipped to navigate the future of these disciplines and make a meaningful impact on the world around them.

Copyrights and Content Disclaimers:

AI-Assisted Content Disclaimer:
The content of this book has been generated with the assistance of artificial intelligence (AI) language models like CHatGPT and Llama. While efforts have been made to ensure the accuracy and relevance of the information provided, the author and publisher make no warranties or guarantees regarding the completeness, reliability, or suitability of the content for any specific purpose. The AI-generated content may contain errors, inaccuracies, or outdated information, and readers should exercise caution and independently verify any information before relying on it. The author and publisher shall not be held responsible for any consequences arising from the use of or reliance on the AI-generated content in this book.

General Disclaimer:
We use content-generating tools for creating this book and source a large amount of the material from text-generation tools. We make financial material and data available through our Services. In order to do so we rely on a variety of sources to gather this information. We believe these to be reliable, credible, and accurate sources. However, there may be times when the information is incorrect.
WE MAKE NO CLAIMS OR REPRESENTATIONS AS TO THE ACCURACY, COMPLETENESS, OR TRUTH OF ANY MATERIAL CONTAINED ON OUR book. NOR WILL WE BE LIABLE FOR ANY ERRORS INACCURACIES OR OMISSIONS, AND SPECIFICALLY DISCLAIMS ANY IMPLIED WARRANTIES OR MERCHANTABILITY OR FITNESS FOR ANY PARTICULAR PURPOSE AND SHALL IN NO EVENT BE LIABLE FOR ANY LOSS OF PROFIT OR ANY OTHER

COMMERCIAL OR PROPERTY DAMAGE, INCLUDING BUT NOT LIMITED TO SPECIAL, INCIDENTAL, CONSEQUENTIAL, OR OTHER DAMAGES; OR FOR DELAYS IN THE CONTENT OR TRANSMISSION OF THE DATA ON OUR book, OR THAT THE BOOK WILL ALWAYS BE AVAILABLE.
In addition to the above, it is important to note that language models like ChatGPT are based on deep learning techniques and have been trained on vast amounts of text data to generate human-like text. This text data includes a variety of sources such as books, articles, websites, and much more. This training process allows the model to learn patterns and relationships within the text and generate outputs that are coherent and contextually appropriate.

Language models like ChatGPT can be used in a variety of applications, including but not limited to, customer service, content creation, and language translation. In customer service, for example, language models can be used to answer customer inquiries quickly and accurately, freeing up human agents to handle more complex tasks. In content creation, language models can be used to generate articles, summaries, and captions, saving time and effort for content creators. In language translation, language models can assist in translating text from one language to another with high accuracy, helping to break down language barriers.

It's important to keep in mind, however, that while language models have made great strides in generating human-like text, they are not perfect. There are still limitations to the model's understanding of the context and meaning of the text, and it may generate outputs that are incorrect or offensive. As such, it's important to use language models with caution and always verify the accuracy of the outputs generated by the model.

Financial Disclaimer

This book is dedicated to helping you understand the world of online investing, removing any fears you may have about getting started and helping you choose good investments. Our goal is to help you take control of your financial well-being by delivering a solid financial education and responsible investing strategies. However, the information contained on this book and in our services is for general information and educational purposes only. It is not intended as a substitute for legal, commercial and/or financial advice from a licensed professional. The business of online investing is a complicated matter that requires serious financial due diligence for each investment in order to be successful. You are strongly advised to seek the services of qualified, competent professionals prior to engaging in any investment that may impact you finances. This information is provided by this book, including how it was made, collectively referred to as the "Services."

Be Careful With Your Money. Only use strategies that you both understand the potential risks of and are comfortable taking. It is your responsibility to invest wisely and to safeguard your personal and financial information.

We believe we have a great community of investors looking to achieve and help each other achieve financial success through investing. Accordingly we encourage people to comment on our blog and possibly in the future our forum. Many people will contribute in this matter, however, there will be times when people provide misleading, deceptive or incorrect information, unintentionally or otherwise.

You should NEVER rely upon any information or opinions you read on this book, or any book that we may link to. The information you read here and in our services should be used as a launching point for your OWN RESEARCH into various companies and investing strategies so that you can make an informed decision about where and how to invest your money.

WE DO NOT GUARANTEE THE VERACITY, RELIABILITY OR COMPLETENESS OF ANY INFORMATION PROVIDED IN THE COMMENTS, FORUM OR OTHER PUBLIC AREAS OF THE book OR IN ANY HYPERLINK APPEARING ON OUR book.

Our Services are provided to help you to understand how to make good investment and personal financial decisions for yourself. You are solely responsible for the investment decisions you make. We will not be responsible for any errors or omissions on the book including in articles or postings, for hyperlinks embedded in messages, or for any results obtained from the use of such information. Nor, will we be liable for any loss or damage, including consequential damages, if any, caused by a reader's reliance on any information obtained through the use of our Services. Please do not use our book If you do not accept self-responsibility for your actions.

The U.S. Securities and Exchange Commission, (SEC), has published additional information on Cyberfraud to help you recognize and combat it effectively. You can also get additional help about online investment schemes and how to avoid them at the following books:http://www.sec.gov

and http://www.finra.org, and http://www.nasaa.org these are each organizations set-up to help protect online investors.

If you choose ignore our advice and do not do independent research of the various industries, companies, and stocks, you intend to invest in and rely solely on information, "tips," or opinions found on our book – you agree that you have made a conscious, personal decision of your own free will and will not try to hold us responsible for the results thereof under any circumstance. The Services offered herein is not for the purpose of acting as your personal investment advisor. We do not know all the relevant facts about you and/or your individual needs, and we do not represent or claim that any of our Services are suitable for your needs. You should seek a registered investment advisor if you are looking for personalized advice.

Links to Other Sites. You will also be able to link to other books from time to time, through our Site. We do not have any control over the content or actions of the books we link to and will not be liable for anything that occurs in connection with the use of such books. The inclusion of any links, unless otherwise expressly stated, should not be seen as an endorsement or recommendation of that book or the views expressed therein. You, and only you, are responsible for doing your own due diligence on any book prior to doing any business with them.

Liability Disclaimers and Limitations: Under no circumstances, including but not limited to negligence, will we, nor our partners if any, or any of our affiliates, be held responsible or liable, directly or indirectly, for any loss or damage, whatsoever arising out of, or in connection with, the use of our Services, including without limitation, direct, indirect, consequential, unexpected, special, exemplary or other damages that may result, including but not limited to economic loss, injury, illness or death or any other type of loss or damage, or unexpected or adverse reactions to suggestions contained herein or otherwise caused or alleged to have been caused to you in connection with your use of any advice, goods or services you receive on the Site, regardless of the source, or any other book that you may have visited via links from our book, even if advised of the possibility of such damages.

Applicable law may not allow the limitation or exclusion of liability or incidental or consequential damages (including but not limited to lost data), so the above limitation or exclusion may not apply to you. However, in no event shall the total liability to you by us for all damages, losses, and causes of action (whether in contract, tort, or otherwise) exceed the amount paid by you to us, if any, for the use of our Services, if any. And by using our Site you expressly agree not to try to hold us liable for any consequences that result based on your use of our Services or the information provided therein, at any time, or for any reason, regardless of the circumstances.

Specific Results Disclaimer. We are dedicated to helping you take control of your financial well-being through education and investment. We provide strategies, opinions, resources and other Services that are specifically designed to cut through the noise and hype to help you make better personal finance and investment decisions. However, there is no way to guarantee any strategy or technique to be 100% effective, as results will vary by individual, and the effort and commitment they make toward achieving their goal. And, unfortunately we don't know you. Therefore, in using and/or purchasing our services you expressly agree that the results you receive from the use of those Services are solely up to you. In addition, you also expressly agree that all risks of use and any consequences of such use shall be borne exclusively by you. And that you will not to try to hold us liable at any time, or for any reason, regardless of the circumstances.

As stipulated by law, we can not and do not make any guarantees about your ability to achieve any particular results by using any Service purchased through our book. Nothing on this page, our book, or any of our services is a promise or guarantee of results, including that you will make any particular amount of money or, any money at all, you also understand, that all investments come with some risk and you may actually lose money while investing. Accordingly, any results stated on our book, in the form of testimonials, case studies or otherwise are illustrative of concepts only and should not be considered average results, or promises for actual or future performance.

Copyright and Other Disclaimers:

This book, "Day Trading with Robinhood: Trade Like a Pro," is an independently published work and is not affiliated with, endorsed by, or sponsored by Robinhood Markets, Inc. or any of its subsidiaries or affiliates. The author and publisher of this book have no association or connection with the Robinhood app, and any opinions, views, or strategies expressed within this book are solely those of the author and do not represent the opinions or viewpoints of Robinhood Markets, Inc. or its affiliates.

The information provided in this book is for educational and informational purposes only and should not be considered as financial, investment, or professional advice. Readers are encouraged to consult with a licensed financial professional before making any investment decisions.

General Disclaimer: The information, strategies, and techniques presented in this book are for educational and informational purposes only. They do not constitute financial, investment, tax, or legal advice. The author and publisher are not responsible for any financial losses or other damages that may result from applying the information contained in this book. Before making any investment or trading decisions, readers should consult with a licensed financial professional.

Risk Disclaimer: Investing and trading in stocks, options, ETFs, and other financial instruments carry inherent risks and may not be suitable for all investors. The value of investments can go up or down, and investors may lose their principal. Past performance is not indicative of future results. The author and publisher of this book do not guarantee any specific outcomes or results from using the strategies and techniques discussed herein.

Testimonials and Examples: Any testimonials, case studies, or examples presented in this book are provided for illustrative purposes only and do not guarantee that readers will achieve similar results. Individual success in trading depends on various factors, including personal financial situation, risk tolerance, and the ability to consistently apply the strategies and techniques discussed.